REFIGURING AMERICA

REFIGURING AMERICA

A Study of William Carlos Williams'
In the American Grain

BRYCE CONRAD

UNIVERSITY OF ILLINOIS PRESS
Urbana and Chicago

Publication of this work was supported in part by grants from the University of Iowa and the Andrew W. Mellon Foundation.

Grateful acknowledgment is given to New Directions Publishing Corporation for permission to quote from the following copyrighted works of William Carlos Williams: *The Autobiography of William Carlos Williams.* Copyright 1948, 1951 by William Carlos Williams. *Collected Poems: Volume I, 1909–1939.* Copyright 1938 by New Directions Publishing Corporation. Copyright © 1982, 1986 by William Eric Williams and Paul H. Williams. *Collected Poems: Volume II, 1939–1963.* Copyright 1944, 1953, Copyright © 1962, by William Carlos Williams. Copyright © 1988 by William Eric Williams and Paul H. Williams. *The Embodiment of Knowledge.* Copyright © 1974 by Florence H. Williams. *I Wanted to Write a Poem.* Copyright © 1958 by William Carlos Williams. *Imaginations.* Copyright © 1970 by Florence H. Williams. *In the American Grain.* Copyright 1925 by James Laughlin. Copyright 1933 by William Carlos Williams. *Paterson.* Copyright © 1946, 1948, 1948, 1949, 1958 by William Carlos Williams. *Selected Essays.* Copyright 1954 by William Carlos Williams. *Selected Letters of William Carlos Williams.* Copyright 1957 by William Carlos Williams. *A Voyage to Pagany.* Copyright 1928 by the Macauley Co. Copyright 1938, Copyright © 1970 by New Directions Publishing Corporation. *Yes, Mrs. Williams.* Copyright © 1959 by William Carlos Williams.

"The Books, the Records" originally appeared in a somewhat altered form as "The Deceptive Ground of History: The Sources of William Carlos Williams' *In the American Grain*" in *William Carlos Williams Review* 15 (Spring 1989): 22–40. A condensed version of "The Poetics and Politics of Sexuality" appeared as "Engendering History: The Sexual Structure of William Carlos Williams' *In the American Grain*" in *Twentieth Century Literature* 35 (Fall 1989).

The only real in writing is writing itself.

WILLIAM CARLOS WILLIAMS
The Embodiment of Knowledge

Contents

1

The Deceptive Ground of History

"I would rather sneak off and die like a sick dog than be a well known literary person in America," William Carlos Williams proclaimed in his chapter on Sam Houston.[1] And ironically, it seemed that America was more than willing to grant Williams his wish with respect to *In the American Grain*. Henry Seidel Canby, writing in the *Saturday Review of Literature* a few weeks after the book's publication in November 1925, pronounced *In the American Grain* "not history, not even good sense," and he declined to discuss the book's historical content on the grounds that "Mr. Williams is a poet and not a historian, and his book is a poet's protest not a historian's unbiased summary. It would be unfair to subject his brooding criticism to close scrutiny."[2] Some weeks later Kenneth Burke reiterated that same verdict in the *New York Herald Tribune Books*, stating, "The purpose is poetry, not history; Williams seeks bravuras rather than facts." Burke located the historical failure of the book in Williams' reliance on "a maximum of 'interpretation' and a minimum of research; his heroes are so busy *living* that they neglect to do anything else, and their inventions, or discoveries, or battles, or policies, become an unimportant by-product."[3] If there was history in *In the American Grain*, it was the particular type that had provided the title for Burke's review: subjective history.

Williams hadn't specifically presented his book as a work of history, but he had made it clear that his work rested upon an understanding of history, exclaiming in one chapter, "I seek the support of history but I wish to understand it aright, to make it SHOW itself" (116). Yet the first reviewers apparently saw little in the book that resembled history as they understood history to be, and they didn't hesitate to voice their objections. Shortly after Canby's piece in the *Saturday Review of Literature,* an anonymous reviewer for *The New York Times Book Review* charged Williams with "wandering into the byways and side issues of uninteresting lives, to envelop a dullness of subject matter in a gracelessly cryptic style." Even though *In the American Grain* possessed moments of "vital and illuminating" writing, the book was "an experiment in the technique of historical writing" whose faults were "a sacrifice to experimentation, perhaps, and highly unfortunate."[4]

Williams undoubtedly read these first three reviews of *In the American Grain*—he carefully followed his critical reception throughout the early stages of his career. And he was responding not only to Burke, but to what he recognized as a general misperception of his book when he quickly sent Burke a perturbed response after reading his piece in the *New York Herald Tribune Books*: "I thought I had salted the original matter with enough historic material to have escaped the bald statement 'Subjective History!' "[5] Williams had indeed done more than merely "salt" *In the American Grain* with historic material. He had not only read but quoted extensively from a wide variety of early American texts, a point he had tried to make explicitly clear in his epigraph to the book, referring to his work as "studies" of past writing, of "letters" and "journals," and "reports of happenings" (v). Yet the critics, intent upon viewing Williams as a poet, seemed unable to see the historical and documentary character of *In the American Grain.*

The only reviewer to go against the grain of these estimates was D. H. Lawrence. There was no question in his mind that *In the American Grain* could claim the status of history. He told readers that "History in this book would be a sensuous record of the Americanization of the white men in America, as contrasted with ordinary history, which is a complacent record of the civilization and Europizing (if you can allow the word) of the American continent." Lawrence overturned the simplistic opposition of poetry and history in favor of one between kinds of historical knowing. Unlike "ordinary history," which told the story of America's conquest by an invading cultural order from Europe, Williams had made history a story of "Americanization," of the spirit of place exerting itself on the European newcomer, thus giving us "a glimpse of what the vast America *wants men to be,* instead of another strident assertion of what men have made, do make, will make, can make, out of the murdered territories of the New World."[6] Lawrence had devoted his own *Studies in Classic American Literature* to creating just such a story out of American literary history, pursuing the emergence of a distinctively American culture through a study of the nation's "classic" literary works. And he recognized Williams' book as the product of a fellow student of American writing, perhaps even hearing an echo of his own book's title in Williams' terming *In the American Grain* a set of "studies."[7]

Lawrence's assessment of *In the American Grain* was the kind that might have helped save the book—save it, that is, by clarifying its complexities. But by the time Lawrence's review appeared in the *Nation*, nearly half a year after the publication of *In the American Grain*, Williams' publishers, Albert and Charles Boni, had already lost faith in the book. Apparently assuming it would be futile to seriously market a work so unanimously panned by reviewers, the Bonis quickly remaindered it, and Williams, as he recalls in his *Autobiography*, found himself ruefully enacting the fate he had posed for himself in the Houston chapter: "I made trip after trip to the publisher's offices until they got so sick of seeing me that all of them would give me a nod and walk by, talking together, and close themselves in before me, leaving me sitting there: a beautiful brushoff. They let me know they did not intend to put more into advertising or promotion and so, bitterly, I had to see my high hopes of success go skittering out the window. In no time at all the thing was remaindered and I began to pick up copies wherever I could" (A, 236).

Williams had good reason to be bitterly disappointed about the treatment of *In the American Grain*, his first book to be issued by a commercial publishing house. He had entertained hopes that the Bonis would give him the financial backing to reach a wider audience than he had previously gained for his poetry, which had appeared only in small privately printed editions, with Williams himself often paying the printing costs. *In the American Grain*, furthermore, had been written with an avowedly public purpose that hadn't characterized Williams' poetry. He wanted to educate Americans about their own history, to help them recognize the distinctive peculiarities of their own culture by studying its origins in the writings and lives of early Americans. But the book won no wide reading. It went out of print soon after its initial publication and remained out of print, virtually forgotten, for nearly fifteen years.

When James Laughlin of New Directions resurrected *In the American Grain* in 1939, he left an indelible mark upon the text—not wanting to loose the book upon the public without some kind of preliminary word, some explanation to potential readers of the difficult verbal terrain they were about to enter, Laughlin asked the poet Horace Gregory to write an introduction.[8] Gregory seemed a happy choice for the task.

He was genuinely and enthusiastically supportive of Williams' writing, having asked Williams to speak at his poetry seminar at Sarah Lawrence College earlier in 1939. Gregory had even played the role of defending Williams against detractors (and he had as many in 1939 as he had had in 1925), being the first to speak on behalf of the vitality of Williams' *Collected Poems* after it had been slammed by the *New Republic* in December of 1938. So it is not suprising that when Gregory asked Williams for information about *In the American Grain*, Williams eagerly responded with a lengthy letter.

The letter is remarkable on several counts. For one, it abounds with factual errors—or, rather, Williams' recollection of the facts continually critiques the factual evidence. He misnames the *Flat Island Book*, which he read for the "Red Eric" chapter, "the famous Long Island Saga." And he becomes increasingly bewildered in his attempts to reconstruct the compositional sequence of *In the American Grain*, confusing the dates on which he was writing the Columbus chapter before finally admitting himself an example of "the frailty of human witnessing." No less fascinating, Williams repeatedly tries to consult "the attic" during his writing of the letter, breaking off the text to run upstairs and peer in the archives, apparently never finding what he was looking for, and finally giving up the search with the exclamation, "Christ only knows where the rest of the stuff is." By the end of the letter, Williams could only say to Gregory, "I hope I haven't confused you too much" (SL, 186–88).

But even though Williams found himself lost among conflicting recollections, he still managed to convey a sense of what he thought most important about *In the American Grain*. Williams directed Gregory's attention to the researched nature of the book, to the many works—from Cortez's letters and Columbus' journal to the writings of Cotton Mather and Benjamin Franklin—he had incorporated into the textual fabric of *In the American Grain*. He knew that if readers were to appreciate his construction of American history, they would have to recognize the documentary materials out of which he had built it. Describing *In the American Grain* as "a study in styles of writing," Williams stressed that he had "tried to write each chapter in the style most germane to its sources or at least the style which seemed to me appropriate to the material," and that "To this end, where possible, I copied and used the original writings" (SL, 187). He indeed seems to have wanted to give Gregory a bibliographical record of the source materials he had used in writing the book, confessing, "I'm sorry I didn't keep a record of all the things I read." The best Williams could do was to mention that "whatever reading I did was done at the N. Y. Public Library in the American History Room" (SL, 186).

Gregory, however, didn't include in his introduction any of the information Williams gave him concerning the historical character of *In the American Grain*. Gregory, in fact, doesn't really talk about the book at all. The only passages of *In the American Grain* he singles out for comment are those invested with "lyricism," the short chapters on Raleigh and Lincoln; otherwise, Gregory spends most of his introduction trying to convince readers that it would be best to approach Williams' book as poetry rather than history. He warns us that "The desire to know history is a near relative of the desire to know truth, and that is where, for most of us, a pit lies waiting" (ix). To avoid that trap, Gregory cautions, "There must be imagination at work to discern the fabulae of history," because "there has been a long established kinship between the historical imagination and poetry" (xi). Regardless of the general brilliance of his insights, Gregory substantially repeats from a different angle what the earlier reviewers had said. By suggesting that the only truth for which we might profitably look in history is ultimately poetry, Gregory reaffirmed the notion that Williams' purpose lay with the latter not the former. And by doing so, Gregory was once again deflecting potential readers of *In the American Grain* away from the grounded historical basis of the text.

Despite Gregory's efforts to champion the book, *In the American Grain* didn't receive a prominent critical recognition until 1950, when Louis Martz asserted its seminal importance in the genesis of Williams' later work. In "William Carlos Williams: On the Road to *Paterson*," Martz appraised *In the American Grain* as the "most significant work of Williams' early career," finding in it a prefiguring of all the concerns that Williams would pursue in *Paterson*.[9] Martz explicitly treats *In the American Grain* as "prose preparation for *Paterson*," and in turn he presents *Paterson* as an *In the American Grain* "on a local scale . . . dealing with events that figure in the grain of northern New Jersey." Williams' technique of quoting "old records" in the poem, Martz perceptively suggests, had origin in Williams' use of "old documents" for *In the American Grain*.[10] Yet Martz's article isn't truly based on a reading of *In the American Grain*. Rather than using the book to approach *Paterson*, Martz uses *Paterson* to interpret the significance of *In the American Grain*, much like an exegete looking for types in the Old Testament after having encountered the antitype of the New. The limitation of this treatment of Williams' book is that it overlooks the history in the text in favor of creating a place in literary history for the text. And Martz, like the critics who preceded him, bluntly dismisses the necessity of seriously reckoning with the book's historical content, asserting, "one thing seems certain: these sketches of figures and events in the development of the New World are not to be regarded primarily as 'history.' "[11]

Very little of what has been written on *In the American Grain* since 1950 has not been influenced, to some degree, by Martz's emplotment of it within a synoptic view of Williams' literary development—an influence made all the more significant by the fact that very little indeed has been written on *In the American Grain* at all. Though widely acknowledged to be an American "classic," the book hasn't been given the careful scrutiny accorded Hart Crane's *The Bridge* or Williams' own *Paterson*, works commensurate to *In the American Grain* in scope and complexity of historical vision. While *The Bridge* and *Paterson* have each been the subject of scores of articles and numerous critical books, *In the American Grain* has had only about a dozen substantial articles or chapters of books devoted to it. And of these, only two—Alan Holder's "In the American Grain: William Carlos Williams on the American Past" (1967), and James Breslin's chapter on *In the American Grain* in his *William Carlos Williams: An American Artist* (1970)—make any notable attempt to address Williams' use of historical material.

Characterizing Williams' book as "a highly selective, impressionistic account of our history, the product of his imagination playing over the documents," Holder adopts Williams' own "strategy of going directly to the documents themselves" to examine the concerns that animated Williams' reading of history.[12] Holder is perceptive on several points, most notably the sexual dynamics of *In the American Grain*. But as a source study, Holder's work is hampered because he often seems more concerned with what Williams left out of *In the American Grain* than what he put into it. Holder tends to look for passages in the historical record that he suggests Williams purposefully overlooks—passages that would give us a more "balanced" and objective view of the past than Williams' "impressionistic" one. Holder, furthermore, is often incorrect in identifying the particular editions and translations that Williams used, thus rendering even more difficult a sharp focus on exactly what material Williams encountered in his documents and how he chose to employ it.[13]

Breslin took issue with Holder's conception of *In the American Grain* and additionally corrected several of Holder's bibliographical errors.[14] Concentrating his efforts at source recovery on four particular chapters—"Red Eric," "The Discovery of the Indies," "The Destruction of Tenochtitlan," and "De Soto and the New World"—Breslin cites, on the basis of textual evidence, exact editions and translations of Williams' sources and also specifies sections of those works that Williams incorporated in the writing of *In the American Grain*. On the basis of this research, Breslin overturns the notion that Williams' use of history is merely subjective or impressionistic, arguing instead that "Williams's method was to cut through a prolixity of detail" in the documents "in order to point up a hidden symbolic pattern" that is "latent" in the source text itself.[15] Yet the problem with Breslin's study is that he offers his description of Williams' methodology for these chapters as a prescription for what Williams should have done throughout the book as a whole. Perhaps moved by the exigency of treating a work as complex as *In the American Grain* within the space of a chapter in his book on Williams' artistry, Breslin valorizes these four chapters as "the best" in *In the American Grain*, downplaying the significance of the many chapters that do not fit his ideal paradigm.

One may easily get lost in the tropological wilderness of *In the American Grain*. Williams' frequent erasures of the semiotic sutures between his text and those he appropriates, the virtual absence of any accompanying bibliographical documentation (nil to what Eliot gives for *The Waste Land*), and the blur of historical fact and verbal creation, make his text a difficult terrain—yet therein lies much of its richness. Williams' book certainly deserves a much wider reading and more vigorous critical discussion than it has received, and I have written the present work in hope of encouraging further studies of *In the American Grain*. Above all else, I have tried to open up the historical and structural elements of the book to view, working through the text in my own way. I have not attempted to create a reader's guide to *In the American Grain*, nor have I followed Williams' chronological sequence of chapters in the movement of my discussion. I have constructed my own narrative here, one designed to mean by interacting with Williams' text and source texts, not necessarily by "interpreting" them in ordinary ways. Rather than applying a single and uniform methodology in my work, I have responded to *In the American Grain* as a book anarchically disruptive of systematic thought.

By the same token, I have not tried to define, a priori or otherwise, just what "history" might or might not be. Recent scholarship on the epistemological basis of the historical understanding could very well be used to dispel the notion that Williams simply fails to approach history "objectively." Work by Arthur C. Danto, Louis O. Mink, and Hayden White has shown how ordinary modes of history writing invent stories about the past according to narrative conventions rather than historio-scientific laws. White, in particular, has worked extensively with the premise that to approach written history as a "verbal artifact that purports to be a model of structures and processes that are long past and cannot therefore be subjected to either experimentation or observational controls" is to show that our histories are "verbal fictions, the contents of which have more in common with their counterparts in literature than they have with those in the sciences." [16] Even in its most objective descriptions of the past, White claims, written history linguistically constitutes its subjects and events, ordering them into narrative schemes of organization. There are no "authentic" histories, White suggests, but only texts that try to "authenticate" themselves as the true story of the past by passing off their own verbal strategies of organization as the structure of the events they pretend to describe. As Lionel Gossman has pointed out, conventional history writing engages in the "referential fallacy," conflating its constituted subjects with their actual referents, creating the illusion that the historian's text truly represents the past itself. [17]

Williams had recognized this fallacy as early as 1919, writing in the prologue to *Kora in Hell*, "Of course history is an attempt to make the past seem stable, and of course it's all a lie. Nero must mean Nero or the whole game's up" (KH, 41). Williams was strongly aware of the irremediable gap between the past and its narrative representations. And in writing *In the American Grain*, he eschews the standard practices by which historians create the illusion of a well-ordered past. Williams doesn't tell a continuous narrative of events about a central subject. Indeed, he specifically attacks conventional history writing for following "governments and never men. It portrays us in generic patterns, like effigies or the carvings on sarcophagi, which say nothing save, of such and such a man, that he is dead. That's history. It is concerned only with the one thing: to say everything is dead" (188). But "History," says Williams, "must stay open, it is all humanity." Williams' idea of an "open" history is not just one that is open to the language of the past, but one that is conscious of itself as language. And rather than attempting to conceal the history-constituting function of his own language, Williams often plainly reveals the fictive and imaginative character of his construction of the past. Yet we shall see that even though Williams explicitly points to certain sources and origins in American history, he just as emphatically erases and disguises others, making history, ultimately, deceptive ground in *In the American Grain*.

But I have not approached *In the American Grain* as a modernist's destruction of the Rankean ideal of truthful representation, nor have I focused on other subjects that one might like to see elaborated here, such as the relation of *In the American Grain* to contemporary reevaluations of American history by Van Wyck Brooks, Paul Rosenfeld, Waldo Frank, D. H. Lawrence, and Hart Crane, or the overall importance of Williams' travels in Europe during 1924 while he was hard at work composing the book. I have consciously marginalized these subjects, often relegating them to my notes, which function not merely as bibliographical entries, but as a running subnarrative to my text. What I hope to have provided here is a map of *In the American Grain* itself, of the peculiar textual contours of this remarkable work. Though I give Williams' epistemology of history a decidedly Emersonian cast, and though I occasionally draw on autobiographical and other writings by Williams to advance my discussion, I have tried to confine my explorations primarily to the book and its sources, being as acutely and painfully aware as Williams himself, in his efforts to put into his *Autobiography* all the crowded sensations and events of his European tour of 1924, that "It can't all be told" (A, 203).

NOTES

1. William Carlos Williams, *In the American Grain*, intro. Horace Gregory (New York: New Directions, l954), 215. All subsequent citations of *In the American Grain*, as well as Gregory's introduction, are parenthetically referenced with page numbers in my text. Citations of Williams' other major works are also parenthetically referenced in my text, and identified by the following abbreviations: A for *The Autobiography of William Carlos Williams* (New York: New Directions, 1967); CEP for *The Collected Earlier Poems of William Carlos Williams* (New York: New Directions, 1951); CLP for *The Collected Later Poems of William Carlos Williams*, rev. ed. (New York: New Directions, 1963); EK for *The Embodiment of Knowledge*, ed. Ron Loewinsohn (New York: New Directions, 1977); GAN for *The Great American Novel*, in *Imaginations*, ed. Webster Schott (New York: New Directions, 1970); IW for *I Wanted to Write a Poem: The Autobiography of the Works of a Poet*, ed. Edith Heal (New York: New Directions, 1978); KH for *Kora in Hell*, in *Imaginations*; P for *Paterson* (New York: New Directions, 1963); SA for *Spring and All*, in *Imaginations*; SE for *Selected Essays of William Carlos Williams* (New York: New Directions, 1969); SL for *The Selected Letters of William Carlos Williams* (New York: New Directions, 1984); VP for *A Voyage to Pagany*, intro. Harry T. Levin (New York: New Directions, 1970); YMW for *Yes, Mrs. Williams: A Personal Record of My Mother* (New York: New Directions, 1982).

2. Henry Seidel Canby, "Back to the Indian," *Saturday Review of Literature* 2 (19 Dec. 1925); rpt. in Charles Doyle, ed., *William Carlos Williams: The Critical Heritage* (London: Routledge & Kegan Paul, 1980), 86, 85.

3. Kenneth Burke, "Subjective History," *New York Herald Tribune Books*, 14 Mar. 1926; rpt. in *William Carlos Williams: The Critical Heritage*, 88, 87.

4. "American Potpourri," *New York Times Book Review*, 7 Feb. 1926, 21.

5. Quoted in Paul Mariani, *William Carlos Williams: A New World Naked* (New York: McGraw-Hill, 1981), 252. Williams had been corresponding with Burke all throughout the time he was writing *In the American Grain*. Ever since Burke had given an acute reading of Williams' poetry in the *Dial* in 1922, Williams had been cultivating him as a literary ally, praising him in *Contact* for helping to establish "an American critical attitude," *Contact* 3 (Spring 1921): 15, and he regarded Burke's review as something of a betrayal.

6. D. H. Lawrence, "American Heroes," *Nation* (14 Apr. 1926); rpt. in *William Carlos Williams: The Critical Heritage*, 90, 91.

7. Lawrence saw *In the American Grain* as the kind of work he had been urging American writers to perform. In "America, Listen to Your Own," Lawrence challenged Americans to turn "to that very America which has been rejected and almost annihilated," to the aboriginal life of the continent: "Americans must take up life where the Red Indian, the Aztec, the Maya, the Incas left it off. They must pick up the life-thread where the mysterious Red race let it fall. They must catch up the pulse of the life which Cortes and Columbus murdered. There lies the real continuity: not between Europe and the new States, but between the murdered Red America and the seething White America. The President should not look back towards Gladstone or Cromwell or Hildebrand, but towards Montezuma," *New Republic* (15 Dec. 1920); rpt. in Edward D. McDonald, ed., *Phoenix* (London: William Heinemann, 1936), 90–91. For a discussion of Lawrence's possible influence on Williams' writing of *In the American Grain*, see Thomas R. Whitaker, *William Carlos Williams* (New York: Twayne Publishers, 1968), 77–78, and Bruce Clarke, "The Fall of Montezuma: Poetry and History in William Carlos Williams and D. H. Lawrence," *William Carlos Williams Review* 12 (Spring 1986): 1–12. For more on Lawrence's engagement with America, see Armin Arnold, *D. H. Lawrence and America* (New York: Linden Press, 1958), and David Cavitch, *D. H. Lawrence and the New World* (New York: Oxford University Press, 1969).

8. Gregory's introduction has quite literally become a part of *In the American Grain*. The essay has been published with every New Directions edition of the book since 1939—and New Directions has been the sole publisher of *In the American Grain* in this country after the Bonis in 1925.

9. Louis Martz, "William Carlos Williams: On the Road to *Paterson*," *Poetry New York* 4 (1951); rpt. in Martz's *The Poem of the Mind* (New York: Oxford University Press, 1966), 134.

10. Ibid., 154, 139.

11. Ibid., 134.

12. Alan Holder, "In the American Grain: William Carlos Williams on the American Past," *American Quarterly* 19 (Fall 1967): 500–501.

13. Holder's treatment of "The Destruction of Tenochtitlan" is characteristic. He cites *Conquest: Dispatches of Cortes from the New World*, ed. Irwin

Blacker and Harry Rosen (New York: Grosset & Dunlap, 1962), an edition Williams plainly didn't use—and Holder quotes only portions of Cortez's letters that, far from appearing in Williams' chapter, are selected to contradict what Holder calls Williams' determination "to have his savages noble, despite their ignoble savagery." Holder even seeks to fortify his critique of Williams' supposedly romanticized portrayal of America's aborigines by reference to Parkman (hardly an "objective" source on Indian matters), arguing that Parkman's account of Indian cruelties in *The Jesuits in North American in the Seventeenth Century* "points up the lack of balance in Williams' book" (508).

14. Breslin, *William Carlos Williams: An American Artist* (New York: Oxford University Press, 1970), 236–37n3, charged that Holder "does not see either the coherence or the profundity of Williams' book," and he also remarked Holder's mistaken source citations for the Tenochtitlan, De Soto, and Rasles chapters. Holder, in turn, responded to Breslin's criticisms when he republished his piece—under the title "Puritan and Redskin: William Carlos Williams's *In the American Grain*"—as the first chapter of his *The Imagined Past: Portrayals of Our History in Modern American Literature* (Lewisburg, Pa.: Bucknell University Press, 1980), defending both his approach to *In the American Grain* (49n2) and, in some cases, his choice of source materials. Though Holder does revise and supplement some of his bibliographical citations on the basis of Breslin's corrections, several errors persist.

15. Breslin, 111.

16. Hayden White, *Tropics of Discourse: Essays in Cultural Criticism* (Baltimore: Johns Hopkins University Press, 1978), 82. In his *Metahistory: The Historical Imagination in Nineteenth-Century Europe* (Baltimore: Johns Hopkins University Press, 1973), White, who has been the most vigorous and prolific thinker in the recent debate over the ontology of history, gives his most comprehensive treatment of written history as linguistic artifact. But the essential background text on history as language is Arthur C. Danto's *Analytical Philosophy of History* (New York: Columbia University Press, 1965), which Danto has subsequently expanded as *Narration and Knowledge* (1985). Also pertinent to the discussion are several articles by Louis O. Mink: "The Autonomy of Historical Understanding," in William Dray, ed., *Philosophical Analysis and History* (New York: Harper & Row, 1966), 160–92; "History and Fiction as Modes of Comprehension," *New Literary History* 1 (Spring 1970): 541–59; and "Narrative Form as Cognitive Instrument," in Robert H. Canary and Henry Kozicki, eds., *The Writing of History: Literary Form and Historical Understanding* (Madison: University of Wisconsin Press, 1978), 129–50.

17. Lionel Gossman, "History and Literature: Reproduction and Signification," in Canary and Kozicki, 29–32.

2

An American Education

"I had a fine afternoon alone with Valery Larbaud, who talked to me of Spanish literature," Williams wrote to Marianne Moore from Paris in late February of 1924. "We also talked of Bolivar and the grand manner in which Spain undertook its new world colonization as contrasted with England's niggardliness. We also spoke of Cotton Mather!!" (SL, 60). Nearly two months later, after a sojourn in the south of France and Italy, Williams recalled his afternoon with Larbaud in another letter to Moore, this time from Vienna: "Valery Larbaud spoke only of Bolivar's sweep of imagination. The English came to America on a 3% basis, but Bolivar saw another Spain in America. He [Larbaud] liked the way the Spaniards 'moved in' to the new world, bringing *lares, penates* and Olympus too with them. I could say little at the sight of the six two-inch-thick volumes on Bolivar which Larbaud threw before me, like pomegranates, on the table. Perhaps I stammered a word about admiring something of the Maya culture" (SL, 63).

Williams' second letter gives us a little more insight into the peculiar personal and cultural dynamic that informed his afternoon with Larbaud. Williams was clearly surprised—if not outright intimidated —by the Frenchman's knowledge of New World history. In the first letter it is *we* who spoke, but in the second it is only Larbaud, while of himself Williams writes, "I could say little," and "Perhaps I stammered a word." Larbaud, furthermore, does more than speak. He produces several hefty volumes on Bolivar, revealing the documentary basis of his judgments. Indeed, what seems to confound Williams is the natural ease with which Larbaud gestures to those densely packed seeds of his knowledge, tossing the volumes on the table "like pomegranates."

Williams was obviously obsessed with his meeting with Larbaud, for he returned to it yet again after the completion of his European journey, making that afternoon in Larbaud's company the setting for his chapter on the French Jesuit missionary Père Sebastian Rasles. And what is suggested in the second letter is made even more explicit here. As Larbaud begins to speak on Bolivar and takes the imposing volumes from the bookcase, Williams experiences a moment of frightened panic. "He presumed too much," Williams writes of the Frenchman. "I am not a student; presently he will ask me questions I cannot answer!" (107). Williams, in fact, claims to have recognized Larbaud's scholarly nature even before the volumes on Bolivar are placed on the table. And that recognition had made him acutely and perhaps painfully aware of his own lack of scholarly sophistication: "He is a student, I am a block, I thought. I could see it at once: he knows far more of what is written of my world than I. But he is a student while I am—the brutal thing itself" (107).

Williams gives us a classic configuration: the juxtaposed sensibilities of the European intellectual and the raw, untutored American. Larbaud commands a knowledge of books—"he was engaged with a treatise upon the great Venezuelan patriot and liberator," Williams tells us as Larbaud reaches for the volumes on Bolivar (108). But Williams is no intellectual. He is "a block," the unrefined matter of the New World, "the brutal thing itself." Larbaud possesses the European's traditional mode of knowledge, *auctoritas,* the sanction of the written word. Williams' knowledge, however, rests upon the less orderly and systematic ground of personal experience, and he fears that he is far out of his depth in attempting to discuss New World history with the Frenchman. Indeed, as the conversation turns to books, specifically the *Magnalia Christi Americana* of Cotton Mather, Williams is apparently forced to disclose the cursory nature of his exposure to that text in comparison to Larbaud's more studied acquaintance with it: "I found that he had read the *Magnalia.* No. HE had read it. I had *seen* the book and brushed through its pages hunting for something I wished to verify" (109–10). Initially intimidated by Larbaud's intellectualism, Williams begins "to heal nevertheless" as Larbaud speaks on New World history, for "Valery Larbaud seemed cultivating my intimate earth with his skillful hands" (108).

"THIS in Paris," Williams exclaims in apparent surprise as he learns that Larbaud had read Mather's *Magnalia* (110). But what actually was said on that afternoon of Saturday, January 26, 1924, in Larbaud's Paris apartment we will never know. We do know, from the diary Williams kept of his European travels that year, that the conversation was conducted in French (a language in which Williams was able to express himself only with considerable difficulty), and that Williams had primarily listened to the "charming" Larbaud, who spoke of Poe, Whitman, Mather, and the Spanish colonization of the Americas.[1] We also know, from Williams' letters to Moore, of Larbaud's preponderant concern with Bolivar, which deeply impressed Williams, who was in the midst of composing his own chronology of personages for *In the American Grain*. Larbaud, like Williams, had been reading books for his task—those imposing "six two-inch-volumes on Bolivar" in this case. But the fact is that none of this circumstantial evidence offers us much assistance in approaching "Père Sebastian Rasles," for what we encounter in the chapter bears little relation to the "facts" of Williams' diary and letters.

The most obvious discrepancy is that the chapter is almost entirely in English. Moreover, not only are Poe and Whitman never mentioned, but Bolivar and the Spanish colonization are dropped in the conversation immediately after they appear. The main topics of the discussion are the works of Cotton Mather and the letters of Sebastian Rasles in *Lettres édifantes*. Yet Rasles is not mentioned at all in the diary and letters. Not only that, but it is Williams who predominantly speaks on these matters while Larbaud progressively lapses in silence, his previous attempts to direct the course of the discussion having been peremptorily dismissed by the increasingly impatient American. Larbaud's sole remark in the last seven pages of the chapter is the terse reply, "They are remote," to Williams' pointed observation that the early battles between the French Catholics and the English Puritans along the New England frontier "have a great importance for the student of today" (128).

What is remote, if anything, is Larbaud's knowledge of the books Williams ironically tells us Larbaud had really read and he himself had only "brushed through." One thrust of Williams' pedagogy for Larbaud and for us is to show the limited vision of the traditional scholar who digests whole tomes but can say nothing incisively detailed about the verbal texture of what he has read. Throughout the chapter Williams becomes more and more exacerbated by the Frenchman's scholarly detachment from the books they discuss. Yet Larbaud's detached perspective on Mather's books and the *Lettres édifantes* cannot be wholly attributed to his cultural and spatial distance from the living fact of the New World—nor can Williams' obvious visceral engagement with those texts be wholly explained by Larbaud's comment that Williams is "from that place" and therefore "caught by a smell" (115). What is at stake here are two contrasting ways of reading history: Williams' self-taught method by which the documents are seen as living sources that constitute the present in addition to the past, and Larbaud's more traditional academic orientation, according to which the documents become quaint relics of a past with no bearing on the present—relics that, as Williams complains, are little more than an object of "enchanting diversion, a curious study" for the scholar (116). What Williams has done in "Père Sebastian Rasles" is essentially to shape Larbaud as a symbolic mask representing the limitations of the conventional intellectual's way of seeing history.

Williams, however, adopts his own symbolic mask. His pretended fear that Larbaud has "presumed too much" and will ask him questions he cannot answer—whatever its apparent basis in the "facts" of the diary and letters—certainly speaks such a mask, for Williams indeed answers more questions than Larbaud can put to him. Williams gives us a playful twist on the American folk motif of the country bumpkin who outsmarts the cultivated city dweller. Rather than Larbaud's gracious scholarly nature cultivating Williams into expression, it seems that Williams plays the role of a mute "block" to test out the ground of Larbaud's pedagogical orientation. After giving us but not Larbaud his thought response to Larbaud's uttered distinction between the Spanish and English appraisals of the New World ("A herd of proofs moved through my mind like stumbling buffalo," 108)—after privileging us with that prolonged inner monologue, Williams makes his entry into the dialogue with the laconic "We have no books, I said" (109). Cunningly, Williams speaks an intentional lie. He knows quite well that we have books because he had been studying them and writing on them for some time. And his writing on those books, in fact, had been published in Europe. The first six chapters of *In the American Grain* had all made their appearance in Harold Loeb's expatriate magazine *Broom* before the day Williams met Larbaud in Paris. Larbaud had undoubtedly read the *Broom* versions of the chapters from "Red Eric" to "Sir Walter Raleigh," for he had taken a keen interest in Williams' work since 1921. He had written warmly on *Kora in Hell* in *Revue de France*, and later on *The Great American Novel* (published by Bill Bird's Three Mountain Press in Paris in 1923) in *Revue européenne*.[2] And his reading of Williams' new work in progress on New World history had certainly played no small part in his extending the summons, through Williams' Paris acquaintance Adrienne Monnier, that Williams should come to see him that afternoon. ("You must talk to Valery Larbaud, she told me. He wants to see you. Why should I? I insist that you go," 107).

Williams' remark, then, that "We have no books" is merely a subterfuge to draw out Larbaud, to verify whether he had indeed read
those *Broom* pieces. That subterfuge is made all the more nakedly apparent for us when Williams tells us, even before the conversation
with Larbaud begins, that Larbaud "knew what I had attempted"
(107). Nonetheless, Williams' artifice goes off without a hitch, for as
soon as Larbaud objects to the statement that we have no books—
"There you are wrong. Two or three are enough, to have shown a beginning. Have not you yourself proven that there is meat"—Williams
instantly marks the success of his ploy: "(so he had read what I intended!)." And having thus made certain that he needn't start from
scratch with Larbaud, that he can presume Larbaud's familiarity with
his ground, with his own historical pedagogy, Williams immediately
breaks into forceful and eloquent speech, delivering one of the most
crucial statements in *In the American Grain* concerning the nature and
importance of historical study:

> I said, It is an extraordinary phenomenon that Americans have lost
> the sense, being made up as we are, that what we are has its ori-
> gin in what *the nation* in the past has been; that there is a source in
> America for everything we think or do; that morals affect the food
> and food the bone, and that, in fine, we have no conception at all of
> what is meant by moral, since we recognize no ground our own—
> and that this rudeness rests all upon the unstudied character of our
> beginnings; and that if we will not pay heed to our own affairs, we
> are nothing but an unconscious porkyard and oilhole for those, more
> able, who will fasten themselves upon us. And that we have no de-
> fense, lacking intelligent investigation of the changes worked upon
> the early comers here, to the New World, the books, the records,
> no defense save brute isolation, prohibitions, walls, ships, fortresses
> —and all the asininities of ignorant fear that forbids us to protect
> a doubtful freedom by employing it. That unless everything that is,
> proclaim a ground on which it stand, it has no worth; and that what
> has been morally, aesthetically worth while in America has rested
> upon peculiar and discoverable ground. But they think they get it out
> of the air or the rivers, or from the Grand Banks or wherever it may
> be, instead of by word of mouth or from records contained for us in
> books—and that, aesthetically, morally we are deformed unless we
> read. (109)

Williams unequivocally stresses the necessity of paying heed to
"the unstudied character" of our verbal beginnings. Only by "intelligent investigation" of the original writings of American history, "the
books, the records," Williams asserts, can we come to recognize "that

what we are has its origins in what *the nation* in the past has been."
For Williams, a history of America must be, in part, a history of writing in America, a study of the ways in which language has been used
to shape our sense of the place and its possibilities. Indeed, *In the
American Grain* is structured to make us look at the roots of our culture
in the writings of early Americans, to force us to read such historical
documents in a manner that conventional approaches to history have
failed to provide. Rather than attempting to make history a narrative
of words merely written *about* the past by a historian, Williams bases
history upon the words of those who first struggled to define life in
the New World. In *In the American Grain*, history thus becomes not a
matter of events, but a matter of language as itself an event. And Williams' book stands not just as a study of historical sources, but also
as an exploration of the ways in which historical knowledge has been
and can be created in America.

Williams thoroughly rejects the conventional historical practice of
attempting to exhume the "true" story of the past. That approach to
knowing presumes that knowledge lies elsewhere, that one must go in
search of knowledge as of a missing object. The search for that object
was exactly what Williams decried in the structure of institutionalized
education, saying that "our schools are based on the principle of a confused mass striving for the unseen summit of a topless cone—and that
alone real" (EK, 50). In his 1939 letter to Gregory, Williams said that
he had written *In the American Grain* as a way of knowing history outside the practices of the institution: "Nothing in the school histories
interested me, so I decided as far as possible to go to whatever source
material I could get at and start my own valuations there: to establish
myself from my own reading, in my own way, in the locality which
by birthright had become my own" (SL, 185). Williams' own way of
reading and knowing history is not solely a matter of geographic locality—it is more insistently one of the locus of self. He structured his
own epistemological principles and pedagogical practices upon the
primacy of the presence of the knower. The very process of writing
In the American Grain helped Williams shape these ideas, and he gave
them an explicit theoretical formulation shortly thereafter (1928–30) in
his book on American education, *The Embodiment of Knowledge* (which
remained unpublished, along with five "philosophical" essays of circa
1915, until 1974).

In *The Embodiment of Knowledge* Williams clearly states what should
already be apparent from a reading of *In the American Grain*: against
the authority of the institution and the sanction of *auctoritas* Williams

posits the individual knower. One does not go in search of the domain
of knowledge, but through the locus of self generates a body of knowledge within one's own body. The act of knowing is literally a process
of incorporation, of embodying. This primacy of the individual over
an exterior authority constitutes "the characteristic American *position* of the intelligence—the pioneer turn of mind." It is opposed by
what Williams calls the characteristic ideology of the academy: "European medieval aspiration toward a peak, aristocratic striving" for the
summit of the "topless cone." The labels *American* and *European* do
not mark any strict geographic reference, but more accurately point
toward two distinct historical modes of knowing: the modern and the
traditional. Geography and history, however, are twin eyes for Williams, often synonymous in his epistemology, and he has stated that
the westward "time-drift" of history has both favored America for
modernist thinking and "brought our culture pattern, what we call
America, to the fore."[3]

Williams, nonetheless, charged the educational system in America
with plodding along according to the old medieval masterbeat of
Europe. The result was that Americans had been distanced from any
sense of immediacy with their own history. As Williams tells Larbaud,
"Americans have lost the sense . . . that what we are has its origin
in what the nation in the past has been." The academy, in fact, was
doubly to blame in that regard, for not only had it failed to make
history available as "a useful body of knowledge made to serve the individual who is *primary*" (EK, 9), but it had neglected to equip Americans with the intellectual tools to possess that body of knowledge for
themselves. Williams' declamations against this state of affairs repeatedly surface in *In the American Grain*: "We are blind asses, with our
whole history unread before us and helpless if we read it," he writes
in "Jacataqua." "Nothing noticed. Nothing taught in the academies.
You'd think that THAT would force us into some immediacy. NEVER"
(179). And in an earlier chapter he cries, "History, history! We fools,
what do we know or care?" (39).

The Rasles chapter, too, is punctuated with such outbursts. "Why
does one not hear Americans speak more often of these important things?" asks Larbaud after Williams' first prolonged discourse
upon the Puritans—a speech of nearly three pages that touches upon
Mather's account of the *Mayflower* pilgrims' first days on shore and
the captivity of Hannah Swarton in the *Magnalia* as well as George
Bishop's book about the Puritans' violent abuses of the Quakers, *New
England Judged by the Spirit of the Lord*. "Because the fools do not believe
that they have sprung from anything: bone, thought, and action," re-

plies Williams. "They will not see that what they are is growing on these roots. They will not look. They float without question. Their history is to them an enigma" (113).

Williams emphatically tells Larbaud that "we are deformed unless we read" and study "the changes worked upon the early comers here, to the New World, the books, the records." Yet it is not enough simply to read. By merely reading without writing, Williams warns in *The Embodiment of Knowledge*, we enter the trap of conventional education and enslave ourselves to a chimerical goal by attempting to contain an endless field of words:

> Why not avoid writing and read? For the wisdom of the ages is inaccessible. Mountains of dead words, cemeteries of words befog the mind. Now another book. It cannot be helped. The conviction that fills the whole body of a man is nearer to him than all the books that have ever been written. And these other books, the great philosophies, the endless treatises of science, the books of religions and the lives of other men—the biographies, the histories—what are they? They are part of the very oppressive, stupid, aimless, ignorant world which has driven him to shelter, to prison within himself, to defeat from which he must escape. HE must escape, weak, comparatively unlettered, by himself. Then, when he is whole and only then will the wisdom of the ages be decipherable. (EK, 105)

Writing is the only means of escape from the "cemeteries of words" that can "befog the mind," for it is writing that gives reading a sense of purpose. Writing, says Williams, enables one "to strike straight to the core of his inner self, by words" (EK, 105)—writing forces the self into clarity and thus brings reading into clarity through the locus of self: "Write. It is surely a deed, as much as digging or a gift to a comrade or a beggar. All one needs to learn from the past is that it existed and not to try to convince. It must be put down each for himself, read each for himself. If it is there it will be gathered—or not. It is in that like fruit on a tree, each will use it or not as he wills. It is—in that it is wholly for himself, to himself—impersonal the only impersonal" (EK, 106).

Williams' methodology suspends all questions of history's objective existence. There is no innate story or form in the past that one must come to know and in pursuit of which one will of necessity become lost among "mountains of dead words," among "cemeteries of words." The library, as Williams suggests in *Paterson*, can become a prison for the dead as well as the living. Words breed words as "Texts mount and complicate themselves, lead to further texts and those to synopses, digests and emendations" (P, 130). Yet it is only the sharp edges of the word itself that can cleave through the mass, the word of the individual who gathers the past "like fruit on a tree." Williams presents a practice clear, simple, radical, and anti-institutional—history "must be put down each for himself, read each for himself."

Like Van Wyck Brooks, Williams sought to reinvent American history. In his *Dial* article "On Creating a Usable Past" (1918), Brooks had attempted to find a way beyond the impasse he had come to in his evaluations of American cultural and literary history in *The Wine of the Puritans* (1908) and *America's Coming-of-Age* (1914). In those works he had assessed the blighting legacy of a New England Puritanism that privileged material and commercial profit as a cultural ideal. Such values were inimical to the artist, Brooks claimed, yet he had been unable to assert an alternative cultural heritage from which American writers might draw sustenance. In his *Dial* article, however, Brooks recognized the possibility of creating an alternative past when he recognized that the very cultural values he condemned had largely determined the writing of American history, that "the interpreters of that past experience have put a gloss on it which renders it sterile for the living mind." Brooks, like Williams, declared the past to have "no objective value; it yields only what we are able to look for in it. And what people find in literature corresponds precisely to what they find in life." Thus if the contemporary American writer is bereft of a living literary tradition, Brooks reasoned, it should be the task of the critic to discover, indeed to "invent a usable past."[4]

But Williams was more influenced by Brooks's denunciations of Puritanism than he was by his approach to writing history. *In the American Grain*—like Lawrence's *Studies,* Paul Rosenfeld's *Port of New York,* and Waldo Frank's *Our America*—espouses the general anti-Puritanism that Randolph Bourne and Van Wyck Brooks had made so much a part of the early twentieth century's rhetoric of history.[5] Yet unlike Brooks and the other writers of his period who attempted to refigure American history, Williams was deeply concerned with questions of how one can know the past.[6] More than any of his contemporaries, Williams shared Emerson's profound engagement with the process of creating historical knowledge. Like Emerson, whose essays again and again assert the primacy of self-education, Williams felt the need to investigate the epistemological basis of the act of knowing itself.[7] And in locating the presence of history in the locus of the perceiver, Williams uses much the same formulation that Emerson had in his essay "History": "We are always coming up with the emphatic facts of history in our private experience and verifying them here. All history becomes subjective; in other words there is properly no history, only biography. Every mind must know the whole lesson for itself—must go over the whole ground. What it does not see, what it does not live, it will not know."[8]

Indeed, in *The Embodiment of Knowledge*, Williams seems to have appropriated much from Emerson.[9] Not only is there a decidedly Emersonian cast to Williams' consideration of such topics as Faith and Knowledge, Beauty and Truth in the five "philosophical" essays appended to the end of the book, but Williams' statement that only when one strikes through the mass of written history and takes for oneself in writing what one will take—that only then will one be "whole and only then will the wisdom of the ages be decipherable," echoes very much the spirit in which Emerson's *Nature* opens: "Our age is retrospective. It builds the sepulchres of the fathers. It writes biographies, histories, and criticism. The foregoing generations beheld God and nature face to face; we through their eyes. Why should not we also enjoy an original relation to the universe?"[10] Emerson was acutely aware that any age that viewed its own present through the lenses of the past, through the "eyes" of "foregoing generations," would lack a vital sense of the creative possibilities of the present. It would see itself as having come too late in history to do what previous ages had seemed to do, namely, to create the world around their own present. But that is precisely what each age must do, Emerson asserts, if it is to live at all, and therefore it must discard inherited formulations of the past lest it be enslaved by them. And that warning is exactly what Williams utters when he cautions about the dangers of reading without the concomitant activity of writing: "Each age wishes to enslave the others. Each wishes to succeed. It is very human and completely understandable. It is not even a wish. It is an inevitability. If we read alone we are somehow convinced that we are not quite alive, that we are less than they—who lived before us. It grows and obsesses us. It becomes a philosophy, a cynicism. We feel that something has died but we are not quite sure what. Finally it seems to be the world, the civilization in which we live. Actually we are enslaved. It is necessary to overcome that" (EK, 107).

"Know then that the world exists for you," Emerson states at the conclusion of *Nature*, and he issues the injunction, "Build therefore your own world."[11] For Williams, as for Emerson, the way to build is to write while remaining rooted in the immediacy of the present, to write so that "WE are the center of the writing, each man for himself but at the same time each man for his own age first" (EK, 107). And this need to center all knowledge of history in the immediate fact of one's present existence is what Emerson's "History" says should be the very

purpose of historical investigation: "All inquiry into antiquity, all curiosity respecting the Pyramids, the excavated cities, Stonehenge, the
Ohio Circles, Mexico, Memphis—is the desire to do away with this
wild, savage, and preposterous There or Then, and introduce in its
place the Here and the Now." [12]

"Here not there," Williams ends his chapter on Samuel de Champlain. Both Williams and Emerson had, of necessity, to equate the
immediacy of the now with the here of America against the then and
there of a distant Europe. Williams was as sharply conscious as Emerson that Americans, particularly American artists, continued to see
themselves and their land through the inherited formulations of the
European mind. Art and learning could not thrive in America because
America had missed out on history. Europe possessed the glorious
achievement of history while America was little more than a wilderness newly crisscrossed by railroad tracks. Europe was the cynosure
of all that had shaped civilization while America was a place where
one could, at best, read in the ancient books, if one could find them,
about all one had been born too late and too far away to experience
for oneself.

Williams knew that formulation well. His own friend and sometime mentor Ezra Pound had left, as he wrote in "Hugh Selwyn Mau-
berly," that "half-savage country" where he had been born "out of
date." The perceived distance between America and Europe was not
merely a matter of geography but equally a matter of time. "London
may not be the Paradiso Terrestre," Pound states, "but it is at least
some centuries nearer it than is St. Louis." [13] To combat this view Williams was "seeking to discover," as he says of Poe, "and discovering,
points of firmness by which to STAND and grasp, against the slipping
way they had of holding on his locality" (219). In writing *In the American Grain*, Williams himself would make an effort to stand by peeling
back this "slipping way" by which Americans possessed America,
peeling it like a false skin donned by some of the earliest American
writers from whose verbal formulations he created his text. He would
find it in Mather's statement in *Wonders of the Invisible World* that the
Puritans were forced to suffer "Exile in a squallid, horrid American
Desart" (82). And he would find it in Franklin's statement in *Information to Those Who Would Remove to America* that America was not a place
for arts "more curious than useful," and that those having talents in
the belles-lettres, painting, and statuary had best remain in Europe
because even "the natural geniuses that have arisen in America with
such talents have uniformly quitted that country for Europe, where
they can be more suitably rewarded" (145).

Against *that* American grain both Emerson and Williams sought to enable Americans to see themselves, to know themselves, elsewhere than on the periphery of Europe and history. By locating knowledge within the perceiving self, they rooted the fact of the Now in the immediate Here of America. It is the locus of self that defines the locus of place. It is the gesture that Williams attributes to Poe: "What he wanted was connected with no particular place; therefore it *must* be where he *was*" (220).

Nowhere was the phenomenon of the American's dispossession from self and place more apparent than in Paris in 1924. In the wake of Harold Stearns's somewhat infamous collection of critical scorecards on the destitute nature of American culture in 1921, *Civilization in the United States* (for which Van Wyck Brooks had written the article on "The Literary Life"), there had been a general exodus of American artists to the Paradiso Terrestre of the Left Bank. Williams was there, too, as he tells us at the opening of the Rasles chapter, "while my bronzed faculties strove to right themselves—among scenes and fashions of this world where all the world comes, from time to time, to shed its nerves—after my brutalizing battle of twenty years to hear myself above the boilermakers in and about New York, where I had embarked so precariously upon my literary career" (105). Williams portrays himself as the temporary New World refugee, recovering in Paris from the clang and clatter of a nation busy with commerce. Yet Paris is no Paradiso for Williams: "I felt myself with ardors not released but beaten back, in this center of old-world culture where everyone was tearing his own meat, *warily* conscious of a newcomer, but wholly without inquisitiveness—No wish to know; they were served." What divides Williams from the expatriate crowd is their lack of curiosity. While they were all nervously feeding at the Parisian trough, he was still nourished by inner sources, by "an awakened realization within myself of that resistant core of nature upon which I had so long been driven for support." No matter where, among "the boilermakers in and about New York" or in the "center of old-world culture," Williams remains centered in the fact of self and his own desire to know, "with antennae fully extended" (105–6).

The only one in Paris who sustained his inner appetite was Adrienne Monnier, "who by her insistence brought me one of my best moments among those days of rushing about and talking and seeing." It was not just the chicken à la Adrienne Monnier she offered Williams, "in the purest tradition of the Parisian art," nor the "wines, the delicious flesh, the poets—all the good things of the world . . . we

must learn again to enjoy." These are but metaphors for that which
feeds the desire to know, which promises, like the Brueghel print of
the fish she shows Williams, the disclosure of the unexpected at every
turn: "the great fish, cut open, discharging from its slit belly other fish
and each fish, slit in turn, discharging other smaller fish, and so on
to the smallest. She laughed with glee. Secretly my heart beat high.
Here was invitation" (106–7).

Monnier offered Williams, along with a promise to "take you to *le
desert*," an invitation from Valery Larbaud to come and discuss New
World history. Here is food indeed, and Williams' decision to accept
the surprising summons to the Frenchman's apartment conveys the
sense of relish and gusto with which Williams approaches the prospect of pursuing his American education in Paris: "Already from the
pot of my brain the odors of foods cooking had begun to rise. This
encouraged me to move" (107).

Williams, however, carefully avoids giving us the impression that
he has set the fare for the afternoon with Larbaud. We have already
seen how Williams plays the untutored "block" before this scholar
who supposedly "knows far more of what is written of my world
than I." Williams even experiences a moment of despair over whether
the American past can sustain him. He recognizes, as Larbaud begins to speak on the Spanish and the English in the New World, that
"here is one at least of this world, moving to meet that other which is
straining for release under my confining ribs—not wishing so much
to understand it as to taste, perhaps, its freshness—Its freshness!"—
but Williams quickly adds his doubt, "if it exist!" (108).

"If it exist." Williams once again voices his hesitation in reference
to his own attempts "to try to find—something, a freshness," in "the
early records" (109). Yet, Williams does indeed know, as does the
reader of *In the American Grain*, that a freshness is there. Williams had
found it in Columbus' awestruck description of the flora and fauna on
the beach at San Salvador, in Cortez's amazement over the beauty of
Tenochtitlan, and in De Soto's penetration of the wilderness. Williams'
doubt is actually part of the symbolic mask he adopts, for our benefit
and Larbaud's, to advance his pedagogy more effectively. Rather than
suggesting that he will be working with an already prepared text in
his ensuing discussion with Larbaud, Williams would have us believe
that his part in the dialogue is generated by spontaneous discoveries.
It is Larbaud, much to Williams' "surprise," who brings up Mather's
Magnalia and *India Christiana*—and it is Larbaud who points to the
Puritans as a possible source of enduring freshness in the American

past: "By the strength of religion alone, they surmounted all difficulties in which science has degraded us again today; all things they explain, with clarity and distinction. It is firm, it is solid, it holds the understanding in its true position, not beneath the surface of the facts, where it will drown, but up, fearlessly into a clear air, like science at its best, in a certain few minds. For our taste, it is perhaps a little grotesque, this explanation—but firm. There is vigor there—and by that, a beauty" (110).

Williams pretends to be caught off guard by this unforeseen turn of events, and caught out of his depth as well. But the real unexpected turn comes as Williams immediately proceeds, on the basis of his own chosen evidence from Mather's books, to overturn everything that Larbaud has just said. We are now given the meal that Williams had been cooking in "the pot of my brain" even before he ever arrived at Larbaud's apartment: a lecture on how the Puritans' basis for knowing the New World was narrowly founded upon their biblical typology of America as a realm of darkness inhabited by the Devil's legions, sequestered from the course of history until that fullness of time when the Puritans would come as the sole bearers of light from the Old World to rebuild Jerusalem in the New World.

Though Williams says it was Larbaud who "had read the *India Christiana* with its two silver trumpets crying, 'a joyful sound,'" it is Williams himself who cites the contents of the book to announce his thesis: "'The American savages were men Satan had whished away (via Asia) at the beginning sound of the two silver trumpets calling from the tabernacle, announcing the advent of the gospel.'"[14] "It is the Puritan," Williams pointedly remarks, and after Larbaud's speech on the vigor and beauty of Puritan thought, Williams begins a prolonged reply with another citation from the *India*: "True enough, I said, there is abundant vigor. But to them it was, America, the seat of them that shall think an evil thought'; the savages were men lost in the devil's woods, miserable in their abandonment and more especially, damned" (110).[15]

The impermeable closure of this epistemological formula for knowing the New World and its aboriginal peoples, this "tied tight littleness" of Puritan thought, Williams argues, "explains their admirable courage, close to the miraculous." In language that paraphrases Mather's account in book 1 of the *Magnalia*—itself a paraphrase of William Bradford's account in *Of Plymouth Plantation*—of the *Mayflower* pilgrims' search for a habitation "that first December," Williams cites their endurance in "Going about from place to place, seeking a lodgment, drowned, frozen, awaking to the howls of savages, dawn and the attack, rushing to the boat for their arquebuses, arrows in their hanging coats, at the mercy of chance and the wind." Such things, Williams concedes, "were of the highest order," but were "permitted only by a lack of full knowledge"—for the courage of the Puritans, "had they been gifted with a full knowledge of the New World they had hit upon, could not have stood against the mass of the wilderness; it took the form, then, for the mysterious processes of their implantation here, of a doctrinaire religion, a form, that is to say, fixed—but small" (111).

In no genre of Puritan writing is this epistemological formula more nakedly visible than in the captivity narrative, for the very form of the genre is prescribed by the formula itself. Redeemed captives were expected to interpret their experience as providential punishment, by exile among Satan's hordes in the wilderness, for some particular sin on their part. The recognition of that sin by the captive was as much a part of one's redemption as actual release from the hands of the Indians, and an explicit avowal of the transgression signaled that one was ready to rectify one's ways and return to the Puritan community of the elect. Williams had read Hannah Swarton's captivity narrative in the *Magnalia*, where Mather inserted it as one of the many Demonstrations of Divine Providence to which book 6 is devoted. Swarton confesses that God had chastized her with captivity among the Indians, and later the French "Papists" in Quebec, because "I had left the publick worship and ordinances of God, where I formerly lived, (viz: at Beverley,) to remove to the north part of Casco bay, where there was no church or minister of the gospel; and this we did for large accomodations in the world, thereby exposing our children to be bred ignorantly like Indians, and ourselves to forget what we had formerly been instructed in; and so we turned our backs upon God's ordinances to get this world's goods."[16] In his initial gesture toward Swarton's narrative, Williams draws a sharp analogy between the bordered confines of the Puritan settlements and the circumscribed nature of the Puritans' curiosity about the New World, telling Larbaud that "They could not afford to allow their senses to wander any more than they could allow a member of their company to wander from the precinct of the church, even from Boston to Casco Bay, FOR WORLDLY PROFIT. This their formula condemned. For that Hannah Swanton [*sic*] was *punished* by captivity and TEMPTATION among the Catholics in Quebec" (111).

Against Larbaud's claim that the Puritan mind evinces a "clarity" that approaches "science at its best," Williams argues that an "*inhuman clarity*" results from the Puritans' Procrustean application of biblical rhetoric to structure their world: "The Kingdom of God; the Devil at fault fighting for souls; Christ the Divine sacrifice; the Bible the guide; the Church its apostle. There it is, concise, bare, PURE: blind to every contingency, mashing Indian, child and matron into one *safe* mold" (111, 112). That mold evidences the Puritans' monotextuality, their entire dependence upon one book for the parameters of their thought, and Williams quotes Mather's remark that the library at Alexandria be- came " 'a truly LEARNED library' " only with the addition of the Bible, pointing to the "turn of the word 'learned' " as "the image of their sophistry" (114).

But the most significant use Williams makes of Mather's writings to refute Larbaud's position is a lengthy excerpt, given largely ver- batim with some excisions, from the *Decennium Luctuosom,* the history of King William's War (1690–97) that Mather later tacked on as the final book of the *Magnalia.* The history, written in 1698, follows the stan- dard Puritan formula of providential interpretation of the hostilities between the Puritans and the French-influenced Indian tribes on the northern borders of the colony. God had used the combined Satanic forces of pagan and Papist as a scourge to punish the backsliding and apostate tendencies among the Puritans. Mather himself explicitly de- livers that metaphor at the close of the *Decennium* by using the occasion of the history as an opportunity to move his audience back onto the straight and narrow. After predicting still more woe to come in the immediate future if the colonists did not make efforts to reform their ways, Mather writes, "Reader, I call'd these things *prophecy;* but I wish I be not all this while writing *history*." [17]

From this document Williams selects an episode that plainly re- veals the Puritans' blindness to their own inability to make humane contact with the Indians. In 1696 Bommaseen, a sachem of the Ken- nebecks, a tribe with which the Puritans had been fighting, entered Boston of his own accord under a flag of truce. He was nonetheless incarcerated as soon as the Puritans got their hands on him, so that, as Mather says, "he might, in a close imprisonment there, have time to consider of his treacheries and his cruelties, for which the justice of Heaven had thus delivered him up." [18] But Mather himself came to the prison to assist Bommaseen and his companions in those consider- ations of their errors, later recording his conversation with the sachem in the *Decennium.* Mather's intent in introducing this purported inter- view into his text is obvious. The Puritans, largely due to their view of the Indians as abandoned by God to the Devil, never experienced any appreciable degree of success in proselytizing their faith among them. With the exception of John Eliot, who translated the Bible into Algonquian in 1663, and Daniel Gookin, who served as the Massachu-

setts colony's first superintendent of Indian affairs, the Puritans had
no missionaries who could speak the Indian languages nor any particular desire to bring the Indians into their community of belief. As a
result, the French Jesuits to the north, who not only spoke the Indian
languages but lived among the tribes, had far outstripped the Puritans
both in coverting the Indians to Christianity and in forming friendly
alliances with them. How ironic, then, that Mather should use his
interview with Bommaseen to convince his readers that the Puritans
rather than the French truly sought the salvation of the Indians.

In the space of two pages, Mather attempts to show himself, "with
all the simplicity and sincerity of a good Protestant," lifting the scales
from Bommaseen's eyes regarding the "poison" of the French Papists.
Claiming that Bommaseen requested the "conference with a minister of Boston" because "he was afraid that the French, in the Christian religion which they had taught the Indians, had abused them,"
Mather describes his own part in the interview—as was his practice when referring to his own works and deeds—only in the third
person. Williams begins his close paraphrasing with the minister's
request that the Indians tell him "What of the things taught 'em by
the French appear'd most suspicious to 'em": "Questioned as to what
the French had taught them, the Indian replied, that the French had
taught them that the Lord Jesus Christ was of the French nation; that
his mother, the Virgin Mary, was a French lady; that they were the
English who had murdered him; and that, whereas he rose from the
dead, and ascended into heaven, all who would recommend themselves to his favor must avenge him on the English as far as they
could" (117).

Such things, at any rate, are what the Puritan formula suggested
the French had undoubtedly taught the Indians, and Mather's recitation of those points is meant to reinforce his audience's sense of a
Satanic league between French Catholic and pagan Indian against the
Puritan colony. But Mather's more immediate purpose is to avenge
himself on the missionary successes of the French Jesuits by showing himself to be the superior proselytizer. Rather than undertaking
a direct refutation of the supposed French indoctrination, Mather endeavors to reveal the good the Puritans have to offer the Indians in its
place:

> The minister knowing their custom to use much similitude in their
> talk, looked about for some agreeable object. His eye lit upon a tank-
> ard of drink which happened to be standing on the table. He said:
> Christ has given us a good religion which might be compared to the
> good drink in the cup on the table. If we take that good drink into

our hearts it will do us good and preserve us from death. That God's Book, the Bible, is the cup. The French having the cup of good drink, put poison in it and had made the Indians drink poison liquor, by which they run mad and begin to kill the English.

It was plain that the English had not put poison in it for they had set the cup wide open and invited all men, for they had translated the Bible into the Indian language. But the French had kept the cup shut fast, the Bible in an unknown tongue, the Latin, and so kept their hands upon the eyes of the Indians when they put it to their mouths to drink. (118)

Williams deviates very little from transcribing Mather's words verbatim, for they quite adequately expose their own closure despite Mather's stress on the openness of the Puritan Bible. Mather emphasizes that the Puritans had "translated the Bible into the Indian language" (Eliot's Algonquian version), but he doesn't mention that the Puritan Bible is not open to interpretation. Indeed, it would hardly occur to Mather to mention this point because he hardly sees himself as an interpreter of the Bible but as a reader of its literal truth. There may well be no intervening priest, yet there clearly is an intervening ideology, one that prevents the Puritan from making contact with anything that lies outside his own narrow definition of the world. Williams draws our attention to the absorbing monstrousness of that definition in Mather's description of the displeasure caused him by the Indians' attempts to touch him:

The Indians, in a rapture of admiration and surprise to find one who had put them in the way of obtaining "pardon for their sins" without paying beaver skins for it, fell on their knees, and, taking the minister's hand in theirs, began to kiss it in an extreme show of affection. But he shook them off with marked dislike of their posture.

He would not suffer the contrite Indians to lay their hands upon him, as the Catholic fathers in the north had done, but drew back and told them to address themselves to God alone. (118–19)

Mather's shunning of the Indians, his horror of actually contacting that which the Puritan formula for salvation denied, is the key gesture of Williams' excerpt from the *Decennium:* it is the Puritans' fear of the Other, of life as found in the New World. The Puritans are a source for Williams—"they were themselves the corn I speak of," he tells Larbaud after describing their first December in the New World (111). But "There was a maggot in them. It was their beliefs" (114). And it is on the basis of those beliefs that Williams identifies the Puritans as "an IMMORAL source" (113). Their formula for knowing America, their fear of touching the native and the unfamiliar, Williams argues, persists today "like a relic of some died out tribe whose practices were revolting" (115). Larbaud counters that "the relic will be beautiful," but for Williams the relic is just as dangerous as the thing itself, for it persists as an "abortion of the mind" to which contemporary Americans are as blind as their Puritan forebears—indeed, more dangerous yet, for contemporary Americans do not recognize it as a part of their historical inheritance: "They will not see what they are is growing on these roots." Williams exposes those roots in Mather's books. And, as if anticipating Larbaud's reaction to the passage in which Mather refuses to let Bommaseen touch him, Williams forcefully drives his point home: "Ah, very fine, you say. But it is very ugly—and it is *that* which has persisted: afraid to touch! But being forced to it every day by passion, by necessity—a devil of duplicity has taken possession of us" (119).

The Puritan legacy that "has taken possession of us" is what blocks our ability to take full possession of America. The Puritans came to the New World already carrying their own world with them, an inaccessible New Jerusalem. As a result, Williams tells Larbaud, the Puritans found "no ground to build on, with a ground all blossoming about them—under their noses. Their thesis is a possession of the incomplete" (114). The Puritans could only incompletely possess the New World, for what they publicly and officially allowed themselves to "know" of it disallowed, except as their own antithesis, the existing life and structure of that world: "The Puritan, finding one thing like another in a world destined for blossom only in 'Eternity,' all soul, all 'emptiness' then here, was precluded from SEEING the Indian. They never realized the Indian in the least save as an unformed PURITAN. The *immorality* of such a concept, the inhumanity, the brutalizing effect upon their own minds, on their SPIRITS—they never suspected" (113).

The "brutalizing effect" of their formula is exactly what made Williams respond so vehemently to Larbaud's statement that there is a beauty in their thought. Williams finds nothing of beauty in the inhuman clarity and logic of their views. Nor are the "cruel amputations" (111) of their formula merely Williams' own cognitive metaphor —they are an all-too-bloody part of the historical record. The Puritans not only butchered Indians and French in the name of piety, but physically tortured English deviants as well. And one of the most convincing proofs Williams offers Larbaud of their brutality of deed is not from Mather, but from a New England Quaker who lived among them, George Bishop. Mather had mentioned Bishop in the *Decennium*, citing him as the author of a book complaining of Puritan persecutions of the Quakers. Such stories, Mather endeavored to demonstrate in his chapter "Quakers Encountered" (Article 29 of the *Decennium*), were the work of the Devil. And Mather's view of the Quakers as little better than the Indians is made starkly apparent as he explains his decision to introduce a chapter on Quakers into his history of the Indian wars:

> For the present, then, we have done with the Indians: but while the Indians have been thus molesting us, we have suffered molestations of another sort, from another sort of enemies, which may with very good reason be cast into the same history with them. If the Indians have chosen to prey upon the *frontiers* and *outskirts* of the Province, the Quakers have chosen the very same *frontiers*, and *outskirts* for their more *spiritual assaults*; and finding little *success* elsewhere, they have been laboring *incessantly*, and sometimes not *unsuccessfully*, to enchant and poison the *souls* of poor people, in the very places where the *bodies* and *estates* of the people have presently been devoured by the salvages.[19]

Mather's association of the Quakers with the Indians gives further testimony to the blindness bred by the Puritan formula. It also masks the underlying issue of Puritan hatred of the Quakers because they, a nonviolent sect, would not assist the Puritans in their righteous wars against the Indians. Yet Williams quotes for Larbaud the Quakers' own perspective, reciting largely verbatim from Bishop's book to expose the "horrid atrocities" the Puritans committed "in the name of their creed," and to which they themselves remained blind:

> There was a book written at that time attacking them: *New England Judged by the Spirit of the Lord*: it contains a relation of the Quakers in New England, from the time of their first arrival there, in 1656, to the year 1660. Wherein their merciless whippings, chainings, finings, imprisonments, starvings, burnings in the hands, cuttings off of ears and putting to death, with other cruelties, inflicted upon the bodies of innocent men and women only for conscience' sake, are described. And a further relation of the Quakers' cruel and bloody suffering from 1660 to 1665, beginning with the sufferings of one William Leddra, whom they put to death. There is also an appendix attacking Cotton Mather.[20] (112–13)

Larbaud's response to this considerable weight of evidence from the books he has supposedly read marks his complete distance from Williams' method of reading the documents. "What superb beauty!" Larbaud exclaims after the citation from Bishop's book. "As with all histories, it begins with giants—cruel, but enormous, who eat flesh. They were giants" (113). To Larbaud's scholarly understanding, these documents contain the clouds of romance as well as the clarity of science. He seems able to see only an abstract and admirable logic or the

generic patterns of myth—because American history apparently begins like "all histories," Larbaud finds a "superb beauty" there. Yet for
Williams, nothing could be less true. "Against his view I continually
protested," he remarks of Larbaud (115). Williams, in fact, becomes increasingly irritated by Larbaud's detachment: "I began to be impatient
of my friend's cultured tolerance, the beauties he saw." And though
he initially displays the graces of a mannered conversant in his replies
to Larbaud—"True enough, I said, there is abundant vigor"—it is not
long before Williams is responding with "No, no" (113) and "No, no,
no" (116) to the Frenchman's comments.

Williams' reading of the Puritans certainly does follow, as he tells
Larbaud at the outset of the discussion, a "rigid tenet" (110). And
Larbaud himself comments that "I find your interest 'très théorique'"
(115). Indeed, Larbaud asks Williams to distinguish between the Puritanism he attacks and the lives of the actual people of the time: "He
smiled and begged me to distinguish in my mind between the rugged
English pioneers and a theoretic dogma that clung to them unevenly,
doubtful how much any of it was a part of any one of them" (114).
Larbaud implies, and rightly so, that the dogma Williams identifies
should not be used to judge the nature of the individual life. A distinction should be made between the public rhetoric of the Puritans and
their private, individual experiences. Yet that very distinction, Williams tells Larbaud, is just what his study of the Puritans is attempting
to achieve. "But that is it, I answered. That is exactly what I pretend to
do, to separate it out, to isolate it. It is an immorality that IS America.
Here it began. You see the cause. . . . I wish to drag this THING out
by itself to annihilate it" (114–15). Williams stresses that his concern
is only with the theoretic dogma in Mather's books and not the Puritans as individuals, but that he is willing to sacrifice those individuals
to attack the "thing" more directly: "I grant you, I said, the stench of
their narrowing beliefs has been made to cling too closely to the men
of that time, but the more reason then to lift it out, to hold it apart, to
sacrifice *them* if necessary, in order to disentangle this 'thing'" (115).

The crux of the disagreement between the French scholar and the
self-taught American pedagogue fully emerges as Williams discloses
his purpose: to annihilate the Puritan epistemological formula. "That
one cannot do," Larbaud objects. History, he suggests, is the past—
it is what had been done and it cannot be changed. But for Williams
history is not the remote realm of that which was. What Williams has
been endeavoring to show Larbaud is the presence of a form contained in the verbal character of Mather's books. It is not the books
themselves that live, he tells Larbaud, but the form that lives in them

"and there hides, as in a lair from whence it sallies now and then to strike terror through the land." Yet Larbaud seems unable to grasp just how Williams can destroy the thing he has named. "And you would be the St. George?" Larbaud asks, suggesting that the enterprise is impossibly remote and mythical.

Williams, however, is not on the track of some chimerical monster. He insistently gestures toward the books themselves as the ground in which the form is planted. "In these books is its seed" (116). Williams has attempted to isolate that seed by searching out its earliest verbal encodings, and he emphatically states that "I speak only of sources. I wish only to disentangle the obscurities that oppress me, to track them to the root and to uproot them" (116). Williams doesn't speak of destroying history itself—he speaks of a selective destruction of particular historical formulations that continue to exist as fossilized conceptual modes that enslave the present. Yet Larbaud cannot encompass that point. "You wish to uproot history, like those young men of the Sorbonne," he says, and Williams hotly replies, "No, I seek the support of history but I wish to understand it aright, to make it sHOW itself" (116).

That statement is of key import for Williams' attack on the Puritans. Most of us, like Larbaud, are likely to have strong reservations about any endeavor that speaks of annihilating a matter of historical record. Such an enterprise conjures up visions of history books being expurgated by censors who don't want us to see for ourselves, of "objectionable" persons and "incorrect" ideologies being erased from texts. But Williams doesn't intend any literal alterations of what has already been recorded. He seeks "the support of history" for his endeavor, and his desire to destroy not particular forms in the past but their continuing power in the present depends upon his making history "sHOW itself" rather than his ability to erase it. The way to destroy those forms is to recognize them, to see where in past writing they first occur, to see the verbal roots of our inherited modes of thought. Williams' attempt to track the formulations of the Puritans "to the root and to uproot them" essentially becomes his initial working out of the process of removing blockage that he would later recommend writers to follow in his essay "Against the Weather" (1939):

> If, as writers, we are stuck somewhere, along with others, we must go back to the place, if we can, where a blockage may have occurred. We must go back in established writing, as far as necessary, searching out the elements that occur there. We must go to the bottom.
>
> If we suspect that, in past writing, archaic forms give the significance a false cast we are under an obligation to go back to that place

where the falsity clings and whence it works. We must unravel it to the last shred; nothing is more important, nothing must stand in the way and no time that is taken to it could be better spent. We have to dig. For by repeating an early misconception it gains acceptance and may be found running through many, or even all, later work. It has to be rooted out at the site of its first occurrence. (SE, 202)

Just as writers may find themselves trapped by "archaic forms" that have gained acceptance through repetition, so a culture may find itself under the hegemony of inherited formulations that blocks its ability to explore what is new and unfamiliar. The inability to recognize those formulations in the place where they first occur in writing simply reinforces their power to persist. The educational system, Williams felt, had done nothing to reveal such places of occurrence to Americans—indeed, could do nothing because the system itself labored under the archaic forms of European academic models. What Williams is after, above all else, in his lecture on Mather's books is to provide an education that would enable Americans to "see that what they are is growing on these roots." That act of seeing, of self-recognition, is the necessary step to removing the historical blockage of Puritan thought and the obstruction it represents to our passage to the New World.

Passage to the New World, of course, is what Williams is ultimately seeking. Pedagogically, his discourse on the Puritans has been a preliminary strategy for gaining that passage, his uprooting of the corrupt seed the necessary step for implanting a better growth. "All that will be new in America," Williams announces, "will be anti-Puritan. It will be of another root. It will be from the heart of Rasles, in the north" (120). The introduction of the French Jesuit missionary Père Sebastian Rasles provides an anti-Puritan model of accommodation —yet it also proves to be Williams' trump card in his argument with Larbaud. The artifice behind his initial fear that Larbaud will ask him questions he cannot answer is now laid completely bare. The French scholar who supposedly knows more of what is written of the New World than does Williams has apparently never heard of the writings of his own countryman, Sebastian Rasles, who lived on the northern borders of the Puritan colony at the end of the seventeenth and beginning of the eighteenth centuries.

Several times during his speeches on Mather's books Williams has suggestively gestured toward the French Jesuits, almost as if he wished to test out Larbaud's acquaintance with the subject. In his reference to Hannah Swarton's captivity among the French in Quebec, and in his relation of Mather's conversation with Bommaseen about what the French had taught him, Williams has given Larbaud ample opportunity to seize upon a topic that one might assume him to have at least encountered if not thoroughly examined. Williams even provides Larbaud with clues that become increasingly explicit. At one point Williams passingly remarks that "there was a Frenchman further north, a Jesuit, of different understanding" (114)—and he later states, "There was, to the north, another force, equal to the Puritans but of opposite character, the French Jesuits; two parties with the Indians between them, two sources opposite" (116).

"THIS in Paris," Williams exclaims when he discovers that Larbaud had read Mather's books. But "THIS in Paris" might more accurately suggest Larbaud's surely startled (if unspoken) reaction to the discovery that Williams had read Rasles's letters, and read them in the original French, in that imposingly voluminous collection of relations by the French Jesuits, *Lettres édifantes et curieuses, écrites des Missions étrangères*. Indeed, once Williams plays his trump, introducing Rasles by name and citing his source—"It is from the *Lettres Édifantes* that I am speaking" (120)—Larbaud is all but effectively reduced to silence, managing only two laconic remarks for the remainder of the discussion. The mere fact that Williams is even acquainted with Rasles's writings in the *Lettres édifantes* carries no inconsiderable weight in his argument with Larbaud, for Williams shows himself to be something of a pioneer in investigating a "source not reckoned with" by most historians writing in English.

The relative obscurity of Rasles has much to do with the inability of the contemporary Puritan writers to reckon with the qualitites of the man at all. Mather had made but one reference to Rasles, and that not by name, complaining in the *Decennium* of the Jesuit "at Narridgaway" who allegedly continued to incite the Indians to attack Puritan settlements after France and England had formally agreed to a cessation of hostilities with the peace at Ryswick in 1696. And Samuel Penhallow, in his *History of the Wars of New England with the Eastern Indians* (1726), had pictured Rasles as nothing more than a cowardly interloper against the Puritans' territorial claims in Maine. Such estimates were left to stand unchallenged as Rasles virtually vanished from histories of the period until Convers Francis' *Life of Rale* (1845) and Parkman's chapter on Rasles in *A Half-Century of Conflict*.[21] But the lack of a more widespread interest in Rasles's life also has much to do with the long inaccessibility in English of the work that contains the man's own words, the *Lettres édifantes*.

The nature of this document, which is still not fully translated into

English, is not without relevance here. The *Lettres édifantes*, a collection of relations by French Jesuit missionaries who served from China to the New World during the seventeenth and eighteenth centuries, began as a publishing venture in Paris in 1702, when the initial volume appeared under the editorship of Père Charles le Gobien, secretary of foreign missions. Nearly seventy-five years later, with the publication of its thirty-fourth volume in 1776, the project came to an end, having survived not only the death of le Gobien and several subsequent editors, but frequent hiatuses in the supply of letters coming back to Paris from the Jesuits in the field. No volumes, for example, were published from 1743 to 1749 because England and France were at war, and the ships carrying reports from the Jesuits were often captured by the English. This fact points to another noteworthy feature of the *Lettres édifantes*: since letters were printed as they arrived in Paris rather than arranged according to chronology or region, unavoidable delays in communications gave a haphazard structure to the whole collection. The two lengthy letters by Rasles, though written but a year apart, appear in two different volumes—his letter of 1722 in volume 17, printed in 1726, his letter of 1723 in volume 23, printed in 1737. Not until after the project was finally completed in 1776 was a more wieldly arrangement of the materials made by yet another editor, Y. M. M. de Querbeuf, who compressed the work into twenty-eight volumes and grouped the letters by region for the Paris printing of 1780–83.[22]

Even with this new edition available, complete sets of the *Lettres édifantes* were rare in America well into the nineteenth century. And for English readers Rasles's letters might have remained lost within the bibliographical density of the collection a good deal longer had not the Reverend William Ingraham Kip purchased a complete set of the *Lettres édifantes* from a Paris bookseller in 1844. Kip translated, along with several other relations, both Rasles's letters in his *The Early Jesuit Missions in North America* (1845), and included as well a brief report by Père de la Chasse, Father Superior of the French missions in New France, that details Rasles's death at the hands of the English force that attacked his village in October of 1724.[23] The only other English translation of the three documents pertaining to Rasles to appear since that time occurs in Reuben Thwaites's seventy-two volume collection *The Jesuit Relations and Allied Documents: Travels and Explorations of the Jesuit Missionaries in New France, 1610–1791*, which includes a number of texts from the *Lettres édifantes* and offers, on facing pages, the original relations (in French, Latin, and Italian) and an English translation.[24]

Kip and Thwaites were the only possible sources in which Williams could have had access to Rasles's writings in English. But remarkably, he used neither one. Remarkably, because in every other instance in which he had a choice to rely on an English translation or to go it alone in an original language with which he was somewhat familiar—the Spanish in the case of Cortez's letters, the French in the case of Champlain's relations—Williams chose to work with an English translation. "Père Sebastian Rasles" is the only chapter in the history to make significant use of a non-English text. In his choice of source editions for *In the American Grain,* Williams otherwise shows himself to have consistently preferred more recent reprintings and translations, accompanied with such textual apparatus as an editor's introduction and explanatory notes. Why, then, did Williams forgo these things with Rasles and delve without guidance into the complicated world of the *Lettres édifantes*?

Williams may have wanted to get as close as possible to Rasles's own words without the use of any interpretive intermediary, just as Rasles had drawn as close as possible to the languages of the Indians, nakedly immersing himself in the peculiar tongues of the tribes among whom he served. In his two letters Rasles includes specimens of these languages—Huron, Algonquian, Illinois, and Abnaki, the later of which he spoke fluently, having lived thirty-three of his thirty-five years in the New World among the Abnakis in Maine. (He had been working for many years on a dictionary of the Abnaki language—the manuscript was seized by the Puritans in their raid on the Abnaki village at present-day Norridgewock in January 1722.)[25] Rasles was open to embodying the unfamiliar, to letting it penetrate his own language rather than fearfully seeking to force the Indians into a tightly bound verbal formula.

In his discussion of Rasles's letters, Williams focuses on the Jesuit's responsiveness to the Indian languages as symbolic of his "close embrace of native things." "For everything," says Williams, "his fine sense, blossoming, thriving, opening, reviving—not shutting out—was tuned. He speaks of his struggles with their language, its peculiar beauties, '*je ne sais quoi d'énergique,*' he cited its tempo, the form of its genius with gusto, with admiration, with generosity" (121).[26] The vigor and beauty Larbaud had argued was present in Mather's writing is supplanted by the vigor and beauty Williams shows to be present in Rasles's appreciation of Indian speech. Rasles did not bring his world with him across the Atlantic as the Puritans did, but gave himself to the unfamiliar to learn, slowly and with difficulty, its unique conceptual lexicon: "He tells of how they laughed at his early attempts at the language. Failing to catch certain gutturals at first, he pronounced but half the words. He speaks of the comparative beauty of the Huron tongue" (123).[27] Rasles did not demand that the Indians learn French

—he demanded of himself that he learn the language of place, *"qui est tout-à-fait différent du génie & du tour de nos langues d'Europe."* [28] Rasles became a master of the highly developed Indian art of oratory, and Williams quotes, in his own translation, one of the several examples of this art that Rasles provides as he relates the reply of an Abnaki speaker to a party of English that had come to sue the Abnakis to remain neutral if war were to break out between France and England: "Know that the Frenchman is my brother, we have the same prayer, he and I, and we live in the same cabin of two fires. If I see you come into the cabin near the fire of my brother, I watch you from my mat. If I see that you carry a hatchet, I would think, what does this Englishman want to do with that hatchet? I get up from my mat to consider what you will do. If he raise the hatchet to strike my brother, I will run to help him" (126).[29]

Rasles learned through these patterns of speech to listen to the voice of the Other. Indeed, for Williams, the act of listening defines Rasles's characteristic posture in relation to the Indians. And Rasles himself reveals that posture as Williams tells of the tribe's seasonal migration to the coast to gather fish after the August corn was harvested:

> it was the habit of the Indians to go to the seashore. It was always, says Rasles, the same formula. He knew what was about to happen. They would gather about their spiritual counselor and offer him a speech, saying that the corn was low, that the tribe must have food and that they begged him to come with them to the shore that they might not be deprived of his spiritual comfort while they were gone. Always he answered with the one word,—
> *Kekiberba* (I am listening, my children).
> When all cried together, *8ri8rie!* (We thank you). (Note, the figure 8 is used by Rasles in his alphabet of the Abnaki language to signify the unique guttural sound characteristic of the Indian dialects.) Then they would break camp. Leaving the church he had built, he would take up his altar of a pine board with him and all would set out upon the trail.[30] (124)

This passage, which Williams renders in English and Abnaki from Rasles's own words, marks a diametric opposition to Mather's description of his conference with Bommaseen. Mather believed he could learn nothing from the Indians, that they had to learn from him. Appropriately, Mather gives Bommaseen his instruction while the sachem is incarcerated, for Bommaseen is imprisoned within Mather's definitions of him from the start, and this "instruction" is more properly a destruction of the man's native talents. Rasles, however, provides an image of a far different type of American education, one in which the Indians instruct a European. By attentively studying "the habit of the Indians"—their speech, their manner of address, their mode of living—Rasles has learned a "formula" that lifts into expression the newness that the Puritans denied, for it is a formula he receives from the Indians themselves: *Kekiberba*—"I am listening, my children." Rasles reveals the basis of his education in the very terms of the new, for he has been listening ever since he set foot upon the New World, listening to its cry, "*8ri8rie!* (We thank you)," gentle as the heart of the forest where he lived and died.

The Indians thank Rasles not for what he gives them but for his receptivity to them—that is his gift. *8ri8rie!*—the word symbolically attests to Rasles's sensitivity to what is strange and difficult in the Indians, for he has heard that which no known alphabet of the European mind can transliterate or contain. Williams parenthetically interjects Rasles's own note, given earlier in the same letter, explaining the relation between the signifier 8 and "the unique guttural sound" that the priest had such difficulty in learning. Williams thus draws our attention to Rasles's incorporation of the New World on the level not just of the word but, more importantly, of speech, of a truly American speech living in the breath, the mere sound rattling in the throat. It is this verbal embodiment of the New World that establishes Rasles as a moral source for Williams, because Rasles expresses the New World as found by conjugating the Indians in his language: "It is *this* to be *moral*: to be *positive*, to be peculiar, to be sure, generous, brave—TO MARRY, to *touch*—to *give* because one HAS, not because one has nothing. And to give to him who HAS, who will join, who will make, who will fertilize, who will be like you yourself: to create, to hybridize, to crosspollenize,—not to sterilize, to draw back, to fear, to dry up, to rot. It is the sun. In Rasles one feels THE INDIAN emerging from within the pod of his isolation from eastern understanding, he is released AN INDIAN. He exists, he is—it is an AFFIRMATION, it is alive" (121).

The "pod" of the Indian's "isolation from eastern understanding" is created by the verbal limits of Europe's established forms of knowing. Rasles cracks those forms "to crosspollenize" and to release the Indian AN INDIAN by releasing himself to learn from the Indian. Rasles, in Williams' hands, becomes a conduit for carrying to us that same "sweet" he drew from the Indians "like honey, TOUCHING them every day" (120). "Reading his letters," Williams tells Larbaud, "it is a river that brings sweet water to us" (121). Rasles gives us the sustaining freshness of the place itself, the place where *he* happened to be.

But food is fact before it is metaphor in early American writing. One must survive in the New World if one is to write about it. In the captivity narrative, especially in its Puritan typology, the experience of hunger and the need to find acceptable food are facts the writer only later gives symbolic resonance. The symbolic treatment of eating in these narratives has much to do with traditional European fears that the captive himself had been potential food for his captors, and that the acceptance of their food—the diet of the Other—would surely be a token that the captive had resigned himself to being symbolically consumed by the Indians. If he ate their food, he would be of them as surely as if they themselves had eaten him—he would become the Other. Yet the captive was forced to it by the exigencies of survival, and one of the most remarkable features of the Puritan captivity narrative surfaces in the redeemed captive's frequent expressions of wonder and bewilderment over how sheer hunger had made the Indian diet, intially rejected as loathsome and disgusting, seem not only palatable but even delicious.

Williams had read of Hannah Swarton's difficulties with food in her captivity narrative in Mather's *Magnalia*. Swarton confesses that a "roasted eel" that was given to her after several days of hunger "seem'd unto me the most savoury food I ever tasted before."[31] And in reading Rasles's letters, Williams noted a parallel preoccupation with the fact of food. He points out that Rasles accepted the Indian diet "with difficulty in some respects at first but in the end with admiration and enthusiasm. '*Ce qui me revolta le plus*,' etc." (122–23). The passage Williams begins to quote here, perhaps suggesting by his "etc." that his students should locate the rest for themselves, reads as follows in the original:

> Ce qui me révolta le plus, lorsque je commençai à vivre avec les Sauvages, ce fut de me voir obligé de prendre avec eux mes repas: rien de plus dégoûtant. Après avoir rempli de viande leur chaudiere, ils la font bouillir tout au plus trois quarts d'heure, après quoi ils la retirent de dessus le feu, ils la servent dans des écuelles d'écorce, & la partagent à tous ceux qui sont dans leur cabane. Chacun mord dans cette viande comme on ferait dans un morceau de pain. Ce spectacle ne me donnait pas beaucoup d'appétit, & ils s'apperçurent bientôt de ma répugnance. *Pourquoi ne manges-tu pas*, me dirent-ils? Je leur répondis que je n'étois point accoutumé à manger ainsi la viande, sans y joindre un peu de pain. *Il faut te vaincre, me répliquerent-ils, cela est-il si difficile à un Patriarche qui sçait prier parfaitement? Nous nous surmontons bien nous autres pour croire ce que nous ne voyons pas.* Alors il n'y a plus à délibérer; il faut bien se faire à leurs manieres & à leurs usages, afin de mériter leur confiance, & de les gagner à Jésus-Christ.[32]

Rasles, like many captives, found it virtually impossible to adjust to the Indians' food and their manner of taking their meals: "*rien de plus dégoûtant.*" Rasles, however, was not a captive, and it is not near starvation that brings him to eat but a desire to adjust to *"leurs manieres et à leurs usages"* to merit the confidence of the Indians and thus convert them to Christianity. Yet to do so, Rasles must conquer himself —*"Il faut te vaincre,"* the Indians tell him. Rasles struggles to become like the Indians in the name of Christ, rather than to resist the Indians and their ways in the name of Christ as the Puritans did. And Williams delivers the metaphor here in terms of food, for Rasles consciously accepts the necessity that he must be symbolically consumed by the Indians, "absorbed in them, LOST in them, swallowed, a hard yeast" (121). But what is most striking is that Williams, in describing the particular hardships Rasles had to accept—especially those of diet —quotes not from the *Lettres édifantes,* but gives instead a very close paraphrase of the opening paragraph of Hannah Swarton's narrative:

> The Indians in Maine at that time were not more than a few thousand, the Abnaki tribe. Their life was hard. Sometimes they had little to eat, often, in certain seasons, nothing. The hardships that Hannah Swanton [*sic*] endured following her captivity, were little more than those of any Indian woman on the march. Speed, speed, or disaster. She must walk or die. The wild world touched them, always, under their cloaks. She tells of her agony, under a heavy load; she crossed swamps on logs, stepping for an hour always from one to two feet from the ground. On this trip they had little to eat for days at a time. Once she had part of a turtle they had killed. Once an Indian gave her a piece of moose liver. Once, on an island in the river with her Indian mistress, she had hailed a passing canoe filled with squaws, who, seeing her condition, gave her a roast eel to feed upon. Whortleberries, roots, and acorns were her fare, "or fish if they could catch any." But this was the life of the savage. It was also his habit, his school. By it he grew round, he grew tough. The wounded were killed. To accept torture with equanimity was a proof of virtue. Skill and courage were revered.
> These things Père Rasles accepted and shared.[33] (122)

It may seem paradoxical that Williams, while charging that the Puritans were "precluded from SEEING the Indian," would use a portion of a Puritan captivity narrative to disclose the details of Rasles's experiences among the Abnakis. Yet Williams has appropriated that very portion of Swarton's narrative that does not conform to the Puritan typological formula. He has essentially located and exploited a structural fault line in the narrative. Swarton's relation opens with a lengthy paragraph that explicitly and graphically tells of her physical struggles for survival among the Indians. With the sole exception of her statement that "my condition was like what the Lord *threat-*

ned the Jews in Ezek. xxiv. 22, 23. We durst not *mourn* or *weep* in
the sight of our enemies, lest we lost our own lives," Swarton initially tells of her experiences in a flat and plain style, without overt
reference to biblical typology. But after this opening paragraph, the
narrative abruptly shifts to a typological mode. For the remainder of
her relation, Swarton heavily interlards her story with biblical quotations designed to illustrate the providential nature of her experience.
Structurally, she imposes a biblical grid to contain her actual lived experience, introducing a rigid and preformulated textual control that
lets through only what is officially permissible for the Puritan to say.
Yet the opening paragraph, like feet sticking out at the end of a bed,
suggests how severely the rest is contained. The tight control exercised over the subsequent narrative permits that paragraph to stand,
as if the control legitimizes the whole and allows the writer to give an
unvarnished account of things that, however intensely experienced,
are not admissible for the Puritan.

In seizing upon this particular section from Swarton's narrative,
Williams has further extracted it from the form in which it is lodged,
freeing it up for his own purpose. This technique of dislodgment is
also to be found in Williams' treatment of other source texts for *In the
American Grain*. Indeed, he uses it again in this very section, appropriating Swarton's words to flesh out Rasles's writing. Citing a passage
in which Rasles describes his travails after he hastily fled a surprise
attack by the English, Williams again incorporates details from the
opening of Swarton's narrative:

> Once when the English would have captured him two of his young
> men came to the chapel-tent in the night and whisked him away. It
> was winter, they had not had time to provide themselves with suffi-
> cient provisions. It was several days to the village. The three suffered
> side by side. They ate the dog that was with them. Then they ate
> their sacks of *loups marins*, boiled at a fire, though Rasles had great
> trouble to swallow his share, *tripes des rocher, excréscences de bois*. They
> ate a certain sort of wood that was cooked and so made partly soft in
> the center,—as Hannah had found and eaten wild pusley at another
> season.[34] (123)

Swarton shared, for a time, the life of the Indians as surely as
Rasles did. But Rasles, unlike Swarton, accepted that life, casting off
the familiar to learn about, to appreciate, and to thrive on whatever
sustenance the New World had to offer. That acceptance makes Rasles,
in turn, food for us, for by not resisting the strangeness and difficulty of the unknown continent, Rasles was able to see the bounty
and abundance of the New World and to convey that bounty to us:

"In the spring the fish come up the river solidly packed, two feet deep —with flesh of the most delicious taste. They gather the fish, eat all they can and dry the rest—that serves them until the corn is ready to harvest. In the spring also, celebrating the Eucharist, Rasles saw the corn planted. In August this was ready to be plucked" (124).[35]

Rasles is able to receive because he allows himself to perceive. Whereas the Puritans allowed themselves to see the New World only within the fixed parameters of their imposed formula, Rasles's openness, his desire to know, exposes to view a richness and abundance to which the Puritans were blind. Their formula itself was their officially sanctioned food, their mode of knowing the New World a perceptual privation in the midst of plenty. Just as the place was to them a horrid and frightening wilderness, the variegated life of the Indian touched them only as "the single horror of his war-whoop terrifying the invader" (124). But Rasles draws sustenance from that which terrified the Puritans most. "He speaks with enthusiasm of the Indian as a fighter," Williams remarks. "He outlines their mode of approach upon a doomed village. —When they have drawn near to the point of attack they say, twenty here, thirty there. To this party that village is given to be *eaten!* It is their term. (He speaks with appreciation of their term)" (127).[36] The Puritans could not see these things because they, like the dispossessed expatriates at the cafes of Paris in 1924, were "wholly without inquisitiveness—No wish to know; they were served." Rasles allowed himself to be served by the New World, and the food he gathered is passed on to us as sustaining metaphor by Williams, who feeds our desire to know.

Williams wrote his chapters for *In the American Grain* in more or less the same chronological order in which they are arranged in the book. When Williams arrived in Paris in January of 1924, his chapter on Raleigh had just come out in the January issue of *Broom,* and when he went to Larbaud's apartment on the twenty-sixth of that month, he was in the midst of composing his "Voyage of the Mayflower," the chapter that directly follows "Sir Walter Raleigh."[37] Larbaud, however, doesn't appear at the actual moment of his occurrence in—or rather concurrence with—the chronology of the history's composition. Williams keeps him waiting in the wings while he finishes with his fulminations against the Puritans' "grotesque designs of violence and despair" (68) in the Mayflower chapter, then he goes on to praise Samuel de Champlain as "a sort of radio distributor sending out sparks to us all" (70) in "The Founding of Quebec," to decry the Puritans' malicious and envious mistreatment of Thomas Morton in

"The May-Pole at Merry Mount," and finally to document the devastatingly violent effects of Puritan dogma in lengthy excerpts from Cotton Mather's record of the witchcraft trials, *Wonders of the Invisible World.* By the time Larbaud enters the history, Williams has thoroughly prepared the ground for his defeat—that is, the topical ground of the French and the English in North America during the seventeenth and early eighteenth centuries. That, of course, is the very ground of "Père Sebastian Rasles," which explicitly gestures back to the preceding four chapters by covering the whole ground from the arrival of the *Mayflower* pilgrims in 1620 to the Puritans' murder of Rasles during a raid on his Abnaki village in 1724.

Though Williams says he was caught off guard by Larbaud at the time of their meeting in Paris, it is Williams who ambushes the Frenchman in their meeting in *In the American Grain,* for the book's structure makes Larbaud's rhetorical stance toward the Puritans seem entirely untenable even before he ever opens his mouth. Williams might have indeed been struck dumb by Larbaud's knowledge of New World history, might have indeed only "stammered a word about admiring something of the Maya culture" on that January afternoon in Paris. And after he returned from the European tour, he quite possibly went back to the New York Public Library and expanded the scope of his research on the early settlement of New England. The Mayflower chapter alone had hardly given Williams an adequate grasp of that history—it had dealt only with the opening pages of Bradford's expansive *Of Plymouth Plantation,* touching only on the actual Atlantic crossing rather than Puritans' experiences with the land. Williams clearly needed to expand that topical ground if he was to refute Larbaud's notion of the Puritan mind being like "science at its best." And the most crushing aspect of this rearguard attack launched *ex post facto* on the Frenchman in Paris is that Williams posits the French themselves as his corrective to the moral deformity of the Puritans.

There is, in fact, much evidence that Williams retrospectively inserted the four chapters following the "Voyage of the Mayflower" into the structure of *In the American Grain,* and that he did so as a consequence of his meeting with Larbaud. The Daniel Boone chapter was the next segment of the book's chronology that Williams turned to work on after he completed the Mayflower chapter during his stay at Villefranche on the French Mediterranean in February of 1924.[38] That "The Discovery of Kentucky" was perhaps intended to follow the "Voyage of the Mayflower" in the book's chronological structure is strongly suggested by the chapter's opening, which explicitly presents Boone as Williams' answer to the Puritans: "There was, thank God, a great voluptuary born to the American settlements against the niggardliness of the damning puritanical tradition; one who by the single logic of his passion, which he rested on the savage life about him, destroyed at its spring that spiritually withering plague" (130). Yet in the final structure of the book, Boone is somewhat preempted by Rasles from his special role as the savagely passionate antidote to "that spiritually withering plague" of "the damning puritanical tradition."

Williams quite frequently fashions bridges between the contiguous chapters of his history. And just as "The Discovery of Kentucky" opens with a gesture back toward the arrival of the Puritans in the New World, near its conclusion the "Voyage of the Mayflower" seems to gesture ahead to the pending geographic jump to the south and Boone's exploration of a more abundant landscape: "If the 'Puritan' in them could have ended with their entry into the New World and the subtle changes of growth at once have started, everything would have been different, but the character of the land was not favorable. They did try to land further south." Or so, at any rate, reads the gesture in the text of the Mayflower chapter that Williams completed at Villefranche and delivered to Ford Maddox Ford's Paris-based *Transatlantic Review*, where it was published in August of that year.[39] But Williams changed the direction of that gesture after he returned from Europe, inserting into the first sentence of the passage a much more explicit interchapter directive: "(See Cotton Mather's 'Wonders of the Invisible World,' the prefatory remarks)" (67). That marker is absent from the 1924 text of the Mayflower chapter, probably because Williams didn't then know that he would be including a chapter based on Mather's record of the witchcraft trials.[40] Williams, in fact, probably didn't know much about the Puritans' writings at all. Larbaud seems to have made him conscious of a gap he needed to fill—a conceptual gap that might have emerged in the structure of the book as a temporal and geographic leap from 1620 Massachusetts to 1769 Kentucky. But that leap is delayed and the temporal ground filled in by four successive chapters that, together with the "Voyage of the Mayflower," prepare the soil for the central thesis of Williams' lecture to Larbaud: "All that will be new in America will be anti-Puritan. It will be of another root. It will be more from the heart of Rasles, in the north."

Williams specifically prepares for Rasles's entry into the history with "The Founding of Quebec," the chapter that immediately follows the "Voyage of the Mayflower." Champlain opens the ground of the New World for the French, not only by founding the city of Quebec, but by quite literally mapping out the contours of "New France, a country almost invented, one might say, out of his single brain" (70). At the same time, Champlain's keen attentiveness to shapes and textures, his "carrying his own head about prying curiously into the wilderness" (73), initiates Williams' search for what he later resoundingly confirms in Rasles—a mode of touching the New World diametrically opposed to the fearful closure of the Puritans. But "The Founding of Quebec" perhaps also prepares for Valery Larbaud's entry into the history, for the chapter takes place as a debate between two contending voices, an argument over how to read the qualities of a man from the documents he has written: "Why cannot I sit here lovingly, quietly and simply thinking of that most delightful man, Champlain, without offending you? Samuel de Champlain, of Brouage, on the Bay of Biscaye, if you remember. His father was an admiral in the navy of Henry of Navarre. Here was a man. Here *is* a man, after my own heart. It is merely in a book? So am I then, merely in a book. You see? Here at least I find the thing I love. I mean here *is* the thing, accurately, my own world, the world in which I myself breathe and walk and live —against that which you present. No, no! I insist. We live in different worlds" (69).

"The Founding of Quebec" opens much like a rehearsal for the dispute in "Père Sebastian Rasles." Williams' animated exclamations —"No, no! I insist. We live in different worlds"—sound exactly like the vociferations that punctuate his lecture to Larbaud. Williams indeed seems to be practicing at how to hush his disputant, for the "you" he addresses here is not allowed to get a word in edgewise, but kept totally speechless by Williams' anticipations of any objections. "See if I am not right," he challenges at one point, and "Do not mistake me though," he cautions at another (69, 72). This silent and silenced "you" is, however, finally allowed to speak at the end of the chapter, and the "I" who has dominated the conversation now becomes the silent party. The positions of speaker and listener are suddenly reversed. Nor is that the only unexpected turnabout, for the voice that speaks at the end of "The Founding of Quebec" catches us completely off guard:

(His friend replies)
To hell with all that: collecting pictures for France—or science—or art! What for the New World? No. I know what you mean. A spirit of resignation. Literature. Books—a library. Good night, then. That's not you. You!
It is why France never succeeded here. It is the Latin, or Gaelic or Celtic sense of historic continuity. Let it go back, Roman, Greek, Phoenician, Egyptian, Arab—Jew; let it go back with roots in every culture of the world. Chinese. It is the weakness of you French—

planting a drop of your precious blood in outlandish veins, in the wilderness and fancying that that addition makes them French—that by this the wilderness is converted! civilized, a new link in the chain. Never. Great as your desire may be. (73–74)

It had seemed that the primary speaker had voiced an American's point of view, finding in Champlain's aesthetic responsiveness to the New World a manifestation of "my own world, the world in which I myself breathe and walk and live—against that which you present." And it had seemed that the "friend" who would reply at the end would have logically been a Frenchman—indeed, perhaps a prototype for the voice of Larbaud, the voice of a cultured scholar who would temper the primary speaker's embrace of Champlain as "a man after my own heart" with a more detached view. But paradoxically, the voice that replies is yet even more savagely American, undercutting the French posturing of the primary speaker, accusing him of having uttered too sophisticated an appreciation of Champlain's qualities, castigating him for displaying "the weakness of you French," for imagining that "a drop of your precious blood" civilizes the wilderness and links it to a great chain of "historic continuity" reaching far back "with roots in every culture of the world."

"The Founding of Quebec" may well be Williams' rehearsal of the strategies by which he appropriates Larbaud to create history. Beneath the masks of "I" and "you," Williams performs a game of vocal posturing, of juggling the verbal positions he so deftly employs to surprise Larbaud in staging the events of their afternoon together in Paris. "That's not you. You!"—Williams unmasks his own posturing in the Champlain chapter. Indeed, he makes no attempt to conceal his artifices, plainly exposing them to view. If Champlain is "merely in a book," declares the primary voice, "So am I, then, merely in a book. You see?" The very act of verbal representation is a kind of dramatic masquerade, Williams suggests, and he even discloses to us his dressing room in the anecdote about Machiavelli that follows the chapter's opening paragraph: "There is a place among the works of Machiavelli where he says that coming home at evening from the fields dusty and tired out he doffs his outdoor clothes, dresses himself for a new part and entering his study becomes a king. It is not too rare a feeling, but at least I understand it" (69). Williams certainly does understand that Machiavellian feeling, and he exploits it to play at voicing the many parts that structure the book, to adopt the numerous disguises by which he enacts the history.

Valery Larbaud could not but enter Williams' history without becoming part of Williams' art. And the same is true not just of Larbaud,

but of the French in general in *In the American Grain*—they fulfill a
very particular role for Williams, providing an anti-Puritan model of
accommodation, and then vanish from the scene. Indeed, no sooner
have the French made their appearance in the history in "The Founding of Quebec," than Williams points to their departure, mentioning
"why France never succeeded here." And even Sebastian Rasles, despite the marvelous resonances Williams sounds from his letters, is
more or less dismissed even before Williams concludes the chapter
named after him. "Père Rasles was, of course, a good man," Williams
tells Larbaud to wrap up the lecture:

> Let it be said that all he did was due to that, as Eliot was a good man
> on the other side. Let it be acknowledged that much the Puritans
> complained of in the Jesuits was justified. And let us say that much
> that Père Rasles might have said against the Puritan-English was also
> true.
>   So one thing cancels the other. A good man is a good man.
>   This leaves two things, two flaming doctrines. As contrasting in-
> fluences, I said, in shaping the aesthetic and the moral fiber of the
> growing race they must be weighed (not for themselves) the Catho-
> lic and Protestant, the qualitites each one has lent in forming our
> morale. (127–28)

Williams unexpectedly brings on John Eliot to "cancel" the discussion of Rasles's personal qualities, claiming "A good man is a good
man," so that he can end the lecture by opposing "two flaming doc-
trines," the Catholic and the Protestant. Williams' call for a "Catholic
America" at the end of the Rasles chapter, his declaration of America
as "the greatest proselytizing ground for the Catholic in the world
today" (129)—issued as it was in full knowledge of life in Calvin
Coolidge's prosperous Protestant nation—is one of Williams' most audacious bits of posturing in the whole book. But Williams will play
almost any part to tease us out beyond the fence lines of an all-too-
settled America.

Larbaud got swept up in that purpose, impressed into the service
of Williams' peculiar historical pedagogy. Although he knew Williams
was writing a series of pieces on New World history, little did Larbaud
imagine, on that afternoon he summoned the American to his Paris
apartment, that Williams would put him into the history itself, essentially turning him into a kind of ventriloquist's dummy that opens his
mouth only to prompt the main act. Larbaud, needless to say, was
none too pleased with that treatment. Williams sent him a copy of
In the American Grain when it was finally finished, but Larbaud never
replied.[41] Larbaud, in fact, even though he had written glowingly of

Williams' earlier work, never wrote another word on Williams.[42] For his part, Williams became equally silent in return. He completely omitted any mention of Larbaud from his *Autobiography*, which otherwise generously details his Parisian stay of 1924. Indeed, Williams seems to have done the very thing that purportedly shocked Larbaud during their conversation in the Rasles chapter—he uprooted him from history. When Vivienne Koch, the author of the first book-length critical study on Williams, asked him about his relationship with the Frenchman, Williams flatly denied ever having met anyone named Valery Larbaud.[43]

NOTES

1. I am indebted to Paul Mariani for providing me with excerpts from Williams' unpublished European diary pertaining to Valery Larbaud, as well as to the composition of *In the American Grain*. Concerning his meeting with Larbaud on January 26, Williams writes, "Larbeau [sic] charming; talked french, told me of interest in the way the Spanish colonized America on a grand scale. Poe, Whitman (predigeus) [sic], Cotton Mather."

2. See Serge Fauchereau's "Valery Larbaud et William Carlos Williams," *Critique* 27 (Juillet 1971): 627–34, for a discussion of Larbaud's critical appreciation of Williams' early work.

3. William Carlos Williams, "The American Spirit in Art," in *Proceedings of the American Academy of Arts and Letters and the National Institute of Arts and Letters*, 2d ser., no. 2 (1952): 51.

4. Van Wyck Brooks, "On Creating a Usable Past," *Dial* 64 (11 Apr. 1918): 337, 338, 339.

5. A number of critics have dismissed Williams' treatment of the Puritans in *In the American Grain*, suggesting that Williams merely espouses the maimed view he acquired from the age of Mencken and Brooks in which the repressiveness of the Puritans was widely attacked as the root of the nation's evils. See, for example, Ernest Earnest, *The Single Vision: The Alienation of American Intellectuals* (New York: New York University Press, 1970), 22–55. Even so professed an admirer of *In the American Grain* as Horace Gregory warns potential readers in his introduction that Williams' treatment of the Puritans is one of the book's flaws, stating that "Dr. Williams' choice of quotation from Cotton Mather echoes the usual cry against the Puritan without revealing the full character of Mather's genius" (xix). Yet Gregory and others have failed to note that Williams shows far more concern with the actual writings of the Puritans than his contemporaries, quoting from Cotton Mather's *India Christiana*, the *Magnalia Christi Americana*, the *Decennium Luctuosom*, and *Wonders of the Invisible World*, as well as from William Bradford's account of the Mayflower group in *Of Plymouth Plantation*.

6. Sherman Paul, in his introductory essay to Rosenfeld's *Port of New York* (Urbana: University of Illinois Press, 1966), discusses the cultural "myth"

that animated these writers, remarking of Brooks and Frank in particular that they "were in fact psychologists rather than historians, and their account of America is more rewarding as psychology than it is as history" (xli). For an overview of the issues involved in the debate over historical "impressionism" in early twentieth-century America, see Frederick J. Hoffman's *The Twenties: American Writing in the Postwar Decade* (New York: Viking Press, 1955), 131–39. Also helpful as background to the period's concern with reevaluations of the American past are Richard Ruland's *The Rediscovery of American Literature: Premises of Critical Taste, 1900–1940* (Cambridge: Harvard University Press, 1967), and Howard Mumford Jones's chapter "A Usable Past," in his *Theory of American Literature* (Ithaca, N.Y.: Cornell University Press, 1948).

7. Williams, however, didn't view himself as a disciple of Emerson—at least not when he turned his mind toward writing *In the American Grain*. When he urged, "Let us learn the essentials of the American situation" toward the end of *The Great American Novel* in 1921, he specifically discounted Emerson's work as a significant part of the American cultural landscape: "We care nothing at all for the complacent Concordites? We can look at that imitative phase with its erudite Holmeses, Thoreaus, and Emersons. With one word we can damn it: England" (211). Williams' failure to distinguish Thoreau and Emerson from Holmes perhaps was the unfortunate result of a skewed historical perspective Williams had received from Brooks. Yet thirty years later in 1951 Williams had completely reversed his position—or rather Emerson's position with respect to Williams' view of America. In "The American Spirit in Art" Williams approvingly quotes Emerson on the importance of forming a national literature, remarking, "to our shame we have never adequately heeded his words" (9). In his 1934 essay "The American Background," Williams positions himself between these two extremes of dismissal and approval with regard to Emerson, claiming "his great vigor" was imprisoned by his allegiance to European literary forms and "the style of the essayists of the older culture" (SE, 155).

8. Ralph Waldo Emerson, "History," in *Selected Writings of Emerson*, ed. Donald McQuade (New York: Random House, 1981), 110–11.

9. Sherman Paul, in his review of *The Embodiment of Knowledge*, points out that Williams' "*Five Philosophical Essays* stands in the same relation to his career that *Nature* stands to Emerson's," *Journal of English and Germanic Philology* 75 (Jan.–Apr. 1976): 310.

10. Ralph Waldo Emerson, *Nature* (1836), in *Selected Writings of Emerson*, 3.

11. Emerson, *Nature* (1836), 42.

12. Emerson, "History," 111.

13. Ezra Pound to Isabel W. Pound, Jan. 1914, *The Letters of Ezra Pound, 1907–1941*, ed. D. D. Paige (New York: Harcourt, Brace and Company, 1950), 30. Pound, nonetheless, was a tireless supporter of American letters, whose obsessive concern with the American scene was indeed quickened by his experience of Europe. See in particular *Patria Mia* (1913), in his *Selected Prose, 1909–1965*, ed. William Cookson (New York: New Directions, 1973), 99–141.

14. One might attribute both citations from the *India Christiana* to Lar-

baud rather than Williams—but the second citation, at least, seems to fit only Williams' stance toward the Puritans rather than Larbaud's. Larbaud, furthermore, makes no quotations from any document in subsequent sections of "Père Sebastian Rasles," while Williams quotes extensively from documents. Williams, however, doesn't always acknowledge his sources, nor does he always quote from them precisely. His apparently exact rendering of Mather's words from the *India*, for example, is actually a paraphrase of the numerous proofs Mather offers for how the Indians came to inhabit America, *India Christiana* (Boston: B. Green, 1721), 22–25.

15. Ibid., 24.

16. Cotton Mather, *Magnalia Christi Americana; Or, the Ecclesiastical History of New-England*, 2 vols. (London: T. Parkhurst, 1702; rpt. Hartford: S. Andrus and Son, 1852; rpt. New York: Russell & Russell, 1967), 2: 357–58.

17. Mather, *Magnalia Christi Americana*, 2: 657.

18. Ibid., 628.

19. Ibid., 644.

20. George Bishop, *New-England Judged by the Spirit of the Lord* (London: T. Sowle, 1703), i.

21. Convers Francis, *Life of Rale*, in Jared Sparks, ed., The Library of American Biography, 2d series, vol. 7 (Boston: Little, Brown, 1845). Francis, a Jesuit, gives a somewhat sympathetic reading of Rasles's life, but Parkman, certainly no lover of Indians, tends to portray Rasles in much the same terms as Penhallow, whose testimony he relies on quite heavily, *France and England in North America*, 2 vols. (New York: Library of America, 1983), 2: 477–501.

22. For more extensive bibliographical information on the *Lettres édifantes*, see Reuben Gold Thwaites, ed., *The Jesuit Relations and Allied Documents: Travels and Explorations of the Jesuit Missionaries in New France, 1610–1791*, 73 vols. (Cleveland: Burrows Brothers, 1900), 66: 298–334.

23. William Ingraham Kip, trans., *The Early Jesuit Missions in North America* (Albany: Joel Munsell, 1873), 1–78.

24. Thwaites, 67: 84–119, 132–247.

25. Rasles's *A Dictionary of the Abnaki Language* was published in 1833 by the American Academy of Arts and Sciences (*Memoirs of the American Academy of Arts and Sciences*, new ser., 1) and became Thoreau's main source of information about the Abnaki language. See Henry David Thoreau, *The Maine Woods*, ed. Joseph J. Moldenhauer (Princeton: Princeton University Press, 1972), 401. Thoreau cites a number of words from Rasles's *Dictionary* in the "List of Indian Words" he appends to *The Allegash and East Branch*.

26. Y. M. M. de Querbeuf, ed., *Lettres édifantes et curieuses, écrites des missions etrangeres*, 28 vols. (Paris: J. G. Merigot, 1781), 6: 162. I cite Querbeuf's twenty-eight-volume version of the *Lettres édifantes* as Williams' probable source not only because it is more widely available than the original edition, but because it is the first printing of the work in which Williams could have found both Rasles's letters as well as Père de la Chasse's letter about Rasles's death—details of which Williams uses in his account—arranged together in one volume.

27. Ibid., 161–62.

28. Ibid., 162.

29. Ibid., 204.

30. Ibid., 214–15, 161.

31. Mather, *Magnalia Christi Americana*, 2: 357.

32. *Lettres édifantes*, 6: 159–60. The following translation is from Thwaites: "The thing which most shocked me when I began to live among the Savages, was being obliged to take my meals with them; for nothing could be more revolting. When they have filled their kettle with meat, they boil it, at most, three-quarters of an hour,—after which they take it off the fire, serve it in basins of bark, and distribute it among all the people who are in their cabin. Each one bites into this meat as one would into a piece of bread. This spectacle did not give me much appetite, and they very soon perceived my repugnance. *Why does thou not eat?* said they. I answered that I was not accustomed to eat meat in this manner, without adding to it a little bread. *Thou must conquer thyself*, they replied; *is that a very difficult thing for a Patriarch who thoroughly understands how to pray? We ourselves overcome much, in order to believe that which we do not see.* Then it was no longer a time to deliberate; we must indeed conform to their manners and customs, so as to deserve their confidence and win them to Jesus Christ" (67: 141).

33. Mather, *Magnalia Christi Americana*, 2: 357.

34. *Lettres édifantes*, 6: 219–21.

35. Ibid., 214.

36. Ibid., 205.

37. In his letter of February 21, 1924, to Marianne Moore, written at Villefranche in the south of France less than a month after his meeting with Larbaud, Williams states, "I've been working on 'The Voyage of the *Mayflower*,' which is now finished at last" (SL, 60). According to his European diary, Williams had completed the Mayflower chapter on February 20, the day before writing to Moore.

38. In his diary for February 23, three days after finishing the Mayflower chapter, Williams records that he "Wrote all a.m. on Boone." "The Discovery of Kentucky," in fact, seems to have preoccupied much of Williams' available time for work on *In the American Grain* during the remainder of his European travels. He was still working on the chapter in mid-June while making his return voyage to America on the *S.S. Zeeland*, recording in his diary for June 17, "Got out of my bunk at 3 and 6 a.m. to write on *Boone*. Think I have it mapped now." (See also A, 206, 233.)

39. William Carlos Williams, "Voyage of the Mayflower," *Transatlantic Review* 2 (Aug. 1924): 50.

40. One might argue, of course, that Williams could have left that marker out of the text he gave to Ford's magazine simply because it wouldn't have made any sense to readers. Why would Williams want to direct them to an essay he hadn't yet published? The marker, however, needn't be taken as a reference to something by Williams—it can also function as a historian's bib-

liographical citation, an editorializing reference to Cotton Mather's *Wonders of the Invisible World*. And Williams' own chapter by the same name is, after all, basically a mere copying of what one can find in Mather's own text.

41. Paul Mariani, *William Carlos Williams: A New World Naked* (New York: McGraw-Hill, 1981), 248.

42. Fauchereau notes Larbaud's silence on Williams after 1924 (634), but in the Rasles chapter.

43. Mariani, 222.

3

Textures of Disorder

Valery Larbaud's positing of a dynamic opposition between the English and the Spanish at the outset of the discussion in "Père Sebastian Rasles" might be something more than Williams' own posturing:

> The English appraised the New World too meanly. It was to them a carcass from which to tear pieces for their belly's sake, a colony, a place to despise a little. They gave to it parsimoniously, in a slender Puritan fashion. But the Spaniard gave magnificently, with a generous sweep, wherever he was able. (This tallies with the bounty of the New World, I said to myself.) They sought to make it in truth a New Spain, to build fine cathedrals, to found universities, to establish great estates. For this I like them, he said. They came as from the King himself to transport nobility, learning, refinement thither in one move. (108)

Larbaud's observation on the Spanish "tallies with the bounty of the New World," Williams silently remarks—but it also tallies with the structure of *In the American Grain*. The chapters from the emerging book that Larbaud had read in *Broom* prior to his meeting with Williams were almost all devoted to the Spanish explorations and conquests of the New World. "The Discovery of the Indies," "The Destruction of Tenochtitlan," "The Fountain of Eternal Youth," and "De Soto and the New World"—Williams' four successive chapters on Columbus, Cortez, Ponce de Leon, and De Soto—form one of the major topical grounds of the book: the Spanish in the Caribbean, Mesoamerica, and North America from 1492 to 1542. Larbaud had perhaps thought that Williams would extend that ground in subsequent chapters of

In the American Grain to develop an explicit opposition between this Spanish root and the English Puritans to the north.

Despite the fact that Williams almost seems to brush aside Larbaud's distinction between the Spanish and the English, moving on to use the French as his opposition to the English—and despite the fact that the Spanish make no significant reappearance in the history after the De Soto chapter—the Spanish do serve Williams with a cultural paradigm that runs against the grain of the English scheme of colonization:

> Under the Spanish the sixteenth-century universities, bishoprics and works of a like order, constituted a project diametrically opposed to what the English understood. What they seemed to have in mind was no colony at all, but within the folds of their religious hegemony an extension of Spain herself to the westward. But the difficulties were too great, too unimaginably novel to the grasp of their minds 'for them to succeed.
>
> From geographic, biologic, political and economic causes, the Spanish conception ended in failure, and the slower, colder, more practical plan of lesser scope out of northern Europe prevailed. North America became, in great measure, a colony of England, so to be regarded by the intellect and fashion of the day. (SE, 135–36)

Williams reiterates here, in his essay "The American Background" (1934), essentially the same distinction between the two cultural groups that Larbaud had proposed, explicitly stating an opposition that is implicitly set up in the early chapters of *In the American Grain*. But Williams additionally gives a possible explanation for why the Spanish vanish so suddenly from the book's historical chronology: the Spanish conception "ended in failure." "The American Background," however, makes no attempt to explore the failure of the Spanish in the New World. Rather than investigating the flux of the New World under the contending colonial claims of Spain, England, and France, the essay focuses on the United States of America, the nation established after 1776. And although "The American Background" does recover much of the historical ground of *In the American Grain*—reexamining Franklin, Washington, Boone, Houston, and Poe—the Spanish do not figure in the essay other than as a momentary rhetorical counter to the English to help Williams set up a conceptual grid for discovering manifestations of a native impetus outside the dichotomy of the two colonial positions:

> Alongside all this, nevertheless, an enterprise neither Spanish nor English, nor colonial by any way of speaking save in its difficulty

and poverty of manner, began widely to form, a new reference by which knowledge and understanding would one day readjust themselves to a changing world. It was America itself which put its head up from the start—to thrive in mode of life, in character of institutions, in household equipment, in the speech, though opposed with might and main everywhere from the official party both at home and abroad. Noah Webster spent a life here building the radically subversive thesis which his dictionary represents. But the same force began pushing its way forward in any number of other forms also. Necessity drove it ahead. Unorthodox, it ran beside the politer usages of the day, never, except in the moment of a threatened national catastrophe, the Revolution, to be given a general sanction. (SE, 136)

Even though Williams concedes that "the Revolution would prove anything but a united movement toward self-realization on the part of America" (SE, 137), he takes it as the first decisive marker of an America "which put up its head from the start," and his historical chronology moves forward from that point.[1] But more than half of *In the American Grain* is devoted to the New World prior to 1776. And the chapters on the Spanish alone constitute nearly a fourth of the book's length. No mere rhetorical maneuver as in "The American Background," the Spanish provide Williams with his strongest affirmations of an America "which put up its head from the start." For although the Spanish conception ends in failure, what defeats it is not a complex nexus of "geographic, biologic, political and economic causes," but, more simply and directly, the spirit of the land itself. The Spanish had to embrace the place boldly and physically if they were to make it "an extension of Spain herself to the westward," and their drive to penetrate to the very core of the New World's life is what enables Williams to ground the beginnings of his history so securely upon them. The conquistadors sought to seize the New World by thrusting themselves nakedly into the unknown—and at times they found themselves, like De Soto, nakedly seized by the very thing they sought to possess.

Hernando de Soto had served as an officer under Pizarro in the conquest of Peru, and he had carried back to Spain a sizeable portion of the spoils from the fall of Cuzco. He knew the riches a conquistador could plunder from the New World and he wanted to carve out his own empire. When he heard the news of the failure of Pámfilo de Narváez's expedition into Florida, De Soto saw his golden opportunity. Or so he imagined it to be, for there had long been rumors of a gilded kingdom hidden somewhere in the interior—El Dorado, the Seven

Cities of Cíbola, something richer than Cuzco, something even more magnificient than Tenochtitlan. The Spanish throne granted him the patent for Florida, making him governor of the territory for life. The place was his—if he could subdue it. And he was certain he could, despite the experience of the Narváez expedition. In 1528, Narváez had headed inland from Tampa Bay with three hundred soldiers. Some eight years and several thousand miles later, the survivors of that force emerged near Culiacán, just north of Mexico City, looking for all the world like the Indians they had thought to conquer. They were only four in number.

Alvar Núñez Cabeza de Vaca, second in command to Narváez, was one of them. De Soto tried to induce him to serve as his second in the new expedition into Florida, but Cabeza de Vaca, after his disastrous experience under Narváez, had resolved never again to serve under the command of another. Cabeza de Vaca's knowledge and experience would have been of inestimable help to De Soto. Certainly the narrative he wrote about his amazing odyssey across the continent —simply titled *La Relación,* but now known in English by the perhaps more appropriate title *Adventures in the Unknown Interior of America*— is the greatest story ever told of how to survive in the New World.[2] De Soto, however, told no story, for he didn't survive. After more than three years of circuitous wanderings through barely passable terrain, the expedition that entered Florida in 1539 came out on the Mississippi in lower Arkansas, dazed and without direction.[3] De Soto was lost, swallowed up in the immensity of America's unmapped space. His original force of six hundred had been cut in half by repeated attacks from the Indians, who now had him surrounded on all sides. "The Governor," writes one of the expedition's survivors, "at seeing himself thus surrounded, and nothing coming about according to his expectations, sickened and died."

De Soto's story, that is, the story of his loss, is told by three separate survivors—an anonymous Portuguese, who identifies himself only as a Fidalgo from Elvas; Luis Hernandez de Biedma, the king's factor to the expedition; and Rodrigo Ranjel, De Soto's private secretary. Though each tells his own version of events, there is a significant difference between the kind of writing one finds in Cabeza de Vaca's narrative and the relations of these survivors of the De Soto expedition. Cabeza de Vaca had to write, of necessity, an autobiographical narrative. His subject is not, ultimately, the governor or the troops, for all such things had ceased to exist. He had to write of himself, of his own transformations. But the three writers of the De Soto expedition were not so mercilessly stripped of such conventional subjects. Only half of De Soto's six hundred perished. The rest got away by building boats and floating down to the Gulf of Mexico, the first Europeans to navigate the Mississippi. And when the first governor died, another had already been named. Even though they emerged from their experience wearing animal skins instead of the helmets and breastplates in which they started, there was still something that resembled an army. As a result, there is nothing personal in the writing of the survivors. They remain members of an expedition, impersonal chroniclers of what befell the governor and the soldiers.[4]

Not only does De Soto have no say in the verbal shape of his story, but neither do the writers themselves, finally, for Williams further depersonalizes their narratives, removing for the most part even any occasional references to "us" or "we." He appropriates their voices to create the voice of She, the voice of the spirit of the land that dictates the story they merely report. Relying on the historian's privilege of synoptic vision, Williams uses the inevitable fact of De Soto's end to create a verbal source in the land itself for the disorder that overwhelms the Spaniard's projected schemes of conquest. De Soto does not simply become lost in the wilderness—he is seduced from his path. She panders to his lust for gold and riches to draw him inexorably across her contours and into her center, the Mississippi. His travels and travails become a kind of savage foreplay. And from the very beginning, She knows the end:

> *She*—Courage is strength—and you are vigilant, sagacious, firm besides. But I am beautiful—as "a cane box, called petaca, full of unbored pearls." I am beautiful: a city greater than Cuzco; rocks loaded with gold as a comb with honey. Believe it. You will not dare to cease following me—at Apalachi, at Cutifachiqui, at Mabilla, turning from the sea, facing inland. And in the end you shall receive of me, nothing—save one long caress as of a great river passing forever upon your sweet corse. Balboa lost his eyes on the smile of the Chinese ocean; Cabeça de Vaca lived hard and saw much; Pizarro, Cortez, Coronado—but you, Hernando de Soto, keeping the lead four years in a savage country, against odds, "without fortress or support of any kind," you are mine, Black Jasmine, mine.—[5] (45)

Though De Soto lacks a voice, by creating the voice of She Williams gives De Soto an ear. She speaks directly to him: "you are mine, Black Jasmine, mine." Yet her language strikes his hearing obliquely, insinuating itself into his consciousness through his contact with the landscape. "The course was north and west," says Williams as he points De Soto inland from the coast, "a march of about a hundred leagues—through obscure and intricate parts: native villages in the

swamps, Caliquen, Napateca, Hurripacuxi, Paracoxi, Tocaste, Cale—
outlandish names" (46).[6] But it is She who breathes the seductive
strangeness of those names into De Soto's ear: "*She*—Who will recognize them? None but you. To the rest without definition but to you
each a thing in itself, delicate, pregnant with sudden meanings" (46).
And although her speeches throughout the chapter are discreetly bordered off from the narrative of events provided by the expedition's
chroniclers, her voice is yet immanent in the very textures of those
appropriated narratives, for She determines the course of events.

De Soto needed a guide, someone familiar with the place and its
manifold languages. Cabeza de Vaca would have served that purpose
well, but De Soto did find someone to take his place—Juan Ortiz, an
unexpected fifth survivor from the Narváez expedition. His story is
almost as remarkable as that of Cabeza de Vaca. Taken captive the
moment he set foot in Florida in 1527, Ortiz was condemned to be,
quite literally, barbecued.[7] He was indeed already partly seared when
the lachrymose entreaties of the chief's daughter saved him from the
flames. Like a prototype of Pocahontas, this Indian maiden delivered
Ortiz from death, eventually supplying De Soto with a Spaniard who
was, in a way, also an Indian, and who could interpret the strange
speech of the place. But it isn't some nameless Pocahontas who provides De Soto with Ortiz in "De Soto and the New World." Williams
appropriates all such facts from the historical record as visible tokens
of the New World's designs upon De Soto. Ortiz is transformed into
her interpreter, the instrument by which She conveys her voice to De
Soto. No sooner does he begin his march into the interior than She
greets his advance by thrusting Ortiz into his path: "*She*—It is de
Soto! all goes forward somehow. But I am before you. It is my country. Everything is in accordance with my wish. Eight men start from
a thicket, naked and tattooed, your lancers rush upon them, but one
falls to his knees crying out, 'Do not kill me. I am a Christian! It is
Juan Ortiz, relic of Narvaez' forces, whom I have nursed tenderly for
you these twelve years, teaching him the wild language. Witness my
love. But I shall take him from you when he is most needed' "(46).[8]
    She has taught Ortiz "the wild language" in preparation for De
Soto's coming. He is a gift that symbolizes her duplicity as well as
Williams' own in presenting the events of his source narratives as the
effects of a cause he himself has created. Through Ortiz, She makes
her directions intelligible to De Soto, leading him "to seek Yupaha, of
which a young slave had told them; a country toward the rising sun,
governed by a woman, where there was gold in quantity" (46).[9] Yet

De Soto, of course, is in a country governed by a woman—a country
that is a woman. And when She has finally brought De Soto to her
loins, She strips Ortiz from him like a casing removed from the seed:
"But I shall take him from you when he is most needed." Ironically,
despite his remarkable survival among the Indians in Florida, Ortiz
didn't survive the De Soto expedition. He died near the Mississippi,
less than three months before De Soto himself gave out. From that
bare fact, Williams generates a narrative pattern that runs throughout
his chapter. She supplies De Soto only to strip him—She strips him
only to supply him. It is her way of "making you solitary—ready for
my caresses" (50).

At first She barely sustains De Soto. The Spaniards are reduced
to short rations as they begin to penetrate the country, "starving for a
month at a time, thankful for a little parched corn, not even ripe, the
cob and all being eaten as it was, and the stalk, too, for want of better"
(46).[10] At Apalachi, where the Spaniards spend their first winter, "they
lived with difficulty on game and other stores, such as they could
take from the natives, miserably, as best as they were able" (46).[11] And
when they resume their march in the spring, going in search of the
imaginary province of Yupaha, they are brought to the verge of starvation: "days, weeks, a month—with small food, such want of meat and
salt that oftentimes, in many places, a sick man would say, 'Now, if I
had but a slice of meat, or only a few lumps of salt, I should not thus
die.' But the Indians, skillful with the bow, would get abundance of
deer, turkeys, rabbits and other game" (47).[12] In the midst of a native
abundance, the Spaniards, unfamiliar with the ways of the country,
suffer harsh privation. But it is all part of her plot. The Spaniards are
forced to endure these prolonged periods of hunger so that they will
all the more readily accept the native sustenance She chooses to offer:
"*She*—For you I come severally as envoys from the chief men upon
the road, bearing baskets of mulberries, a honey comb, marten skins
and the hides of deer, and in calabashes the oil of walnuts and bear
fat, drawn like olive oil, clear and of good taste" (48).[13]

The De Soto expedition is reduced to relying on the native foods of
the country, and that dependency ultimately forces the Spaniards to
adopt the native methods of interacting with the country. They must
accept the place on her terms. By the time they reach the Mississippi,
at the beginning of their fourth year in the country, they have "learned
to catch rabbits with Indian snares" (54).[14] In Williams' design, the
New World attempts to initiate De Soto into her tribe by removing
the accoutrements and tools by which he would impose his designs
upon the land. "And if, to survive," She tells De Soto, "you yourself

in the end turned native, this victory is sweetest of all" (51). And food proves simply one of the devices She employs to achieve that end. The provisions She offers "from the chief men upon the road" are actually a decoy to put the Spaniards off guard as they approach Mabilla. "'Unprepared, we believed ourselves on a footing of peace, so much so that some of us, putting our arms in the luggage, had gone without any'" (48).[15] And at Chicaca, the Spaniards are once again offered food under the pretext of friendship: "The Indians, at peace, came frequently with turkeys and rabbits and other food—but secretly they were plotting other matters" (50).[16]

At both Mabilla and Chicaca, the expedition loses the bulk of its armor and weapons as the Indians set fire to both towns after deceiving the Spaniards with an apparently amicable reception.[17] "Thus, to anger you, I have possession of all the baggage, the clothes, pearls and whatever else you have besides lost in the conflagration," She tells De Soto during the battle at Mabilla. And from the fire at Chicaca, the Spaniards emerge virtually stripped, forced by her plot to enter a "new world naked" (SA, 95): "*She*—Naked, armless, acold you draw off, in the morning, to Chicacilla, protecting yourself as best as you can—there to retemper the swords and await what will happen. Some are reduced to straw mats for their only cover, lying now this way, now to the fire, keeping warm as they are able" (50).[18]

But De Soto's nakedness is symbolic in yet other ways. Not only has he been stripped of his European tools of conquest, but also disabused of his European notions of warfare, nakedly initiated into the craft of the country. At the Mississippi, She once again tries to beguile him with an offering of food as the chief of the province presents De Soto "great quantity of fish, and loaves like bricks, made of pulp and plums." This time, however, De Soto is watchful, his senses attuned to the deceptive signals of the environment after his experiences at Mabilla and Chicaca: "Making the gifts had been a pretext, to discover if any harm might be done; but finding the Governor and his people on their guard, the chief began to draw off from the shore, when the crossbowmen, who were in readiness, with loud cries shot at the Indians, and struck down five or six of them" (51–52).[19] That response is exactly what She had hoped to elicit. "Well, done, Spaniard! like an Indian," She replies. De Soto has learned her lessons well, finally mastering the devices of the country as surely as his soldiers do in learning to catch hares with Indian snares. He has come, literally and metaphorically, to a great crossing, the crossing of the Great River. For that She had stripped him—as a European. And for that She will clothe him—as an Indian:

She—Now you are over, you have straddled me, this is my middle.
Left to right, the end is the same. But here in the center I am not
defeated. Go wander. Aquixo, Casqui, Pacaha. Take what you will.
Clothe your men, yourself you will never clothe as I clothe you, in
my own way. They have suffered, they have gone nearly bare. At
Pacaha I have provisioned them in advance.

.   .   .

Shawls, deer skins, lion and bear skins, and many cat skins were
found. Numbers who had been a long time badly covered here
clothed themselves. Of the shawls they made mantles and cassocks.
Of the deer skins were made jerkins, shirts, stockings and shoes; and
from the bear skins they made very good cloaks, such as no water
could get through. They found shields of raw cowhide out of which
armor was made for the horses.[20] (52–53)

The Spaniards who had come as conquerors have symbolically become those they had come to conquer. "Look, then, Soto," She bids
him, "upon this transformed army." His divorce from the Old World
has become irrevocable. "Where is she now, Doña Ysobel, your help-
mate, years since in Cuba?" She asks. With part of the wealth he had
received from the fall of Cuzco, De Soto had paid a generous marriage
pledge for the hand of Ysabel de Bobadilla when he returned to Spain.
Ironically, he had looted the New World to buy a bride from the Old
World, bringing her with him across the Atlantic to Cuba at the start
of the expedition. But now a river has been crossed. De Soto shall
have a new bride: "The chief of Pacaha bestowed on him two of his
sisters telling him that they were tokens of his love, for his remem-
brance, to be his wives. The name of one was Macanoche, that of the
other Mochila. They were symmetrical, tall and full; Macanoche bore
a pleasant expression; in her manners and features appeared the lady;
the other was robust" (53). [21]

She is many. "For you I come severally," She tells De Soto. She
is Tuscaloosa, "tall of person, muscular, lean and symmetrical." She
is Macanoche. She is Mochila. She is the Indians of Aquixo, "painted
with ochre, wearing great bunches of white and other plumes of many
colors" (51). She is large, of multiple disguises. She is the Great River,
so wide that "a man standing on the shore could not be told whether
he were a man or something else, from the far side" (52). She is space,
and She swallows De Soto.

He had no direction to follow, other than to turn inland. The
other conquistadors had sought bordered objectives. Ponce de Leon
was insular, confining his schemes of conquest mainly to Puerto Rico.
Cortez had a well-marked path before him. He marched directly to

Tenochtitlan without wandering from his course. But De Soto faced the enormity of a continent. "Now it is no sea-ringed island," She tells him, "now it is no city in a lake: Come, here is room for search and countersearch" (54). Even though "it was his object to find another treasure like that of Atabalipa, lord of Peru," there was no trail to lead him there. He simply had to plunge into the vastness of the place.

The expedition did indeed trace a circuitous course. And even though Williams presents the Mississippi as De Soto's predestined end, De Soto arrives there only by misdirections and indirections. His efforts at linear progress are continually frustrated by the composition of the landscape: "Crossing a stream after nine last days of forced marching they came out into a pine grove on the far bank. Here all direction was lost. 'He went about for the road and returned to us desperate'" (47).[22] In search of a country rich in gold, De Soto finds himself instead struggling to move through a savage proliferation of the unfamiliar, engulfed in a vertiginous landscape:

> And what? Silences, death, rotting trees; insects "so tnat the sails were black with them and the men laughed in spite of their forlorn condition, to see each others' faces so swollen and out of shape in the morning"; alligators, reptiles, a wild rose "like that of Spain, but with less leaves, because it grew in the woods." Sun, moon, stars, rain, heat, snow; water to the neck for days; blue-butterflies among the green palmetto leaves; grapes and others that grow on vines along the ground; plums of two sorts, vermillion and gray, of the form and size of walnuts, having three or four stones in them; wolves, deer, jackals, rabbits,—.[23] (48)

Williams purposefully creates the dizzying swirl of this landscape so that one image will emerge out of it with startling clarity: the Mississippi. There, as in a vortex, the generative power of the landscape is concentrated. And there She brings De Soto to a halt:

> after struggling seven days through a wilderness having many pondy places with thick forests, they came out upon the Great River.
> He went to look at the river: swift and very deep; the water flowing turbidly, bringing from above many trees and much timber, driven onward by its force. (51)

Williams focuses this initial description of the Mississippi within De Soto's consciousness.[24] De Soto is made witness to the river's strength as soon as he arrives. It is a power he can neither master nor escape. Even though he builds boats to cross the river, his crossing marks his defeat: "this is my middle," She tells him, "here in the center I am not defeated."

Williams invests the latter stages of the expedition's wandering route with a poignant significance. For nearly a year after crossing the Mississippi, De Soto attempted to traverse the country to the west, only to find himself turning back to the river once again, at a loss how to proceed. Williams appropriates that doubling back to suggest that although De Soto crosses the Mississippi, he cannot go beyond it. Not only does the terrain on the western side prove utterly impassable, but with the death of Juan Ortiz, De Soto finds virtually any attempt at movement bewildered:

> without an interpreter, not knowing whither he was traveling, Soto feared to enter the country, lest he might get lost. The death was so great a hindrance to our going, whether on discovery or out of the country, that to learn of the Indians what would have been rendered in four words, it now became necessary to have the whole day; and oftener than otherwise the very opposite was understood to what was asked; so that many times it happened the road traveled one day, or sometimes two or three days would have to be returned over, wandering up and down, lost in the thickets.
> For four days marching was impossible because of the snow. When that ceased to fall, he traveled three days through a desert, a region so low, so full of lakes and bad passages, that at one time, for a whole day, the travel lay through water up to the knees at places, in others to the stirrups; and occasionally, for the distance of a few paces there was swimming. And he came to Tutelpinco, a town untenanted and found to be without maize, seated near a lake that flowed into the river with a great current.[25] (54–55)

De Soto is more than just bogged down and already beginning to sink into the landscape—he is sucked back toward the Mississippi. "Nearer, nearer," She says in response to the excerpt. And De Soto cannot but draw nearer, as if carried by "a great current." Yet it is no longer with a sense of resistance that De Soto approaches. The river, like the voice of She, has insinuated itself into his mind. Williams fixed the initial sighting of the river within De Soto's consciousness in preparation for the moment at which De Soto would see the Mississippi as the one thing to emerge clearly for him out of the vast profusion and confusion of the landscape. Indeed, Williams had already envisioned that moment before he ever began writing "De Soto and the New World." In *The Great American Novel* he had imagined De Soto's discovery of the Mississippi as taking place within the Spaniard's own interior geography: "Here he had confronted the New World in all its mighty significance and something had penetrated his soul so that in the hour of need he had turned to this Mighty River rather than do any other thing. Should it come to the worst he had decided what to do. Out of the tangle around him, out of the mess of his own past the river alone could give him rest. Should he die his body should be given to this last resting place. Into it Europe should pass as into a new world" (GAN, 204). *In the American Grain* achieves that moment with a subtle manipulation of source documents rather than direct pronouncement as Williams inserts the insistently repetitive phrase *The river, the river* into the excerpts that tell of De Soto's resignation of any further efforts to escape the country:

> At Guachoya he sent Juan de Anasco with eight of the cavalry down the river to discover what population might be there and get what knowledge there was of the sea. He was gone eight days and stated, when he got back, that in all that time he could not travel more than fourteen or fifteen leagues, on account of the great bogs that came out of the river, the canebrakes and thick shrubs that were along the margin, and that he had found no inhabited spot.
>
> The river, the river.
>
> The Governor sank into deep despondency at the sight of the difficulties that presented themselves to his reaching the sea; and, what was worse, from the way in which the men and horses were diminishing in numbers, he could not sustain himself in the country without succor. Of that reflection he pined.[26] (55–56)

Frustrated even in his attempts to gain any intelligence of the surrounding country, De Soto looks to the river itself as his destination. He "sinks" into despondency. The metaphor belongs to the Fidalgo. And he uses it again to speak, in fitting style, De Soto's epitaph in the wilderness: "The next day, the twenty-first of May, departed this life the magnanimous, the virtuous, the intrepid captain, Don Hernando de Soto, Governor of Cuba and Adelantado of Florida. He was advanced by fortune, in the way she is wont to lead others, that he might fall the greater depth" (57).[27] Indeed, the facts as well as the metaphors for De Soto's descent into the river belong to the Fidalgo. The report of how De Soto's corpse was wrapped in shawls filled with sand and "committed to the middle of the stream" (58) to conceal the death from the Indians comes verbatim from the record.[28] Even the catalogue of fish in the river comes verbatim from the Fidalgo. But Williams shifts the narrative placement of that catalogue, creating a startling revelation by moving the inventory from where the Fidalgo had tidily put it at the end of his earlier chapter about the expedition's first arrival at the Mississippi to round off that section of his relation with a description of the various fish in the river.[29] De Soto's descent becomes an affirmation of native forms, a celebratory fertilization of America's teeming multiplicity:

Down, down, this solitary sperm, down into the liquid, the formless, the insatiable belly of sleep; down among the fishes: there was
one called bagre, the third part of which was head, with gills from
end to end, and along the sides were great spines, like very sharp
awls; there were some in the river that weighed from a hundred
to a hundred and fifty pounds. There were some in the shape of a
barbel; another like bream, with the head of a hake, having a color
between red and brown. There was likewise a kind called peel-fish,
the snout a cubit in length, the upper lip being shaped like a shovel.
Others were like shad. There was one called pereo the Indians sometimes brought, the size of a hog and had rows of teeth above and
below. (58)

In "De Soto and the New World" the Mississippi becomes the am-
nion of the continent, the originating center for an evolution of American forms. Mark Twain and Sherwood Anderson, among others, had
also realized the river's generative possibilities in their production of
American narrative forms. But Williams takes that generative metaphor a step further—or more properly, many steps backward. In his
writing, an evolution of American literary forms begins as an involution, a descent back to origins. "We struggle to comprehend an
obscure evolution," Williams had written in *The Great American Novel*,
"when the compensatory involution so plainly marked escapes our
notice" (GAN, 215). *The Great American Novel* had relentlessly attacked
the very nature of prose narrative to evolve stories from set beginnings, constantly doubling back upon itself in a tortuous search to
discover the beginning. Williams perfects that movement in "De Soto
and the New World," leading De Soto back to a beginning at the end
by deconstructing De Soto's own attempt to impose an evolutionary
narrative upon America.

Yet Williams was well aware that conventional historical narrative was especially based on an evolutionary premise: the historian's
imperative to identify one set of events as the consequence of a preceding set of occurrences. And "De Soto and the New World" actually
ends with a deft parody of one of the historian's traditional concerns. Rather than follow the fate of the survivors who managed to
escape the country, Williams closes by quoting the Fidalgo's passage
about the disposition of De Soto's effects: "Luís de Moscosco [*sic*]
ordered the property of the Governor to be sold at public cry. It consisted of two male and three female slaves, three horses, and seven
hundred swine. From that time forward most of the people owned
and raised hogs" (58).[30] Playing on De Soto's symbolic role as sperm in
the fertile trough that produces a fish "the size of a hog," Williams lets

that final sentence resonate as his own parodic gesture toward what evolved as a consequence of De Soto's demise.

While Williams was working on *In the American Grain*, Waldo Frank was engaged in writing *Virgin Spain*. But there is more than just a temporal concurrence between the composition of these two works, for Frank was developing his historical paradigm of America as "the grave of Europe" even as Williams was giving dramatic enactment to a similar notion in his chapters on the Spanish. In "The Port of Columbus," the closing chapter of *Virgin Spain*, Frank created an imaginary meeting between Cervantes and Columbus at Palos de la Frontera, the port from which Columbus had sailed on his first voyage in 1492. Columbus repeatedly directs Cervantes to gaze westward across the Atlantic upon "the golden-towered America" that Spain had built in the New World, pronouncing it "but the Grave of Europe." And as he discloses the collapse of the towers to Cervantes in a final apocalyptic vision, Columbus triumphantly announces, "Now shall be the birth of the World which I discovered." Spain will not prove to be the conqueror of the New World, says Columbus, but rather a begetter of seed, "A mother of beginnings."[31]

For Williams as well as for Frank, the New World is born out of the death of the Old—the end marks the beginning. De Soto quite literally finds America to be the grave of Europe, but his death transforms him into a "solitary sperm" penetrating the place. Not surprisingly, Frank greatly admired Williams' chapters on the Spanish, particularly "The Discovery of the Indies." In the Columbus chapter Williams had done more than simply use the idea of the beginning born from the end as a conceptual metaphor for his narrative. He had used it as a structural principle for ordering his deployment of the various documents by Columbus that make up the chapter. "Waldo Frank," says Williams, "was the only person who recognized the technical difficulty and wrote me a letter praising the ending. I had managed after all kinds of rewriting to tell about the three voyages and at the same time to keep the discovery that occurred in the first voyage for a dramatic ending. It meant turning everything around, ending with the beginning" (IW, 42).[32]

Williams had still not managed to achieve that reversal of the conventional chronology of historical narrative in the version of "The Discovery of the Indies" he published in the March 1923 issue of *Broom*. That version does, however, terminate with the discovery of 1492 just as the final version in *In the American Grain* does, ending with Columbus' marvelous and marveling description of the flora and fauna on the beach at San Salvador, excerpted from his journal of the first voyage. But that moment doesn't emerge as the beginning released at the end as Williams wanted it to do. It is, quite simply, the end, because the *Broom* version begins by setting a narrative time frame prior to the discovery, indeed prior to Columbus' ever having sailed from Spain:

> A dense waterboundary over beyond the Azores needed a ship through it. Having failed to secure a footing for the adventure in every capital, ridiculed, driven about from place to place, in rags finally, his mind burning, the martyr's fervor eating now back of his breastbone, his son at his side—the Italian joins the mob about their Catholic Spanish Majesties encamped before Granada. There he watches his opportunity, for the last time to make his proposal.
>
> He hears the talk: Christ in the ascendant! but Spain ruined, sees the Moor come out and kiss the royal hands, fanfare of trumpets! Spaniards shouting! passage of the priests in robes—but no money. India . . . rich, but far. So then it comes to him:
>
> CHRISTOPHORO! him that carried Christ across the river.
>
> Being a practical shipmaster, besides the flame, he makes his plea: To the west. To India. In the name of Christ: gold, jewels, spices—.[33]

Much like a conventional practitioner of the craft, Williams places us at a specific moment in time from which the subsequent portions of his narrative will seem to unfold of their own accord without overt manipulation by the historian. He provides enough compressed summary of events preceding that moment to give a sense of Columbus' expectations and motives, and he limits his own temporal perspective to that of his protagonist, betraying no knowledge of the eventual outcome of Columbus' plans. Thus there is no rupturing of that narrative time frame as Williams splices onto this opening passage his excerpts from Columbus' journal of the first voyage, letting Columbus himself narrate the westward crossing leading up to the moment of discovery that ends the *Broom* piece. In short, Williams creates for us the illusion of reality, summoning us to imagine that we, too, are venturing into the unknown as we read the chapter—that we, too, can experience the glorious moment of discovery as if it were happening for the first time.

Such a "beautiful illusion" didn't satisfy Williams, yet he found it was hard to shake free of it. "I wrote and wrote and wrote," he says, "but it wouldn't come out" (A, 183). "The Discovery of the Indies" took him more than a year to complete, going through as many as ten different versions before it reached its final form. Though it was the first chapter of *In the American Grain* on which he began work in the fall of 1922, he was still working on it when he left for Europe in

January of 1924, struggling with it even as the *S.S. Rochambeau* carried him across the Atlantic away from America. Yet that eastward ocean journey might well have proved instrumental in helping him resolve the technical difficulties of the chapter. For in the final version of "The Discovery of the Indies," Williams begins his excerpts from Columbus' journal of the first voyage not with the westward venture into the unknown but with the return voyage to Europe in 1493, when the New World was behind Columbus both temporally and geographically—when the discovery was no longer a matter of either immediate or pending experience, but rather a fact of memory for the Italian.

From that point in history Williams leads us chronologically forward, eliding great blocks of time and compacting events, from Columbus' triumphant reception in Madrid in 1493 to his utterly devastated state in Jamaica in 1503, when his fourth and final voyage had collapsed in shipwreck and he himself had shipwrecked in spirit. Columbus' fortunes had undergone a startling reversal during these years. In the spring of 1492, the Spanish throne had named him perpetual viceroy and governor of whatever territories he might find to the west —in the fall of 1500, after his third voyage, he had been branded a traitor, arrested, and carried back to Spain in chains and disgrace. By 1503 he was a broken man, barely able to keep his ships afloat. He had to face the bitterness of his fate, and in the letter he wrote from Jamaica that year he begged the Spanish throne not to restore his rights and privileges, but to grant him sanction for a pilgrimage to Rome.

Williams seizes on that request to conjecture that if Columbus "had undertaken that holy pilgrimage of which he had spoken, the flower might, again, in that seclusion, often have appeared to him in all its old-time loveliness, as when he himself floated with luck and in sunshine on that tropic sea toward adventure and discovery" (16). The excerpts from the journal of the first voyage leading up to the moment of discovery no longer proceed within a received historical chronology. The discovery becomes a rediscovery for Columbus, a journey back through memory, a descent into the past much like that Williams would later envision in *Paterson*:

> The descent beckons
> as the ascent beckoned
> Memory is a kind
> of accomplishment
> a sort of renewal
> even
> an initiation, since the spaces it opens are new places
> inhabited by hordes

                              heretofore unrealized,
          of new kinds—
                    since their movements
                        are toward new objectives
              (even though formerly they were abandoned)
          No defeat is made up entirely of defeat—since
          the world it opens up is always a place
                      formerly
                        unsuspected. A
          world lost,
                  a world unsuspected
                          beckons to new places
          and no whiteness (lost) is so white as the memory
          of whiteness.   (P, 77–78)

    Williams had to create a plot that would drive Columbus back
into the spaces of memory. But it was probably less his own Atlantic
crossing to Europe that suggested the shape of that plot to Williams
than it was his work with De Soto. The technical difficulties of "The
Discovery of the Indies" were still unresolved when he worked out
the basic form of "De Soto and the New World."[34] In the *Broom* version of the Columbus chapter, Williams had forgone his own privilege
of synoptic vision, attempting to capture the spontaneous drama of
Columbus' first voyage by more or less simply reproducing the journal
of 1492 up to the moment of discovery. He hadn't taken into account
Columbus' projected schemes of conquest nor their eventual collapse.
But in the final version of the chapter, Williams does exactly what he
had done with De Soto—he creates a plot that is staged as a complex
interplay between two opposing plots, between Columbus' efforts to
impose a preformulated narrative design upon the New World and
the New World's efforts to frustrate and destroy that design. Columbus and the New World wrestle for control of the narrative direction
of the chapter, though to the synoptic eye of the historian the outcome of that struggle is a matter of historical inevitability: "Heroically,
but pitifully, he strove to fasten to himself that enormous world, that
presently crushed him among its multiple small disguises. With its
archaic smile, America found Columbus its first victim" (10).

    Williams, however, doesn't attempt to create an audible voice for
the New World as he does in the De Soto chapter. There he had taken
what might have been spoken by himself as historian and delivered
it through the speaking mask of She, disguising his own involvement
in constructing the drama. She had spoken the synoptic prologue

that opens the chapter, laying bare De Soto's inevitable fate in advance, essentially describing the very plot of the chapter itself. In "The Discovery of the Indies," Williams speaks the synoptic prologue, revealing not only Columbus' fate but the historian's own structural mechanism of leaving the telling of the beginning until the end:

> The New World, existing in those times beyond the sphere of all things known to history, lay in the fifteenth century as the middle of a desert or the sea lies now and must lie forever, marked with its own dark life which goes on to an immaculate fulfillment in which we have no part. But now, with the maritime successes of that period, the western land could not guard its seclusion longer; a predestined and bitter fruit existing, perversely, before the white flower of its birth, it was laid bare by the miraculous first voyage. For it is as the achievement of a flower, pure, white, waxlike and fragrant, that Columbus' infatuated course must be depicted, especially when compared with the acrid and poisonous apple which was later by him to be proved.
>
> No more had Columbus landed, the flower once ravished, than it seemed as if heaven itself had turned upon this man for disturbing its repose. But the initiative taken, the course broached, the story must go on. He left a handful of colonists in the islands while he, himself, returned to Spain with the news and for aid. (7)

In *Broom*, Williams had been a mere scene-setter, but here he becomes the director of a grand historical symphony. The New World is "a predestined and bitter fruit existing, perversely, before the white flower of its birth" because Williams chooses to give us the "bitter fruit" before he reveals "the white flower of its birth." The discovery, the "ravishing" of that flower, becomes the unseen cause of the storm of troubles that overwhelms Columbus. Like his fated progenitors in another Edenic garden, Columbus tasted a forbidden fruit—he disturbed the "repose" of the New World, violated its "immaculate fulfillment" as a world "beyond the sphere of all things known to history." Now he must experience "the acrid and poisonous apple," for "the initiative taken, the course broached, the story must go on."

Columbus is caught in the ineluctable machinations of the plot, for Williams drops him into the diachronicity of events at the exact moment when the response of the New World in "its multiple small disguises" first seems to visibly manifest itself in Columbus' writings. From Columbus' journal entries for the two-month-long return voyage to Spain in 1493, Williams selectively quotes only the portions describing the violent storm that nearly swamped the ships just off the Azores:

Sunrise the wind blew still harder, and the cross seas were terrific. Continued to show the closely reefed mainsail to enable her to rise between the waves, or she should otherwise have been swamped. Now I feared that we should perish. I should have borne this misfortune with less distress had my life alone been in peril, but what caused me boundless grief and trouble was the thought that just now when our gainsayers were to be convinced and the discovery of a New World victoriously to be announced, that just now the Divine Will should wish to block it with my destruction.

Of this mind, I resolved, that even if I should die, the ship be lost, to find a means of not losing a victory already won. I wrote on a parchment, with the brevity which the time demanded, how I had discovered the lands I had promised to find, describing the route I had followed and how your Highness had possession of all that had been found by me.

This folded and sealed, I had a cask brought, and having wrapped the writing in waxed cloth surrounded by a large cake of wax, I enclosed all in a barrel stoutly hooped, which I threw into the sea. All believed it some act of devotion.[35] (8)

What Columbus sees as the workings of "the Divine Will," Williams gives us to read as evidence of the New World's counterplot. He achieves essentially the same kind of duplicity he had in handling his excerpts from the De Soto narratives, letting Columbus himself describe the presence of a force he cannot consciously identify. Yet that force nonetheless has the power to force a narrative redirectioning upon Columbus, and he does indeed momentarily redirect his narrative here, temporarily abandoning the recording of the journal to inscribe another text he hopes will survive him. But Columbus himself survives, and more than just the fury of the storm—he narrowly escapes capture by pirates in the Azores and, later, accusations from the Spanish throne "of playing traitor to Castile, of having tried to bargain with the Portuguese sovereign" after the storm forces him into Lisbon harbor. That he does escape on each occasion, however, is only because the New World's plot allows him to do so: "there was too much still for him to endure for catastrophe to have overtaken him so early; some savage power had him in its care, preserving him for its later pleasure" (9).

Yet Columbus believes nothing stands between him and the fulfillment of his designs. Having made the discovery and successfully returned to Spain, where "his triumph was acclaimed, his captives were paraded in Madrid, his gold was witnessed, his birds, monkeys and native implements were admired," Columbus imagines he holds the New World securely in his hands: "now he saw before him the illusive bright future of a great empire founded, coupled with a fabulous conquest of heathendom by the only true church. Much had been promised him. He had succeeded in the sternest hazard, the great first step; should not the rest prove easy? It rose before him like a great gilded mountain" (9). Williams gives an even more explicit confirmation of Columbus' certainty that he alone controls the narrative direction of the history by having Columbus recall to mind the agreements issued him by the Spanish throne prior to his having sailed from Palos. With "the great first step" of his projected scheme already accomplished, Columbus sees himself following the undeviating lines of a course that had been set long before he ever laid eyes on the New World:

> that henceforth I should be called Don, and should be Chief Admiral of the Ocean Sea, perpetual Viceroy and Governor of all the islands and continents that I should discover and gain in the Ocean Sea, and that my eldest son should succeed, and so from generation to generation forever.
>
> . . .
>
> Item: that of all and every kind of merchandise, whether pearls, precious stones, gold, silver, spices, etc., of whatever kind, name and sort which may be bought, bartered, discovered within the said Admiralty, your Highnesses grant from henceforth to the said Don Cristóbal, the tenth part of the whole . . . granted, in the town of Santa Fe de la Granada on the 17th day of April, in the year of our Lord Jesus Christ, 1492. I, the King. I, the Queen.[36] (9–10)

"Unhappy talk," Williams responds. "What power had such ridiculous little promises to stay a man against that terrific downpour on the brink of which they were all floating? How could a king fulfill them? Yet this man, this straw in the play of elemental giants, must go blindly on." Williams suggests that the repercussions of Columbus' having ravished the New World, of having symbolically raped the virgin territories of a world outside the sphere of history, go far beyond Columbus' own particular fate. His act unleashes a "terrific downpour." American history begins as a cataclysmic upheaval, a rupturing of the known dimensions of the world.[37] Columbus cannot be blamed for his blindness to the enormity of the situation. "How could he have realized that against which he was opposed?" Williams asks (10).

Nor is Columbus the only "straw in the play of elemental giants." The men who oppose him are also swept up in the cataclysm. Bobadilla and his other "instinctive enemies" simply happen to be "not so backward on their part. With malicious accuracy, finding him more and more alone, they sensed everything and turned it to their own advantage, being closer to that curious self-interest of natural things than he." Yet within the scheme of "The Discovery of the Indies," they, too, are but straws finally, mere tools that pry Columbus loose from the validating titles of his projected scheme, leaving him unprotected against the embrace of the New World: "when riding a gigantic Nature and when through her heat they could arrogate to themselves a pin's worth of that massive strength, to turn it against another of their own kind to his undoing,—even they are natural and as much a part of the scheme as any other" (10–11). As he does with De Soto, Williams appropriates whatever blocks the advance of Columbus' planned course as evidence of the New World's opposition.

Though Williams wanted to cover all four of Columbus' voyages, he seems to have never made an attempt to use any of the material in his source volume pertaining to the second voyage. Indeed, Williams makes a sizeable temporal elision in his selection of excerpts, jumping from the portions of the *Journal of the First Voyage* for the return voyage to Spain in 1493 and the "Articles of Agreement" signed by the Spanish throne in 1492 all the way to the letter Columbus wrote in 1500 while being carried back to Spain in irons after his arrest by Bobadilla at Española put an abrupt end to the third voyage. By 1498 Ferdinand and Isabella had finally lost faith in the Italian. He had shown himself not only an ineffective administrator of colonial government in the Indies, but unable to produce the gleaming mounds of gold for the coffers of Spain that he had been promising the sovereigns ever since his initial return. Nor were they at all pleased that he had made slave trading, in lieu of profits from gold, the basis of Española's economy, and they sent out Francisco de Bobadilla to relieve Columbus of his duties as governor.

Columbus' mode of temporal vision radically shifted from the projective to the retrospective when he was shocked out of his schemes and titles by his arrest at Española. He was compelled to review the course of his career, to copy his plot from life rather than dictate it to experience. And Williams explicitly introduces his excerpts from the letter of 1500 in terms of Columbus' revisioning of his past: "Bewildered, he continued, voyage after voyage, four times, out of his growing despair; it seemed that finally by sheer physical effort a way must be found—till the realization of it all at last grew firmly upon him":

> Seven years passed in discussion and nine in execution, the Indies discovered, wealth and renown for Spain and great increase to God

and to his Church. And I have arrived at and am in such a condition that there is no one so vile but thinks he may insult me.

What have I not endured? Three voyages undertaken and brought to success against all who would gainsay me; islands and a mainland to the south discovered; pearls, gold, and, in spite of all, after a thousand struggles with the world and having withstood them all, neither arms nor counsels availed, it cruelly kept me under water.

If I were to steal the Indies or land which lies beyond them from the altar of St. Peter and give them to the Moors, they could not have greater enmity toward me in Spain.[38] (11)

By making this chronological jump in his selection of excerpts and situating Columbus at the end of his career, Williams is able not only to let Columbus himself fill in the gap, but also to suggest Columbus' capacity for seeing the New World through the reevaluating lenses of memory before he posits Columbus' memorial return to the moment of first discovery. Williams, in fact, creates the impression of an even larger temporal leap forward here by fusing his brief excerpts from the letter of 1500 to his lengthier selections from the letter of 1503—the so-called *Lettera Rarissima* written from Jamaica after the collapse of the fourth voyage—so that the two letters seem to form one continuous narrative written at the later date. He is thus able to provide Columbus a single, terminal recognition of the forces that oppose him, a devastating revelation of that to which he was previously blind:

> Up to the period of reaching these shores, I experienced most excellent weather, but the night of my arrival came on with a dreadful tempest, and the same bad weather has continued ever since. On reaching the island of Española, I despatched a packet of letters, by which I begged as a favor that a ship be supplied me at my own cost in lieu of one of those that I had brought with me, which had become unseaworthy, and could no longer sail. The letters were taken, and your Highnesses will know if a reply has been given them. For my part I was forbidden to go on shore.
>
> The tempest was terrible throughout the night, all the ships were separated, and each one driven to the last extremity without hope of anything but death; each of them also looked upon the loss of the rest as a matter of certainty. What man was ever born, not even excepting Job, who would not have been ready to die of despair at finding himself as I then was, in anxious fear for my own safety, and that of my son, my brother and my friends, and yet refused permission either to land or to put into harbor on the shores which by God's mercy I had gained for Spain sweating blood?[39] (12–13)

Columbus himself seems to have grasped that the elements and government had teamed against him, that he had been driven from

the island which was to have been the seat of his power as much by the
fury of the storm as by the authority of Spain's decree. Even more significant, Columbus recognizes an analogue for his fate in the position
of the ships. He, too, has been "driven to the last extremity without
hope of anything but death." The storm that has caught his fleet is
but a metaphor for the larger storm that has overtaken his fortunes
—to narrate the events of the tempest at sea is equally to tell of the
disruption of his schemes, to realize that what is really lost is not the
ships but the land he "had gained for Spain sweating blood." Williams
again captures Columbus' narrative movement from the condition of
the ships to the condition of his life in the subsequent description of
the storm that carried him off from Española:

> Twenty-eight days did this fearful tempest continue, during which I
> was at sea and saw neither sun nor stars, my ships lay exposed, with
> sails torn, and anchors, rigging, cables, boats and a great quantity
> of provisions lost. Other tempests have been experienced, but never
> of so long a duration as this. I myself had fallen sick, and was many
> times on the point of death, but from a little cabin that I had caused to
> be constructed on deck, I directed our course. My brother was in the
> ship that was in the worst condition and the most exposed to danger;
> and my grief on this account was the greater that I had brought him
> with me against his will.
>
>   Such is my fate, that the twenty years of service through which I
> have passed with so much toil and danger, have profited me noth-
> ing, and at this very day I do not possess a roof in Spain that I can
> call my own: if I wish to eat or sleep, I have nowhere to go but to
> the inn or tavern, and most times lack wherewith to pay the bill.[40]
> (14–15)

Twenty-eight days of storm have done to the ships what twenty
years in the service of Spain have done to Columbus—both have been
stripped bare. The ships have lost "anchors, rigging, cables, boats and
a great quantity of provisions," while Columbus has lost even "a roof
in Spain that I can call my own." He is as exposed and unprotected
as his fleet. But Columbus, in his own text, tries not to punctuate his
accounts of storm with descriptions of the tempestuous disordering
of his life. Though he sees himself, like Job, at the mercy of powers
beyond his control, he still attempts to keep some control over the
writing of the letter. On each occasion that the letter begins to sound
more like a lament from the ashpit of Uz than a report of his voyage, he sharply breaks off the perceived digression to get on with the
progression of his narrative: "But to return to the ships," Columbus
remarks after he decries the injustice of being forbidden to land at

Española. Only after he has completed the report of the voyage does Columbus finally permit himself, at the conclusion of the letter, to recite his larger grievances and sufferings.

Williams, however, has taken Columbus' effort to control the course of his narration and turned it against him. The verbal marker "But to return to the ships" that Columbus left behind in his attempt not to stray from the immediate matter of the voyage serves Williams with the means to lead Columbus further off course. Directly following the passage in which Columbus speaks of losing the lands he "had gained for Spain sweating blood," Williams inserts nearly a page of excerpts from Columbus' lamentations at the end of the letter before he allows him "to return to the ships" (14). Columbus is made to digress rather than progress in telling the events of the voyage at hand, lapsing into a recounting of the Bobadilla affair once again, and finally into a synopsis of the devastation that has claimed him:

> I was twenty-eight years old when I came into your Highnesses' service, and now I have not a hair upon me that is not gray; my body is infirm, and all that was left me, as well as to my brothers, has been taken away and sold, even to the frock that I wore.
>
> I would implore your Highnesses to forgive my complaints. I am indeed in as ruined condition as I have related. With regard to temporal things, I have not even a *blanca* for an offering; and in spiritual things, I have ceased here in the Indies from observing the prescribed forms of religion.[41] (13–14)

The shifting of these passages from the conclusion of the letter underscores Columbus' inability to progress even when he does at last "return to the ships," for Williams gives the ships little opportunity to encounter anything other than tempest. He takes the series of violent storms that overswept Columbus during his exploration of the coast of Central America from November 1502 to May 1503 and combines them into a single furious blast, excising all other intervening material and denying Columbus even the safe harbors and occasional periods of respite he had had at the time of events:

> Never was the sea so high, so terrific and so covered with foam; not only did the wind oppose our proceeding onward, but it also rendered it highly dangerous to run in for any headland, and kept me in that sea, which seemed to me as a sea of blood, seething like a cauldron on a mighty fire. Never did the sky look more fearful; during the day and night it burned like a furnace and every instant I looked to see if my masts and sails were not destroyed. These flashes came with such alarming fury that we all thought the ships must have been

destroyed. All this time the waters from heaven never ceased, not to say that it rained, for it was like a repetition of the deluge. Twice had the ships suffered loss in boats, anchors, rigging, and were now lying bare without sails . . . still raining. The sea very tempestuous and I was was driven backward under bare poles. . . .

I anchored at an island, where I lost, at one stroke, three anchors; and at midnight, when the weather was such that the world appeared to be coming to an end, the cables of the other ship broke, and it came down upon my vessel with such force that it was a wonder we were not dashed to pieces; the single anchor that remained to me was our only preservation. After six days, when the weather became calm, I resumed my journey, having already lost all my tackle; my ships were pierced with borers more than a honeycomb and the crew entirely paralyzed with fear and in despair. There the storm returned to drive me back. . . . I continued beating against contrary winds, and with the ships in the worst possible condition. With three pumps, and the use of pots and kettles, we could scarcely clear the water that came into the ship, there being no remedy but this, against the shipworm, I determined on keeping the sea, in spite of the weather, when we miraculously came upon land.[42] (15–16)

Even when the storm does seem to abate, Williams himself renews the tempest, inserting the phrase *There the storm returned to drive me back* as if it were Columbus' own. The fourth voyage collapses almost at a single blow with an apocalyptic finality, for Columbus is given no chances to recoup his losses. It is his own language, nonetheless, that delivers the eschatological tropes for an elemental chaos so terrific "that the world appeared to be coming to an end." He is swept away by "a sea of blood" and torrential rains that come "like a repetition of the deluge." But it is Williams' impaction of these passages that declares the finality of their impact on Columbus. The boats, anchors, rigging, and tackle that were actually lost over the space of eight months are carried off in a week of unremitting violence, and Columbus emerges with ships that are little more than bare timbers, the hulls "pierced with borers more than a honeycomb" and barely kept afloat with "the use of pots and kettles."

Williams leaves no doubt of the storm's effect upon Columbus, for he makes Columbus admit defeat with the defeat of his fleet, juxtaposing the concluding words of the letter with the arrival of the devastated ships at land: "Weep for me whoever has charity, truth and justice. I did not come out on this voyage to gain myself honor and wealth; for at that time all hope of such a thing was dead. I do not lie when I say, that I went to your Highnesses with honest purpose of heart, and sincere zeal in your cause. I humbly beseech your Highnesses, that if it please God to rescue me from this place, you will graciously sanction my pilgrimage to Rome and other holy places. May the holy Trinity protect your Highnesses' lives, and add prosperity" (16).[43]

Columbus has truly been driven back by storm—back to places he possesses only in memory, back to spaces of memory in which he might once again have possessed the flower of his first voyage. But the storm is more than just a device for Williams to turn Columbus back upon his tracks, to redirect his course toward origins rather than projected outcomes. The sustained passage of elemental violence Williams inflicts upon Columbus also strips him clean for the ensuing moment of discovery, forcing him, like De Soto, to enter a "new world naked." Williams' success in rendering the purity of the first voyage balances, in part, upon this paradox of regenerative violence. It takes a "Catastrophic Birth" to produce a beginning: "By violence lost, recaptured by violence / violence alone opens the shell of the nut" (CLP, 8).

Following hard on the heels of the excerpts from the later letters, the peculiar qualities of the journal emerge with striking clarity. Plot gives way to isolate, detailed notations. Rather than a verbal repassage through past events, in which several months are narrated in a paragraph or even several years gathered in a single sentence, the writing of the journal represents an immediate verbal passage into the unknown, a day-by-day movement through time in which consciousness is rooted in the uncertainties of the moment. The first voyage blots out all familiar frames of reference. Williams begins his excerpts from the journal not with the departure from Palos on August 3, but with the westward turning from the Canaries toward the open sea on September 8. And in the entry for the following day, Columbus remarks the loss of the known: "This day we lost sight of land, and many fearful of not seeing it again sighed and shed tears" (17).

Though Williams makes occasional minor elisions in the journal's account of the westward crossing, one element he never cuts—and quite often adds to the text from material provided in the editor's footnotes—is the terror of the crew over the prospect of never being able to regain the familiar.[44] Williams purposefully dramatizes that fear to establish Columbus' openness toward experiencing the unknown in contradistinction to his crew's anxious glances back toward Spain. Indeed, just at the moment when the crew seems on the verge of mutiny, Williams inserts into the text his own conjectured dialogue between

Pedro Gutierrez[45] and Columbus concerning the uncertainty of the voyage:

> *Peter Gutierrez*: So that, virtually, you have staked your life and the lives of your companions, upon the foundation of a mere speculative opinion.
>
> *Columbus*: So it is: I cannot deny it. But consider a little. If, at present you and I, and all our companions, were not in this vessel, in the midst of this sea, in this unknown solitude, in a state uncertain and perilous as you please; in what other condition of life should we pass these days? Perhaps more cheerfully? or should we not rather be in some greater trouble or solicitude, or else full of tedium? I care not to mention the glory and utility we shall carry back, if the enterprise succeeds according to our hope. Should no other fruit come from this navigation, to me it appears most profitable inasmuch as for a time it preserves us free from tedium, makes life dear to us, makes valuable to us many things that otherwise we should not have in consideration. (22–23)

Far from striking terror into Columbus, the indeterminacy of the voyage becomes its own reward, for it offers escape from the predictability of the familiar and "preserves us free from tedium." Regardless of its outcome, the voyage delights Columbus because it holds the world of habitual experience in abeyance and "makes valuable to us many things that otherwise we should not have in consideration." Williams endows Columbus with a capacity of double reckoning. He comprehends the peril and fear felt by his crew "in this unknown solitude," but what terrifies them sharpens his perceptions.

Columbus, of course, was a habitual double reckoner in measuring his distance from the familiar. He had his own stratagem, born on the same day the ships lost sight of home, of recording a double set of figures—one denoting the true number of leagues they had sailed, the other a lesser number made public to the crews: "we made nineteen leagues, and I decided to reckon less than the number run, for should the voyage prove of long duration, the people would not be so terrified and disheartened" (17).[46] The members of the crew are allowed to plot themselves closer to home, but Columbus knows where he stands in the advance. He is, literally and metaphorically, in Williams' own favored position, the position Williams claims for the poet in *Kora in Hell*: "The poet should be forever at the ship's prow" (KH, 28). Columbus becomes, in the end, exactly what Williams wanted—an analogue of the writer as discoverer, his senses whetted for contact. The impact of the New World upon him is sudden and spontaneous, a rich abundance of diverse textures conjugated in his language. The entries in his journal burst into flower with fierce heat:

> Bright green trees, the whole land so green that it is a pleasure
> to look on it. Gardens of the most beautiful trees I ever saw. . . .
> I saw many trees very unlike those of our country. Branches grow-
> ing in different ways and all from one trunk; one twig is one form
> and another is a different shape and so unlike that it is the greatest
> wonder in the world to see the diversity; thus one branch has leaves
> like those of a cane, and others like those of a mastic tree; and on a
> single tree there are five different kinds. The fish so unlike ours that
> it is wonderful. Some are the shape of dories and of the finest colors,
> so bright that there is not a man who would not be astounded, and
> would not take great delight in seeing them. There are also whales. I
> saw no beasts on land save parrots and lizards.
>
> On shore I sent the people for water, some with arms, and others
> with casks; and as it was some little distance, I waited two hours for
> them.
>
> During that time I walked among the trees which was the most
> beautiful thing which I had ever seen.[47] (26)

Williams performs his own double reckoning with the moment
of discovery. Though he situates it within Columbus' memory, the
opening of "The Destruction of Tenochtitlan" replaces it within history: "Upon the orchidean beauty of the new world the old rushed
inevitably to revenge itself after the Italian's return." The discovery
becomes symbolic of Williams' sense of a double inheritance in American history. Columbus' penetration "beyond the sphere of all things
known to history" is paradoxically a flowering and a deflowering,
both "the achievement of a flower, pure, white, waxlike and fragrant"
and a rape of the New World's "immaculate fulfillment." Columbus
may have been possessed of a "streamlike human purity of purpose"
(11) in his first Atlantic crossing, yet the larger consequences of the
discovery were anything but pure: "The main islands were thickly
populated with a peaceful folk when Christ-over found them. But the
orgy of blood which followed, no man has written" (41).[48] And despite
his fine sensitivity to the landscape, Columbus himself, as Williams
well knew, played no small part in depopulating it—"traffic in girls:
nine years old, reads the Italian's journal" (41).[49]

Williams confronts the paradox of this double inheritance in "The
Fountain of Eternal Youth," one of the bloodiest and most violent
chapters of *In the American Grain*. "History begins for us with murder
and enslavement, not with discovery," Williams announces. And he
goes on to suggest that perhaps it would have been better if Columbus

had never made it back to Spain: "Listen! I tell you it was lucky for Spain the first ship put its men ashore where it did. If the Italian had landed in Florida, one twist of the helm north, or among the islands a hair more to the south; among the Yamasses with their sharpened bones and fishspines, or among the Caribs with their poisoned darts —it might have begun differently" (39).[50]

The Spaniards were indeed ruthlessly murderous in their colonization of the New World, and there was perhaps no Spaniard with more blood on his hands than Ponce de Leon. His wholesale slaughter of the natives of Puerto Rico makes the Puritans' violence against the Indians seem almost nugatory in comparison:

> The Spaniards killed their kings, betrayed, raped, murdered their women and children; hounded them into the mountains. Ponce with his wife and children in the *Casa Blanca* was one of the bloodthirstiest. They took them in droves, forced them to labor. It was impossible to them—not having been born to baptism. How maddening it is to the spirit to hear:—Bands of them went into the forests, their forests, and hanged themselves to the trees. . . . Caravels crept along the shore by night. Next morning when women and children came down to the shore to fish—fine figures, straight black hair, high cheekbones, a language—they caught them, made them walk in bands, cut them down if they fainted, slashed off breasts, arms—women, children. Gut souls. (41–42)

Given this utter devastation of the New World's human landscape, it seems odd that Williams would attempt to use the Spanish to affirm the New World's native spirit in his history. But Williams gives a peculiar twist to the notion of a double inheritance in the American past. "We are the slaughterers," he says, but at the same time, "We are, too, the others." We are double: "It is the tortured soul of our world" (41). We possess not just the lands of the defeated, but their souls as well— or, rather, their souls possess us: "Fierce and implacable we kill them but their souls dominate us. Our men, our blood, but their spirit is master. It enters us, it defeats us, it imposes itself" (40). Place does not belong to us as much as we belong to place, claimed by it through the very duality of our history: "No, we are not Indians but we are men of their world. The blood means nothing; the spirit, the ghost of the land moves in the blood, moves the blood" (39).

"A curious thing about the Spirit of Place," Lawrence observes in his *Studies in Classic American Literature*, "is the fact that no place exerts its full influence upon a new-comer until the old inhabitant is dead or absorbed."[51] Williams, perhaps echoing Lawrence, seems to use Ponce's annihilation of the natives to assert their influence. Like the

Caribs whom Ponce exterminated—"they whose souls lived in their bodies, many souls in one body; they who fought their enemies, ate them" (39)—the Spaniards, Williams suggests, incorporated the souls of those they vanquished. Ponce and the other conquistadors certainly didn't kill coldly and antiseptically with the brutal logic of the Puritans—nor did they try to civilize the place by planting a mere "drop" of blood in "outlandish veins" like the French. The savagery of the place seems to have entered the Spaniards' veins as a primal desire to bathe the ground in blood, to spill it almost ritualistically like the Aztec priests in the temple at Tenochtitlan. Williams might indeed echo Lawrence here, for in his first published version of "The Spirit of Place" Lawrence had posited a "great mystic-magnetic polarity" between the Spaniards and the peoples they conquered in the New World, claiming that "the impulse to religious cruelty" which characterized the Spanish Inquisition "*came* to the Spaniards from America, and was exercised secondarily by them in Europe."[52]

Yet Williams, though he may have taken his cue from Lawrence, probably derives his posture in "The Fountain of Eternal Youth" from a much deeper connection. The bloody ground of Puerto Rico is actually the blood ground of Williams' own New World genealogy, the place of his mother's birth. Pound had always berated Williams for imagining himself a "real" American. "And America! What the hell do you a bloomin' foreigner know about the place?" Pound scoffed. A British father and French-Spanish mother from Puerto Rico had spared Williams, Pound felt, from what Pound himself had to bear: "the virus, the bacillus of the land in my blood, for nearly three bleating centuries." And he advised Williams to "thank your bloomin gawd you've got enough Spanish blood to muddy up your mind, and prevent the current American ideation from going through it like a blighted collander."[53] Williams, however, seems to have used his Spanish heritage as a way of asserting the land in his blood in *In the American Grain*. His Spanish blood from Puerto Rico, in fact, might well explain not just his stance in "The Fountain of Eternal Youth," but why Williams chose to do a chapter on Ponce de Leon at all. With Columbus, Cortez, and De Soto, Williams had a substantial body of historical source texts with which to work. With Ponce, he had none.

To tell the story of Ponce's quest for the chimerical fountain, Williams used a book that can hardly be called a historical source, Frederick Ober's *Juan Ponce de Leon*. Written in 1908, Ober's life of Ponce, like its companion volumes in his Heroes of American History series, is little more than a juvenile adventure story with a historical setting. Williams' choice of such a puerile fiction is entirely at odds with his preference for using original documents as the textual basis of *In the American Grain*. Then again, Williams had little choice but to go against the grain of his history if he were to do a chapter on Ponce. There are no original documents concerning Ponce's career in the Indies—his history is mainly apocryphal, having grown with its telling over the centuries, from Garcilaso de Vega to Las Casas, from Oviedo to Herrera, from Gomara to Barcia, from Washington Irving to Frederick Ober, much like the expanding web of stories that make up Faulkner's *Absalom, Absalom!*[54]

Though Williams parodies the romantic excesses of Ober's style, the real source for the chapter would seem to be Williams himself. He has selected not so much a source text as a source ground—the ground of his New World origins, Puerto Rico—for his symbolical masquerade as one of the "others," one of the defeated, in order to destroy the destroyer. "Do these things die?" he asks. "Men who do not know what lives, are themselves dead. In the heart there are living Indians once slaughtered and defrauded—Indians that live also in subtler ways" (42). Williams makes them live in those subtler ways, appropriating the legend of Ponce's search for the Fountain of Youth to fabricate the revenge of the New World on Ponce:

> An old Indian woman among his slaves, began to tell him of an island, Bimini, a paradise of fragrant groves, of all fruits. And in the center of it a fountain of clearest water of virtue to make old men young. Think of that! Picture to yourself the significance of that—as revenge, as irony, as the trail of departing loveliness, *fata morgana*. Yet the real, the thing destroyed turning back with a smile. Think of the Spaniard listening. Gold. Gold. Riches. And figure to yourself the exquisite justice of it: an old woman, loose tongued—loose sword—the book, her soul already half out of her with sorrow: abandoned by a Carib who had fled back to his home having found Borequien greatly overrated. Her children enslaved.[55] (42–43)

Ponce wants to find what Williams accords De Soto—life-giving waters, a beginning in the end. But the kind of double reckoning Williams employs with his source documents to create De Soto's transformation into a fertilizing spermatozoa can cut both ways. In his search for a regenerative beginning, Ponce unwittingly becomes both a tale chaser and a tail chaser: "no end—away from the beginning—tail chaser" (44), Williams wryly remarks. And he gives Ponce, in the end, a death that ironically mocks the beginning of the Spaniard's career in the New World, spilling his blood upon the ground as he goes in search of the fountain: "the Yamasses put an arrow into his thigh at the first landing—and let out his fountain. They flocked to the beach, jeered him as he was lifted to the shoulders of his men and carried away. Dead" (44). Even in their worst defeats of the New World, the Spanish provide Williams the opportunity to offer his strongest affirmations of place.

Ponce de Leon is "the destroyer of beauty, drawn on by beauty" (43)—a perfect model of the conquistador's role in *In the American Grain*. Yet Williams forces all the conquistadors to play this role. He shows no interest in investigating their unique qualities as individuals, treating them essentially like puppets of one generic ilk. Only Columbus—an Italian in the service of Spain, and more an explorer than a conqueror—receives a distinctive physiognomy of character in Williams' chapters on the Spaniards. But Cortez, Ponce, and De Soto perform only one function. They penetrate the New World's life, striking in toward its richest beauty. Each one enters the history, in his turn, to fulfill the part Williams explicitly spells out for them at the opening of "The Destruction of Tenochtitlan":

> Though men may be possessed of beauty while they work that is all they know of it or of their own terrible hands; they do not fathom the forces which carry them. Spain cannot be blamed for the crassness of the discoverers. They moved out across seas stirred by instincts, ancient beyond thought as the depths they were crossing, which they obeyed under the names of King or Christ or whatever it might be, while they watched the recreative New unfolding itself miraculously before them, before *them*, deafened and blinded. Steering beyond familiar horizons they were driven to seek perhaps self-justification for victorious wars against Arab and Moor; but these things are the surface only. At the back, as it remains, it was the evil of the whole world; it was the perennial disappointment which follows, like smoke, the bursting of ideas. It was the spirit of malice which underlies men's lives and against which nothing offers resistance. (27)

The conquistadors can be little else than puppets, for not only do they not act of their own volition, "they do not fathom the forces which carry them." Only the historian can see beneath "the surface" to glimpse those "instincts, ancient beyond thought" that impel the conquistadors "beyond familiar horizons." Williams seems to echo Lawrence's notion of a "great mystic-magnetic polarity" between the Spaniards and the New World more strongly here than anywhere else in the book—but Williams doesn't share Lawrence's interest in depth psychology, at least not in "The Destruction of Tenochtitlan."[56] The apparent Lawrentian imprint on this passage is itself but "the surface only," and indeed Williams' entire chapter works upon a manipulation of surfaces. Far from establishing a basis upon which to explore the submerged depths of Cortez's mind, Williams rather dismisses any need to look any further into them. Cortez the man has already been explained. He is a surface only, with no more depth than the mask of the conquistador Williams demands he wear. Cortez is merely "a conqueror like other conquerors," Williams goes on to say, simply "one among the rest" (27).

If Cortez is "a man of genius superbly suited to his task" (27), it is only because the task Williams allots him is so narrowly defined. He is to lead Williams into the very heart of Tenochtitlan, and to stand "deafened and blinded" as he watches "the recreative New unfolding itself miraculously before" him. And Cortez is, in fact, superbly suited to that task, for his fierce determination to conquer the city overcame every possible barrier in his path. Cortez didn't even have an offical patent from the Spanish throne for the conquest of Montezuma's domain. Nor would he wait to receive one. Against the opposition of Diego Velasquez, governor of Cuba, and Fonseca, bishop of Burgos and president of the Council of the Indies, Cortez crossed the Gulf from Cuba and landed near Cempoala on the Mexican coast with fewer than six hundred soldiers and only sixteen horses. He was resolved to perform the bold stroke, to take Tenochtitlan, to act the part of governor of the territory, hoping that then Charles V would officially grant him title to the role he had already arrogated to himself in deed. Nothing would deter him. He beached his ships and burned them to prevent his troops from turning back. He pressed into the interior against the express wish of Montezuma and the resistance of native armies that at times numbered above fifty thousand. He even succeeded in taking the city. Posing as a friendly visitor to the Aztec emperor, Cortez held him hostage for several months, extorting from Montezuma a fortune in gold and precious stones as tribute for the Spanish throne.

Even when the kind of treacheries that helped sink Columbus seemed to have robbed him of everything, Cortez wouldn't be stopped. In 1521 Velasquez sent out none other than Pámfilo de Narváez, later leader of the ill-fated expedition into Florida, to attack Cortez from behind and arrest him as an interloper. Cortez had to leave the city under keeping of a small Spanish garrison while he went to head off Narváez on the coast. Cortez not only subdued Narváez, he also managed to win over most of Narváez's troops to his side, an act of sheer military genius.[57] But when Cortez returned to Tenochtitlan he found the Aztecs in revolt. They forced him out, and it truly seemed that everything—both the city and the wealth he had pirated from it—was irrevocably lost during his hectic retreat across the causeways on *la noche triste*. Yet Cortez refused to yield. He regrouped his forces on the lake shore, spent several months building brigantines for a renewed assault, and then kept the city under siege for two years, inching his way inside, waging pitched battles for control of the causeways.

Cortez finally received his commission from Charles V in 1523. He had proved victorious not just in the field but on paper as well. His detailed relations to the emperor were an essential part of his plot, for his success in winning recognition from the throne depended on his marshaling words as decisively as he deployed his troops. His object, in both regards, had been to achieve what a conqueror must have: a narrative of conquest. The sword of the general had served up material of a familiar shape for the pen of the writer.

Ironically, Cortez would have been poorly suited to Williams' task had he not been something more than the conqueror Williams makes him. In the letter Cortez wrote while the boats were being built for his second assault on the city, the man who had pushed at the borders of geography suddenly discovered that he had arrived at the boundaries of his language. He had come to meet perhaps his sternest trial—to provide Charles V with "a just conception of the great extent of this noble city of Temixtitan, and of the many rare and wonderful objects it contains." Faced with the prospect of delivering an aesthetic rather than military possession of Tenochtitlan, Cortez declared himself in need of reinforcements, for "it would require the labor of many accomplished writers, and much time for the completion of the task." But Cortez had brought no armada of writers, nor did he have, like Marco Polo, a Rustichello to help him. He found himself, for the space of ten pages, journeying through unfamiliar verbal territory, momentarily forced to become a travel writer more than a general in his attempt to describe a city so marvelous that "even we who have seen these things with our own eyes, are yet so amazed as to be unable to comprehend their reality."[58]

That role is precisely what Williams appropriates from Cortez. Williams cleaves the man in two, taking for himself the words of the startled traveler, and leaving to Cortez the deeds of the general. Cortez, in fact, is denied a voice altogether—like Ponce and De Soto, he is mute, "deafened and blinded" by the beauty of the New World. But Ponce and De Soto are mute because they never wrote their own stories. Cortez is mute because Williams has lifted the man's own words. And Williams hides any signs of the theft—for the most part. In almost each set of excerpts he places a brief phrase in quotation marks—not, however, to attribute the words to Cortez or any other particular speaker, but apparently merely to show that some sort of record is near at hand. In his extract describing the gifts Cortez received when he arrived at Tenochtitlan, Williams puts only the phrase *of so costly and unusual workmanship that considering their novelty and wonderful beauty no price could be set on them* in quotation marks (31), just as he later puts only the phrase *everything which the world affords* in quotation marks in the extracts concerning the marketplace (32).[59] But if this seems like a peculiar method of citing bibliographical source material, Williams proves even more bizarre in the penultimate paragraph of the chapter. There he sows quotation marks carelessly, perhaps even flagrantly throughout the excerpts that describe the interior of Montezuma's palaces. There are quotation marks often needlessly thrown in to divide off passages that are continuous in Williams' source. Yet even here we are left to surmise exactly whose writing Williams is quoting. The only time Williams lets Cortez speak in his own person is at the end. And then only to say " 'It grieved me much but it grieved the enemy more' " (38), regarding his decision to burn Montezuma's beautiful aviaries as a way of reducing the Aztecs to submission.[60]

But what else would one expect of such a crafty double reckoner? Williams takes what he wants and leaves the rest to the conqueror, pushing his military exploits to the periphery. The initial march from the coast inland—to which Cortez devotes nearly forty pages—is reduced to two sentences: "The advance was like any similar military enterprise: it accomplished its purpose. Surmounting every difficulty Cortez went his way into the country past the quiet Cempoalan maizefields, past the summit of Popocatepetl, until, after weeks of labor, he arrived upon the great lakes and the small cities in them adjoining Tenochtitlan" (29). Williams completely elides any mention of the fierce battles Cortez fought on his way to the city, of the Tlascans and others he won to his purpose by promising to free them from the yoke of Montezuma's authority, of the various subterfuges the Aztecs employed to halt the advance, and of the other episodes that properly belong to Cortez and the story of his military feats. By the same token, Williams shuffles the two-year siege of the city into a single paragraph at the close of the chapter. "And then the end," he flatly states to introduce the conclusion. Cortez's painstakingly detailed accounts of the battles for control of the causeways are compressed into a rapidly flashed series of pictures. For Williams, it is "merely a matter of detail and of time as to what form the final catastrophe would take" (37).

Williams' narration of the city's destruction becomes a narrative wrapper, the necessary historical packaging around the interior paragraphs of the chapter that speak his real concern—the act of the city's construction, the building up of Tenochtitlan rather than its tearing down. Cortez, nonetheless, had shown himself just as capable of enacting the former as the latter in his writing. Though he had felt illequipped to give Charles V a just conception of Tenochtitlan's beauty, Cortez quite splendidly reveals his sense of wonder as he piles up, almost breathlessly, a catalogue of names for the incredible abundance in the marketplace of the city. Even in his overall approach to verbally organizing the city's spatial layout Cortez is hardly at a loss for effective strategies. He deftly uses the penetrating vision of a conquistador to present his description as a narrative movement from outside to inside, exterior to interior. He begins by mapping out the city's geographic position on the lake and works his way slowly inside, through the marketplace to the temples, and finally into Montezuma's private apartments. Williams has had to make very few alterations other than to cut and paste sections of Cortez's description into place, fitting them into a larger design of the city as verbal artifact. "The Tenochtitlan chapter," he says, "was written in big square paragraphs like Inca masonry. I admired the massive walls of fitted masonry—no plaster —just fitted boulders. I took that to be a wonderful example of what I wanted to do with my prose; no patchwork" (IW, 42–43).

Williams artfully joins the movement from exteriors to interiors in Cortez's description of the city to the larger plot of Cortez's penetration inland to the city. Cortez truly becomes "drawn on by beauty," for Williams searches out and lays bare the points of contact between Cortez and the New World that impel the Spaniard to strike more and more deeply into the vital life of the place. Our first glimpse of him is on the coast, where he first glimpses the wondrous textures of the New World. Williams gives an almost page-long verbatim excerpt from his source, a detailed inventory of the many gifts Montezuma sent to Cortez with the advice "not to risk coming up into the back country" (28). Yet the allurement of "a gold necklace of seven pieces, set with many rubies, a hundred and eighty-three emeralds and ten fine pearls, and hung with twenty-seven little bells of gold" and the many other gifts enumerated in the passage far outweighs Montezuma's request.[61] "But Cortez was unwilling to turn back," Williams remarks; "rather these things whetted his appetite for the adventure" (29).

Cortez is drawn inland—to make contact again. Though Williams compresses the narration of Cortez's inland march to a mere two sentences, the day on which Cortez arrives at the outlying cities on the lake is recapitulated at length. Here, on the perimeter of Tenochtitlan, the "recreative New" indeed begins "unfolding itself miraculously before" the Spaniard:

> Cortez now passed over his first causeway into one of the lesser lake cities, built of well-hewn stone sheer from the water. He was overcome with wonder. The houses were so excellently put together, so well decorated with cloths and carven wood, so embellished with metalwork and other marks of a beautiful civilization; the people were so gracious; there were such gardens, such trees, such conservatories of flowers that nothing like it had ever been seen or imagined. At the house where the Conqueror was entertained that day and night he especially noted a pool built of stone into the clear waters of which stone steps descended, while round it were paven paths lined with sweet-smelling shrubs and plants and trees of all sorts. Also he noted the well-stocked kitchen garden.[62] (30)

The primary fact of Cortez's approach to the city is the perceptual act. The movement of the Spaniard's "eye" is as important as the movement of his "I." Cortez "especially noted," and "Also he noted" —Williams repeats the formula to impress the textures of the place on Cortez's senses. He makes the moment of aesthetic vision an event in the history as surely as Cortez's actual entry into the city is an event. "There it lay!" cries Williams as the city appears on the horizon. Indeed, he transforms Cortez's act of crossing over the causeway and entering the city into an aesthetic event, focusing the unfolding scene in the Spaniard's eye:

> There it lay! a city a large as Cordova or Seville, entirely within the lake two miles from the mainland: Tenochtitlan. Four avenues or entrances led to it, all formed of artificial causeways. Along the most easterly of these, constructed of great beams perfectly hewn and fitted together, and measuring two spears-lengths in width, the Christian advanced. Running in at one side of the city and out at the other this avenue constituted at the same time its principal street. As Cortez drew nearer he saw, right and left, magnificent houses and temples, close to the walls of which, each side, moved parallel rows of priests in black robes, and between them, supported by two attendants, Montezuma, on foot, down the center of the roadway.[63] (30)

Cortez does not simply enter Tenochtitlan—he sees, as he draws nearer, an edifice of words, words that Williams has taken from Cortez himself and "perfectly hewn and fitted together" to construct the balanced symmetry of the things seen "right and left," of "magnificent houses and temples," of the "parallel rows of priests" between which Montezuma, "supported by two attendants," comes "down the center of the roadway." Cortez is literally drawn in by the beauty of Tenochtitlan. Montezuma puts "a golden chain" around Cortez's neck and leads him "by the hand" into "the center of the city," where the Spaniard is immediately showered with an abundance of "rich gifts . . . precious metals, gems, male and female apparel of remarkable elegance, ornamental hangings for bedchambers, tapestries for halls and temples, counterpanes composed of feathers interwoven with cotton, and many beautiful and curious artifices of so costly and unusual workmanship that considering their novelty and wonderful beauty no price could be set on them' " (30–31).[64] Cortez is overcome not just with wonder but with a material profusion that inundates the senses. Yet Cortez's arrival at his quarters in the center of the city is only the end of his physical journey—now begins the real adventure of the eye.

"Scarcely an element in the city's incredible organization but evidenced an intellectual vigor full of resource and delicacy," says Williams (32). The streets, the aqueducts, the marketplace, the temples, the rooms of Montezuma's private retreats—each feature reveals in succession its "incredible organization" before the eyes of Cortez, extending the already established movement of the plot as a penetration into the interior. From the public space of the marketplace, "where daily sixty thousand souls engaged in buying and selling" (32), Cortez moves into the private space of the temples, into the "sacred precinct" of the main temple and down its halls from which "through very small doors, opened the chapels, to which no light was admitted, nor any person except the priests, and not all of them" (33). And from the inner sanctum of the temple, the blood and seed root of the Aztecs' life, Cortez penetrates to the spaces exclusively constructed for the delight and amusement of Montezuma, the "barbaric chieftain" about whose "suave personality" the "most airily expansive moods of the race did flower, just as the black permanence of tribal understanding stood rooted in the priesthood" (35).

Against these vital spatial disclosures, Williams juxtaposes the uncomprehending responses of Cortez, the "terrible hands" of the conquistador. As soon as Montezuma has led Cortez into the city, Williams has Montezuma draw him aside and disclose his own flesh to the Spaniard, inviting him to touch it, to know the reality of the New World by feeling it with his hands, telling him, " 'They have told you that I possess houses with walls of gold and many other such things and that I am a god or make myself one. The houses you see are of stone and lime and earth.'—Then opening his robe: 'You see that I am composed of flesh and bone like yourself and that I am mortal and palpable to the touch' " (31).[65] But Cortez is unable to touch this man, this place, in the way they offer themselves to him. He can only demand that they acknowledge his reality. To Montezuma's "smiling sally, so full of gentleness and amused irony, Cortez could reply nothing save to demand that the man declare himself a subject to the Spanish King forthwith and that, furthermore, he should then and there announce publicly his allegiance to the new power" (31).[66]

But Cortez's response to Montezuma's playful disclosure of self is not nearly as devastating as his response to the disclosure of the Aztecs' religious practices. His entry into the inner sanctum of the temple brought Cortez to the place of the Aztecs' most essential bond to the ground: "Here it was that the tribe's deep feeling for a reality that stems back into the permanence of remote origins had its firm hold. It was the earthward thrust of their logic; blood and earth; the realization of their primal and continuous identity with the ground itself, where everything is fixed in darkness" (33–34). Cortez essentially uproots the flower of Tenochtitlan by casting down the Aztec idols. The Aztecs' ritual worship of their originating tie to the earth is embodied in the flesh of these idols as certainly as the flowering of their race is embodied in the flesh of Montezuma. "The figures of these idols themselves," Williams points out, "were of extra-human size and composed, significantly, of a paste of seeds and leguminous plants, commonly used for food, ground and mixed together and kneaded with human blood, the whole when completed being consecrated with a bath of blood from the heart of a living victim" (34).[67] Cortez lays his hands upon the idols, but only to push them down from their pedestals, "at the same time purifying the chapels and setting up in them images of Our Lady and the saints" (34). The changing of the gods marks the death of Tenochtitlan. The vital life of the city withered almost as soon as Cortez arrived, as Williams suggests, because Tenochtitlan was "so completely removed from those foreign contacts which harden and protect, that at the very breath of conquest it vanished" (32). Yet Cortez had pierced to the very root of the flower.

Williams certainly doesn't try to equivocate about the city's destruction, to conjecture how Tenochtitlan might have been spared had one thing or another gone differently at the time of events. He plainly admits the fact of loss, specifically titling his chapter to announce, before all else, the destruction of Tenochtitlan. No matter that Cortez didn't want to destroy it, or that he later "tried to rebuild the city" (38), or that Montezuma, "by a sudden, daring stroke . . . might have rid himself of the intestine enemy who was each day, each week, striking deeper at the nation's life" (34). Tenochtitlan was destroyed. Yet for Williams, that fact simply proves that Tenochtitlan wasn't just some fantastic vision, some *fata morgana* like Ponce's Fountain of Eternal Youth. As Williams' comment in "The American Background" emphasizes, Tenochtitlan should be remembered as something actual— actual enough to have been destroyed: "One is at liberty to guess what the pure American addition to world culture might have been if it had gone forward singly. Perhaps Tenochtitlan which Cortez destroyed held the key. That is also beside the point, except that Tenochtitlan with its curious brilliance may still legitimately be kept alive not as something which *could* have been preserved but something which was actual and was destroyed" (SE, 142–43).

Though it is tempting to speculate what might have emerged from Tenochtitlan if Cortez had not conquered the city, Williams refuses to indulge in fantasies of the might-have-been. His insistent concern is that the city indeed existed at the time of Cortez's arrival as a purely American cultural artifact, that its structure and order were an unadulterated expression of the spirit of the place where it grew. Williams needed to keep that aspect of Tenochtitlan "legitimately" alive to show his contemporaries that there is a ground to build on in America. In that sense Tenochtitlan does hold the key to Williams' vision of a uniquely American culture, for the city symbolizes culture as the act of cultivating the local:

> The burning need of a culture is not a choice to be made or not made, voluntarily, any more than it can be satisfied by loans. It has to be where it arises, or everything related to the life there ceases. It isn't a thing: it's an act. If it stands still, it is dead. It is the realization of the qualitites of a place in relation to the life which occupies it; embracing everything involved, climate, geographic position, relative size, history, other cultures—as well as the character of its sands, flowers, minerals and the condition of knowledge within its borders. It is the act of lifting these things into an ordered and utilized whole which is culture. It isn't something left over afterward. That is the record only. The act is the thing. It can't be escaped or avoided if life is to go on. It is in the fullest sense that which is fit. (SE, 157)

The position Williams voices here in "The American Background" had already been acted out in *In the American Grain*. Williams had worked the soil of history to show that rather than an object to be imported, like bringing "the tower of the Seville Cathedral to Madison Square," culture is a process of cultivating the place where one is (224). And in his chapter on Poe, Williams implicitly glances back to

Tenochtitlan as he delivers his answer to our traditional way of seeing America in terms of what it culturally lacks:

> What it lacked, really, was to be cultivated. So they build an unrelated copy upon it; this, as a sign of intelligence,—vigor. That is, to bring out its qualities, they cover them. Culture is still the effect of cultivation, to work with a thing until it be rare; as a golden dome among the mustard fields. It implies a solidity capable of cultivation. Its effects are marble blocks that lie perfectly fitted and aligned to express by isolate distinction the rising lusts which threw them off, regulated, in moving through the mass of impedimenta which is the world.
>
> This is culture; in mastering them, to burst through the peculiarities of an enviroment. It is NOT culture to *oppress* a novel environment with the stale, if symmetrical, castoff of another battle. (224–25)

Williams' "golden dome" that "implies a solidity capable of cultivation" is Tenochtitlan. The cultural act of lifting the unique qualitites of a place into expression is verbally enacted in Williams' excerpts from Cortez. The marketplace gathers together "everything that could be found throughout the whole country," arranging "each kind of merchandise in a separate street or quarter of the market assigned to it exclusively," so that "the best order was preserved" (33).[68] No mere place of commerce, the marketplace of Tenochtitlan performs the transformative gesture of art—it enunciates the distinctive character of its environment. Even more so Montezuma's palaces. The Aztec emperor not only has one palace " 'in which are kept the different species of water birds found in the country,' " and another " 'in which are kept lions, wolves, foxes and a great variety of other animals of the cat kind,' " he has " 'every object in his domain imitated in gold and silver being wrought so naturally as not to be surpassed by any smith in the world; the stonework executed with such perfection that it is difficult to conceive what instruments could have been used, and the feather work superior to the finest production in wax and embroidery' " (36, 35).[69]

To the inventive imagination rooted in the realities of its environment, all facts become artifacts. And for Williams, Montezuma himself is the highest expression of the Aztecs' genius for cultivating the ground: "The whole waking aspirations of his people, opposed to and completing their religious sense, seemed to come off in him and him alone: the drive upward, toward the sun and stars. He was the very person of their ornate dreams, so delicate, so prismatically colorful, so full of tinkling sounds and rhythms, so tireless of invention. Never was such a surface lifted above the isolate blackness of such profound savagery" (35). But Montezuma is not simply "lifted above" the "profound savagery" of the Aztecs' life—he is the product of it, its flowering. His "drive upward, toward the sun and stars," is rooted in "the earthward thrust of their logic," their ritual shedding of blood and seed upon the ground.

Was rooted, that is. Williams knows Montezuma's marvelous city is forever gone. "The whole world of its unique associations sank back into the ground to be reënkindled, never"—but Williams adds a pivotal qualification to this loss: "Never, at least, save in spirit; a spirit mysterious, constructive, independent, puissant with natural wealth; light, if it may be, as feathers; a spirit lost in that soil" (32). That spirit is exactly what Williams reenkindles to write "The Destruction of Tenochtitlan," descending into the soil of the Aztecs' deepest belief to express his own profoundest belief in the basis of culture: "The earth is black and it is there: only art advances" (34).

NOTES

1. Dickran Tashjian, "History and Culture in 'The American Background,' " *William Carlos Williams Review* 11 (Spring 1985): 13–19, argues that this essay "significantly qualified and enlarged the sense of history that had framed *In the American Grain*," and that in writing the piece "Williams perceived a cultural dialectic that would allow a synthesis of old and new," thus overcoming the dichotomous structure of the earlier history (13, 17). But Tashjian fails to point out that the essay actually greatly reduces both the temporal and geographic scope of *In the American Grain* to pursue that synthesis.

2. Alvar Núñez Cabeza de Vaca, *Adventures in the Unknown Interior of America*, trans. Cyclone Covey (Albuquerque: University of New Mexico Press, 1983). Williams knew of Cabeza de Vaca, and in fact mentions him by name at the opening of "De Soto and the New World" as one who "lived hard and saw much" (45). Williams most probably read the excerpts from Buckingham Smith's 1851 translation of Cabeza de Vaca's narrative that appeared as "De Vaca's Journey to New Mexico" in *Old South Leaflets*, no. 39, a reprint series that provided Williams with a number of his source materials, and that I discuss more fully in my concluding chapter. It seems odd, perhaps inexplicable, that Williams doesn't do more with Cabeza de Vaca in *In the American Grain*, for the Spaniard seems tailor-made for Williams' purposes. Charles Olson, certainly no less interested in the dynamics of New World history than Williams, would later suggest the potential of Cabeza de Vaca's life in "Cabeza de Vaca, An Idea for an Opera," in Donald Allen, ed., *The Fiery Hunt and Other Plays* (Bolinas, Calif.: Four Seasons Foundation, 1977), 45–48.

3. Williams erroneously cites 1548 as the year of the expedition's entry into Florida (45).

4. The only one who might have written in a more personal way was

Ranjel, for he prepared his report from a diary he kept during the course of events. But neither the diary nor even the report itself is extant, unfortunately, and Ranjel's narrative exists only in the epitome given by Oviedo in his *Historia General y Natural de las Indias*. Though Williams relies primarily upon the Fidalgo's relation in constructing his chapter, he also draws supporting details from Biedma and, to a lesser extent, from Ranjel. The only possible volume in which Williams could have found all three narratives printed together was Edward Gaylord Bourne's *Narratives of the Career of Hernando de Soto in the Conquest of Florida*: "The True Relation of the Vicissitudes that Attended the Governor Don Hernando De Soto . . . by a Fidalgo of Elvas" and "Relation of the Conquest of Florida . . . by Luys Hernandez De Biedma," trans. Buckingham Smith; "A Narrative of De Soto's Expedition, Based on the Diary of Rodrigo Ranjel, His Private Secretary," trans. Edward Gaylord Bourne, 2 vols. (New York: A. S. Barnes, 1904; rpt. New York: Allerton, 1922; rpt. New York: AMS Press, 1973). Williams perhaps chose Bourne's volume simply because he was familiar with the historian's name from the source he used for the Columbus chapter—but in doing so, Williams drew on the most comprehensive collection of De Soto materials then available.

5. Both quotations in this passage are from the Fidalgo's narrative (Bourne, 1: 71, 215).

6. The phrase *through obscure and intricate parts* is from Biedma's relation (Bourne, 2: 11).

7. Buckingham Smith, in the annotations to his translation of the Fidalgo's narrative originally made for the Bradford Club, provides the following etymological note: " 'Barbacoa,' of which we have not the elements, is from the Yucayo, and in its simplest signification appears to mean scaffolding raised on posts, such an arrangement as was made for burning Ortiz, mentioned in Chapter IX.; or a crib, such as was used for storing the crop; or staging put up in the fields, whereon the natives watched, that birds should not take the grain. From it, through the Spanish, comes the word into the English 'barbacue.' " *Narratives of De Soto in the Conquest of Florida* (New York: John B. Moreau, 1866; rpt. Gainesville, Fla.: Palmetto Books, 1968), 222.

8. See the Fidalgo, 26–27.

9. Ibid., 50–51.

10. Ibid., 37.

11. Plundering the Indians' stores of maize was indeed one of the expedition's main ways of obtaining food. But Williams fabricates the difficulty of the Spaniards' first winter to advance his own plot. The Fidalgo gives a quite contrary report of the first winter at Apalachi: "The Campmaster, whose duty it is to divide and lodge the men, quartered them about the town, at the distance of half a league apart. There were other towns which had much maize, pumpkins, beans, and dried plums of the country, whence were brought together at Anhayca Apalache what appeared to be sufficient provision for the winter" (47).

12. The Fidalgo, 56–57.

13. Williams conflates the Fidalgo's descriptions of the gifts from two separate such receptions by the natives (73, 74).

14. The Fidalgo, 145.

15. Though Williams appears to quote directly from a single source, the quotation is his own amalgam from the Fidalgo (93) and Biedma (19).

16. The rabbits are from Biedma (22), but Williams supplies the turkeys.

17. At Chicaca, the Indians actually did set fire to their own town during the night, causing heavy losses among the unsuspecting Spaniards who were quartered there. (The details for Williams' dramatic rendering of the battle scene are from Biedma, 23, and the Fidalgo, 103–5.) But at Mabilla, it was actually the Spaniards who fired the town, despite the fact that their own goods lay within. The cacique of the province, Tuscaloosa, had invited the Spaniards to enter as his guests, but the advance party discovered the ambush and managed to withdraw before the rest of the troops reached the town. Yet the Indians the Spaniards had previously enslaved as carriers had deposited all the expedition's effects just outside the perimeter of the town, and Tuscaloosa's people seized them while the advance party retreated. The Spaniards resolved to burn Mabilla anyway, explains the Fidalgo, "because they considered the loss less than the injury they might receive of the Indians from within the houses, where they had brought the things together" (97). Williams, nonetheless, suggests that the firing of Mabilla is the work of She as much as is the burning of Chicaca. Indeed, he not only has She voice the dramatic narration of the battle scene, in details taken largely from Ranjel (Bourne, 2: 126), but Williams additionally says that because the loss of pearls in the fire made De Soto resolve to push on farther into the country in hopes of replacing them with yet other wealth, "to Tuscaloosa must be given credit, in effect, for a great victory" (49).

18. The details here are from the Fidalgo, 106, 107.

19. The whole of this lengthy episode is taken verbatim from the Fidalgo, 113–14.

20. Williams quotes verbatim from the Fidalgo, 122.

21. Williams again quotes verbatim from the Fidalgo, 129.

22. The quotation is adapted from Biedma, 12.

23. Though drawn from De Soto's chroniclers, the composition of this landscape is peculiarly Williams' own. The image of sails black with insects is not from De Soto's inland trek, but from the Fidalgo's description of the survivors' journey down the Mississippi in the brigantines they built under Luís de Moscoso's command (208–9). The description of the wild rose is from Ranjel's narrative (96–97). The additional observations of plants and animals are taken from the Fidalgo's concluding chapter—more of an appendix actually, a convention very prevalent in early American writing, a catalogue of the species seen during one's travels (222). That section of the Fidalgo's relation is itself a composite landscape, one not emplotted in a story but rather listed as the elements of an inventory, but Williams has incorporated it here into the diachrony of his narrative.

24. The Fidalgo, too, had seen the river from De Soto's perspective, re-marking, "He went to look at the river, and saw that near it there was much timber of which piraguas might be made" (112). The Fidalgo imagines the river for De Soto as merely an obstacle, implying his first thought was for building boats. Williams keeps De Soto as the framing consciousness but erases the thought of boat building, replacing it with the Fidalgo's later description of the river's great power.

25. Williams quotes, with some elisions, verbatim from the Fidalgo, 146–47.

26. Except for his insertion between the two paragraphs, Williams quotes verbatim from the Fidalgo, 153–54.

27. The Fidalgo, 161.

28. Ibid., 162.

29. Ibid., 124.

30. Ibid., 163–64.

31. Waldo Frank, *Virgin Spain* (New York: Boni & Liveright, 1926), 298, 299. Frank sets up his pairing of Cervantes with Columbus in an earlier chapter, "The Will of Don Quixote," in which he presents Cervantes as the culminating figure of the western quest to fuse the world into wholeness, to find what Frank terms the medieval principle of the Unity of the One. He calls Cervantes' Don Quixote "the last prophet of our historic Order" (225). Frank further develops his notion of America as "The Grave of Europe" in his subsequent book, *The Re-Discovery of America* (New York: Charles Scribner's Sons, 1929), 56–66.

32. For Williams, mentioning Waldo Frank's admiration for "The Discovery of the Indies" would become virtually synonymous with mentioning the difficulties he encountered in writing the chapter. See, for example, Williams' *Autobiography* (183), and Linda Wagner, ed., *Interviews with William Carlos Williams* (New York: New Directions, 1976), 65.

33. William Carlos Williams, "The Discovery of the Indies," *Broom* 4 (March 1923): 252.

34. Williams was working on "The Discovery of the Indies" and "De Soto and the New World" simultaneously, and in fact completed both chapters on the same day, February 13, at Villefranche, as he notes in his diary: "I finished the Columbus and De Soto pieces finally."

35. Christopher Columbus, *Journal of the First Voyage*, trans. Sir Clements R. Markham, in Julius E. Olson and Edward Gaylord Bourne, eds., *The Northmen, Columbus, and Cabot, 985–1503* (New York: Charles Scribner's Sons, 1906), 238–39, 241–42. Williams does here what typifies his handling of the journal. He stitches together selected excerpts from several days of entries to form what seems to be a single, extended entry by Columbus. In addition, he puts the text back into the first person. There are actually no extant copies of the journal itself, and its contents have come to us only through the work of various epitomizers. Ferdinand Columbus used portions of the original text in writing his father's life, and Las Casas also had a copy of the text he used in

writing his *Historia de las Indias*. Bourne, editor of the Columbus materials in Williams' source document, draws upon yet another epitome, first published in 1825 by the Spanish historian Navarrete from a manuscript in the archives of the Duke del Infantado. (It is not certain who prepared this manuscript, though Navarrete conjectures the handwriting to be Las Casas'.) This version is not only longer and more detailed than the other epitomes, but it gives an exact transcription of Columbus' own words for the entries from October 12 to October 28, 1492. The rest of the entries, however, are written by the epitomizer himself, who paraphrases the words of "the Admiral," referring to Columbus throughout the text by his official title. Williams erases the presence of the epitomizer from his selection of excerpts, creating the impression that Columbus' own manuscript has survived to tell the story. Williams, furthermore, avails himself here, as he frequently does, of Bourne's scholarship by incorporating materials from the editor's notes into "The Discovery of the Indies." He takes Columbus' account of sealing a parchment in a barrel during the height of the storm from Bourne's lengthy citation from Ferdinand Columbus, who provides that section of the journal in the exact words of his father. And one last point regarding the peculiar permutations the already complicated matter of the journal undergoes in Williams' treatment—Columbus never used the phrase *New World* in relation to the lands he discovered, and indeed believed, even after his fourth voyage, that he had reached the Orient. Williams, however, needed to have a Columbus who was conscious of having discovered a New World, and he inserts the phrase into his excerpt here.

36. The first quotation is from Columbus' prologue to the *Journal of the First Voyage,* wherein he reiterates the titles officially granted him by the Spanish throne. The second is excerpted from "Articles of Agreement between the Lords, the Catholic Sovereigns, and Cristóbal Colon," trans. George F. Barwick, in Olson and Bourne, 79, 80.

37. Claude Lévi-Strauss, too, speaks of Columbus' discovery of a world that had been "spared the agitations of 'history' for some ten or twenty millennia" as the beginning of "a terrible ordeal" for the European mind, an epochal shattering of humankind's conceptual vision of self, world, and history, *Tristes Tropiques*, trans. John Russell (New York: Criterion Books, 1961), 78–79. Edmundo O'Gorman, *The Invention of America* (Bloomington: Indiana University Press, 1961), gives a brilliant reading of this cognitive torsion in his study of New World cartographic representations.

38. Christopher Columbus, "Letter of Columbus to the Nurse of Prince John," trans. George F. Barwick, in Olson and Bourne, 372, 371. Williams' handling of this letter, which Columbus addressed to Doña Juana de Torres, nurse of the lately deceased royal heir to the throne, is indicative of his treatment of much of his source material on Columbus. He not only excises material that doesn't suit his purposes—such as Columbus' growing mystical conviction that he was God's chosen messenger to reveal the realm "Of the new heaven and earth which our Lord made, when Saint John was writing the

Apocalypse" (371)—but reorders the arrangement of certain passages to more explicitly juxtapose Columbus' major accomplishments with the ignominy of his present state. In addition, Williams introduces into the text phrases such as *a mainland to the south discovered* to circumvent the tangled matter of Columbus' geographical conceptions. In his subsequent selections from the letter, after Columbus' recitation of the Bobadilla affair, Williams has Columbus speak of undertaking "that holy pilgrimage which has long been in my heart" (12). Columbus actually doesn't mention anything about a pilgrimage in this letter —but Williams inserts the remark to help set up his own later conjecture about what would have happened if Columbus had made a pilgrimage to Rome.

39. Christopher Columbus, "Letter of Columbus on the Fourth Voyage," trans. R. H. Major, in Olson and Bourne, 389–90.

40. Ibid., 392–93.

41. Ibid., 417–18.

42. Ibid., 399–400, 406, 407.

43. Ibid., 418.

44. Williams uses Bourne's note on Ferdinand Columbus' *Historia del Almirante* for that purpose in the entry for September 9 just previously cited, *Journal of the First Voyage*, 94. Other notable instances occur in the entry for September 23, in which Williams takes information from Bourne's note on Las Casas' *Historia* (100), and in the entry for October 10, in which he draws on information Bourne provides from Oviedo's *Historia* and Peter Martyr's *De Rebus Oceanicis* (108).

45. Gutierrez, however, is not Williams' own invention. He is referred to twice in the *Journal of the First Voyage* and identified alternately as "a gentleman of the King's bed-chamber" (109), and as "keeper of the king's drawing-room, and servant of the chief butler" (210).

46. Columbus, *Journal of the First Voyage*, 94.

47. The combustive heat of this passage, which Williams gives as occurring on Saturday, October 13, is partly the result of Williams' compression—he combines together the choicest and most marvelous wonders that Columbus noted over the course of five days, from Saturday to the following Wednesday. And in his rendition of Columbus' entry for Friday, October 12, Williams cuts the original text by half, gleaning the passages in which Columbus describes the shape and features of the natives who gather to meet him on the beach, and trimming statements such as, "It appeared to me to be a race of people very poor in everything," and, "They should be good servants and intelligent, for I observed that they quickly took in what was said to them, and I believe that they would easily be made Christians, as it appeared to me that they had no religion," *Journal of the First Voyage*, 111.

48. Williams plays on the Genoan's name. *Christophoro* literally means "Christ-bearer"—"him that carried Christ across the river," as Williams had put it in the *Broom* version of "The Discovery of the Indies."

49. Williams appears to have in mind something he had read in Columbus' "Letter to the Nurse of Prince John" rather than the journal: "A hundred

castellanos are as easily obtained for a woman as for a farm, and it is very general, and there are plenty of dealers who go about looking for girls; those from nine to ten are now in demand, and for all ages a good price must be paid" (378). Columbus seems to offer this comment as a complaint about the state of affairs in Española—yet it was he who instituted slave trading as a mainstay of the island's economy.

50. Williams seems to play here on a remark from Las Casas' *Historia* that Bourne provides as a note to the entry for October 7 in *The Journal of the First Voyage*: "If he [Columbus] had kept up the direct westerly course and the impatience of the Castilians had not hindered him, there is no doubt that he would have struck the mainland of Florida and from there to New Spain, although the difficulties would have been unparalleled and the losses unbearable that they would have met with, and it would have been a divine miracle if he had ever returned to Castile" (107).

51. D. H. Lawrence, *Studies in Classic American Literature* (New York: Viking Press, 1964), 35.

52. Lawrence, "Introduction to Studies in Classic American Literature, Spirit of Place," *The English Review* 27 (Nov. 1918): 327, 328.

53. "To William Carlos Williams," 10 Nov. 1917, Letter 137, *The Letters of Ezra Pound, 1907–1941*, 123–24. Williams himself quotes this letter in the prologue to *Kora in Hell* (KH, 11–12), turning its cutting edge back upon Pound in their long-standing exchange of verbal blows over what Williams termed, in a later letter to Pound, "your old gag of heredity, where you come from where I come from" (SL, 69).

54. Williams does, in fact, rely upon biographies by historians in several later chapters of *In the American Grain* as well. Yet in such cases, he generally selects texts that are more legitimately historical in purpose than Frederick Ober's *Juan Ponce de Leon* (New York: Harper & Brothers, 1908). Indeed, there is some evidence that Williams actually tries to conceal the signs that might point to Ober's text, altering the proper names that could serve as indicators of his source. "Bezerillo," the variant Ober gives for the name of Ponce's infamous hound, is transformed to "Berrescien," and "Agueybana," Ober's spelling of the name for the Carib chief who led his people into the hills during Ponce's extermination campaigns is rendered "Aboujoubo" by Williams. While such permutations might evidence nothing more than a certain carelessness in transcribing source material, Williams' choice of names for the island of Puerto Rico could well be an effort to place the would-be searcher on the trail of a source as phantom as the fountain itself. He refers to the island once by its original Indian name, Boriquen, once by its modern name, Puerto Rico, and once by the name Ponce had originally given it, San Juan, delivering the latter in an orthography—"San Ion"—commonly found in sixteenth- and seventeenth-century English translations of the Spanish historians. But all three forms can be found in Ober, who tries to give his swashbuckling tale an authentically historical flavor. Ober, in fact, proves to be a richly accommodating source for Williams, providing an eclectic and unique knowledge of

Puerto Rico's past. Williams' references to the Carib gods, "Mabouya, in the forest, Oumekon, by the sea" (39), for example, draw on information peculiar to Ober alone (238), which he acquired while doing ornithological research in the Caribbean during the late nineteenth century. (See his *Camps in the Caribees: The Adventures of a Naturalist in the Lesser Antilles,* Boston: Lee and Shepard, 1880.) And Ober's first-hand knowledge of the island terrain produced the lush jungle descriptions ("Rousseau has it," Williams mockingly remarks) replete with "thick vines in flower attended by ensanguined hummingbirds which darted about from cup to cup in the green light" and "flamingoes, pelicans, egrets, herons" that Williams uses for parodic effect in his chapter (40, 42; Ober, 244–45).

55. Ober, 168.

56. Bruce Clarke, in his "The Fall of Montezuma: Poetry and History in William Carlos Williams and D. H. Lawrence," *William Carlos Williams Review* 12 (Spring 1986): 1–12, gives an excellent discussion of how Williams' and Lawrence's approaches to history converge at the figures of Montezuma and Cortez. But I think it safe to say that "The Destruction of Tenochtitlan" doesn't follow Lawrence's own lines of interest. In his first version of "Spirit of Place," Lawrence identified the Quetzcoatl legend and Montezuma's reception of Cortez "with mystic sympathy, mystic desire" as the key to understanding the conquest of Mexico (325). Williams, however, omits any mention of the Quetzcoatl legend. Furthermore, neither Cortez nor Montezuma is the focus of Williams' chapter. The real protagonist is Tenochtitlan. Just as he would later write of a city as a man in *Paterson,* Williams makes Tenochtitlan a living character in his chronology of men. And it is interesting to note that "The Destruction of Tenochtitlan" was one of the few chapters Lawrence chose to quibble with in his otherwise laudatory review of the book. "Was Tenochtitlan really so wonderful?" he asked, and he advised Williams to go back to the books: "(See Adolf Bandelier's 'The Golden Man,')" (*William Carlos Williams: The Critical Heritage,* 91). Yet Lawrence's reference is peculiar. Adolphe F. Bandelier's *The Gilded Man* (New York: D. Appleton and Company, 1893), the book Lawrence apparently had in mind, makes no mention of Tenochtitlan.

57. Williams, with a characteristic twist, takes the motto that Cortez had said Narváez had had his troops carry into battle against him—"*viva quien vence,*" long live the victor—and uses it as the sardonic cry that ends his chapter. See *The Despatches of Hernando Cortes,* ed. and trans. George Folsom (New York: Wiley and Putnam, 1843), 134.

58. Folsom, 110.

59. Williams does not put these phrases in quotation marks because they are so in his source—nor does he even render the quote itself with precision in either case, omitting the internal punctuation from the first, and changing the wording of the second, which reads "all kinds of merchandise that the world affords" (Folsom, 108, 112). These sorts of alterations are indicative of Williams' treatment of the larger excerpts in which these two phrases occur.

60. Characteristically, Williams doesn't quote Cortez exactly. The Span-

iard writes, "Although it grieved me much, yet as it grieved the enemy more, I determined to burn these palaces" (Folsom, 280).

61. The inventory Williams quotes doesn't come directly from Cortez's own letters, but from Peter Martyr's *De Insulis Nuper Inventis*. Cortez had perhaps described the gifts in a letter he wrote to Charles V just prior to the inland march. But that letter isn't extant, though it is generally agreed Martyr had copied the inventory of gifts from it. In his introduction to Cortez's letters, Folsom had provided his own translation of that passage from Martyr, and Williams quotes from there (36–37).

62. Williams loosely paraphrases Cortez in this passage (Folsom, 83).

63. Williams combines here two separate passages from Cortez: one in which Cortez narrates his reception by Montezuma on the causeway, and the passage in which Cortez begins his description of the city (Folsom, 108, 111).

64. Williams doctors the record to create this sense of Cortez's seduction by the city. Cortez is careful to write that he first placed a necklace "of pearls and glass diamonds" around Montezuma's neck before receiving the Aztec's ceremonial gift (Folsom, 86)—but Williams omits that report. In addition, he gives a richer and more lavish sense of the gifts Montezuma bestows on Cortez at his quarters. Cortez had mentioned only in passing that Montezuma presented him "with many and various jewels of gold and silver, featherwork, and five or six thousand pieces of cotton cloth, very rich and of varied texture and finish" (Folsom, 87). But the presentations Williams delivers here are from Cortez's minutely detailed and lengthy inventory of the wealth he had levied in tributes for Charles V from the city and its provinces over several months (Folsom, 109, 108).

65. Montezuma did, according to Cortez, take him aside for a private interview as soon as the Spaniards were settled in their quarters. But Williams radically alters Cortez's report of what was said on that occasion. He entirely omits Montezuma's story of how it was long known that one would come from the East to subjugate the Aztecs, thus discarding what most historians see as the key to explaining Cortez's success in subduing the city: the legend of Quetzcoatl and Montezuma's voluntary submission to the invader (Folsom, 87–88). The one part of Montezuma's speech Williams does quote resonates with meanings quite different from those it has in its original context. There Montezuma playfully offers himself to Cortez's touch to disabuse the Spaniard of the marvelous lies that the Tlascans, the Aztecs' implacable enemies, had told Cortez about Montezuma to gain favor with the conqueror (Folsom, 88).

66. By omitting the legend of Quetzcoatl, Williams is able to make Montezuma's submission to Cortez seem more a strategic attempt to consolidate his own power in dire circumstances than an acknowledgment of Cortez's authority: "Whatever the Aztec may have felt during the weeks of Cortez' slow advance upon his capital from the seashore, nothing at the present moment seemed to disturb his aristocratic reserve. He had thought and he had made up his mind. Without semblance of anger, fear or impatience; without humility or protest but with the force bred of a determination to face at any cost

a situtation fast going beyond his control, he spoke again. He explained that his people were not the aborigines of the land but that they had emigrated there in times past and ended by accepting the Spanish Monarch as his rightful and hereditary master" (31–32). Montezuma's admission that the Aztecs "were not aborigines of the land" is as close as Williams comes to touching the Quetzcoatl legend.

67. Williams compresses Cortez's own description (Folsom, 117–18).

68. Cortez's inventory of the marketplace at Tenochtitlan is a remarkable moment in early American writing. Almost like a prototype of Whitman, Cortez recites a voluminous catalogue of names that seems a verbal celebration of New World abundance. Williams gives a sizeable excerpt in his text (32–33), but Cortez's catalogue is actually twice that length (Folsom, 112–14).

69. The lengthy descriptions of Montezuma's palaces (35–36) are excerpted verbatim from Cortez's even lengthier descriptions (Folsom, 120–23).

4

The Poetics and Politics of Sexuality

When Lawrence described Williams' book as "a glimpse of what the vast America *wants men to be*," he was right in more than one way. *In the American Grain* almost exclusively features the relation of men to the New World. From Eric the Red to Abraham Lincoln, Williams overwhelmingly populates the American past with male figures, naming men rather than women as the subjects of his various chapters. There is essentially only one female figure in the book: the landscape itself, She, the female essence of the New World. "One is forced upon the conception of the New World as a woman" (222), Williams writes in his chapter on Poe. But it is Williams who presses that conception upon his book, patterning American history after the image that had provided him with the cover illustration for *Kora in Hell*: multiple spermatozoa surrounding a single ovum. Many men, but only one woman, like a continent. They gather upon her shores, and at times, like De Soto, plunge into her body, achieving the objective Williams had pursued in *Contact,* and that kindled his writing of *In the American Grain*: the "implantation of the sperm."[1]

Such ritualized inseminations of the land are Williams' metaphor for the germination of a distinctively American culture, a life that grows from the unique conditions of the American environment. The aboriginal life of the New World, Williams endeavors to show in "The Destruction of Tenochtitlan," was rooted in just such a ceremonial fertilization of the female earth. But *In the American Grain* is primarily concerned with the possibility of creating an indigenous American culture out of the newcomers from Europe. The "peculiar condition of destiny" that marks American history for Williams is "the implantation of an already partly cultured race on a wild continent" (213). The European newcomer had another ground to look back to across the Atlantic, and it was that "home" he often tried to reproduce in the New World, without adapting to the unique conditions of place. But Williams conducts American history as a search for those men who broke through that conceptual barrier and seeded themselves in the ground, symbolically fertilizing the native female element like De Soto —or literally fertilizing it like Morton in his pagan revels with Indian maidens at Merry Mount.

Williams' conception of the New World as a woman is, of course, hardly unique. As Annette Kolodny has shown in *The Lay of the Land*, it is perhaps the oldest and most pervasive metaphor in American writing.[2] What distinguishes *In the American Grain* is the way it apprehensively uses the metaphor to envision the American past according to imperatives of gender rather than of genre. Though the early chapters of the book seem to be structured in terms of a conceptual opposition among the main cultural groups from Europe that sought to establish themselves in the New World, their underlying structure is based upon a sexual opposition between an invading male principle and a native female principle—the same opposition by which Williams would explain his own genesis as an American poet in a letter he wrote in 1946 to an Australian editor, Flexmore Hudson, to clarify his position on the nature of literary creativity.

The course of intellectual history, Williams argues, has largely been determined by a process of androgynetic development: "Minds beget minds, there's no use denying that. Newton begat Einstein just as Newton himself was got androgynously out of Archimedes."[3] With respect to literary history, what Williams comprehends as androgynetic development resembles the paradigm put forth by T. S. Eliot in "Tradition and the Individual Talent" and, more recently, by Harold Bloom in *The Anxiety of Influence*—male writers give birth to themselves by choosing their own literary paternity, by selecting from the past the work of other writers that will symbolically father their own.[4] Williams sees this process as one that denies a fertilizing contact with what he terms the "supplying female"—it generates writing "father to father. No mother necessary." As a result of this female absence, Williams claims, androgynetic development tends to produce "literary sterility," an enervation of the inventive imagination's power to generate new literary forms.[5]

But it is Pound rather than Eliot whom Williams poses in the letter as the exemplar of this androgynetic mode of development—and not simply because in 1946 Pound, having just been brought back to America, tried for treason for his profascist broadcasts in Italy during the war, and confined to St. Elizabeth's Hospital in New York, seemed better proof of "literary sterility" than did Eliot. Pound, Williams felt, had wanted to become his literary father, to shape his artistic genesis within the same partiarchal literary tradition of Europe by which Pound had fathered himself. "My mind balks," says Williams in the letter.[6] And he had indeed rebelled against this symbolic father, developing a theory of literary creativity that replaced a sterile and didactic father with a fecund and iconoclastic mother.[7] Pound had gone off to Europe to seek his paternity in tradition, repeatedly summoning Williams to follow in his footsteps—but Williams chose to remain in America, insistently equating his native ground with the female principle that he was certain could alone provide his source of fertilization as a writer.

His fertilization. Though Williams describes the inseminating act of culture in terms of the "implantation of the sperm," the New World is not a passive woman upon whose body the male inscribes his narrative. She resists inscription within history—history, that is, as represented by the rigidly fixed literary forms that Williams associates with the "father to father" sterility of Europe's ruling literary canons. Indeed, it is her power to rupture those forms that makes her a supplying female, the one who fertilizes the male. That is the founding mythos of *In the American Grain*—the birth of a poet out of fertilizing contact with the female body. And it is in this sense that Williams makes Columbus the first American poet, and his description of the beach at San Salvador the first American poem.

But Columbus is also America's "first victim." The spirit of place turns upon him for his symbolic act of rape. Williams creates the New World as a woman who can castrate the determining power of an invading Old World patriarchy. Ponce is cut down by an arrow in his thigh. De Soto, too, is critically wounded in the thigh. In his account of the fighting at Mabilla, Williams invents the detail of an arrow piercing De Soto's "thigh between the edges of the armor"—an arrow sent by She, which "has upon its barbs a kiss from my lips" (49). To become sperm, De Soto must lose his conquering phallus. "Come, black-beard, tireless rider, with an arrow in the thigh" (54), She tells him. She opens herself to him only because the means by which he would extend his authority has been severed. To perform the inseminating acts for an American culture, Europe must be symbolically castrated of its power to inscribe a narrative upon the ground. She will marry, Williams suggests, but she will not be raped.

Williams privileges those men who resign male will and marry the ground, giving themselves fully to place. Like De Soto, they are symbolically consumed, sexually incorporated into the New World. Living in isolation among the Indians, Rasles is "swallowed, a hard yeast." Boone too, is swallowed, going solitary into the unexplored wilds of Kentucky for three months "to enjoy ecstasy through his single devotion to the wilderness with which he was surrounded." Boone penetrates inland—not to conquer, but to be taken: "The beauty of a lavish, primitive embrace in savage, wild beast and forest rising above the cramped life about him possessed him wholly. Passionate and thoroughly given he avoided the half logic of stealing from the immense profusion" (136). Boone is "thoroughly given"—he possesses the New World by yielding himself to be completely "possessed" by it in "a lavish, primitive embrace." His "single devotion to the wilderness," makes him Williams' emblem of marriage between man and the New World: "There must be a new wedding. But he saw and only he saw the prototype of it all, the native savage. To Boone the Indian was his greatest master. Not for himself surely to be an Indian, though they eagerly sought to adopt him into their tribes, but the reverse: to be *himself* in a new world, Indianlike. If the land were to be possessed it must be as the Indian possessed it. Boone saw the truth of the Red Man, not an aberrant type, treacherous and anti-white to be feared and exterminated, but as the natural expression of the place, the Indian himself as 'right,' the flower of his world" (137–38).

Williams accords to Boone the greatest role in the book—the man who marries the earth, who recognizes the Indian as his master, as the natural flowering of place. Yet Boone fails to sound the resonances of Rasles, the man who may have indeed supplanted him in that role during Williams' writing of the book. The primary reason Boone lacks Rasles's depth is the absence of his verbal relationship to the land, of the language that would evidence his conjugation of the New World. Williams, however, couldn't get directly at Boone's words—he could only imagine the man's verbal character because Boone himself had left no written testament, nor had his speech ever been accurately rendered in writing. The closest approximation of Boone's voice that Williams could find was in the brief narrative "The Adventures of Col. Daniel Boon," which John Filson had appended to his *The Discovery, Settlement, and Present State of Kentucke* (1784). Though purportedly dictated to Filson by Boone, the language of the piece is obviously Filson's, the style mannered and literary.[8] And when Williams attempts to turn the narration of his chapter over to Boone himself, preparing the stage for the man's entry with a flourish, announcing Boone's call to Kentucky in ringing tones—"It touched the great keynote of his character, and the hour and the man had come" (133)—the passage Boone speaks falls totally flat. Williams, chagrined, breaks off the excerpt and apologizes to the reader for the dismal performance: "Thus opens the so-called autobiography, said to have been written down from Boone's dictation, late in his life by one John Filson. But the silly phrases and total disregard for what must have been the rude words of the old hunter serve only, for the most part, to make it a keen disappointment to the interested reader" (133).

Williams nonetheless tries to persist with his wonted practice of wholesale verbatim excerpting, providing a full page and a half more from Boone's narrative, before finally chucking the document altogether in utter frustration. "But only impatience is kindled by the silly language of the asinine chronicler," Williams testily remarks as he pulls the plug on Filson. Instead of "the rude words of the old hunter," Filson gives Williams only a romantic gloss on the raw and primitive. And Williams finds himself stuck in the position of arguing with his source text rather than lifting it into expression: "But when Filson goes on to declare Boone's loneliness 'an uninterrupted scene of sylvan pleasures' it is a little too much to bear. Constant exposure to danger and death, a habitation which he states had been discovered by the savages, the necessity of such stratagems as the resort to the canebrake rather than to take the risk of being found in his cabin, have nothing of sylvan pleasures in them. Boone had too much strong sense to feel anything but patience amidst the scenes of his solitude" (135).

Boone's role in the book doesn't begin to assume flesh until Williams abandons Filson and any attempt to recover, or rather uncover, Boone's own words. Indeed, Boone's verbal absence allows Williams to speak the part of an ideal figure—not by creating a voice for Boone, but by using Boone's silence to release his own voice. Boone's solitary venture into the wilderness, his sensual delight in the landscape, his aversion to the settled spaces, his reverence for the Indians—a mere handful of details provides the historical basis for Williams to kindle his own poetic imagination and to clothe Boone in an engendering language of his own manufacture:

> because of a descent to the ground of his desire was Boone's life important and does it remain still loaded with power,—power to strengthen every form of energy that would be voluptuous, passionate, possessive in that place which he opened. For the problem of the New World was, as every new comer soon found out, an awkward one, on all sides the same: how to replace from the wild land that which, at home, they had scarcely known the Old World meant to them; through difficulty and even brutal hardship to find a ground

to take the place of England. They could not do it. They clung, one
way or another, to the old, striving the while to pull off pieces to
themselves from the fat of the new bounty.

Boone's genius was to recognize the difficulty as neither material
nor political but one purely moral and aesthetic. Filled with the wild
beauty of the New World to overbrimming so long as he had what he
desired, to bathe in, to explore always more deeply, to see, to feel,
to touch—his instincts were contented. Sensing a limitless fortune
which daring could make his own, he sought only with primal lust
to grow close to it, to understand it and to be part of its mysterious movements—like an Indian. And among all the colonists, like
an Indian, the ecstasy of a complete possession of the new country
was his alone. In Kentucky he would stand, a lineal descendant of
Columbus on the beach at Santo Domingo, walking up and down
with eager eyes while his men were gathering water. (136–37)

Boone expresses his "primal lust" on a level "purely moral and
aesthetic." His "ecstasy of a complete possession" becomes Williams'
reply to the Puritan thesis of "a possession of the incomplete." Rather
than fearfully pilfering "from the fat of the new bounty," Boone sensu-
ously "bathes" in "the wild beauty of the New World," letting it fill him
"to overbrimming." Williams endows Boone with the qualitites of a
poet—of America's prototypical poet, Christopher Columbus. Boone
emerges "a lineal descendant of Columbus on the beach at Santo Domingo," the progeny of a uniquely American genealogy based upon an
aesthetic embrace of the ground. Indeed, at the outset of the chapter
Williams explicitly frames Boone's discovery of Kentucky as a repetition of Columbus' discovery, portraying Kentucky in terms of a virgin
land not yet violated by history: "Kentucky, the great wilderness beyond the western edge of the world, 'the dark and bloody ground' of
coming years, seemed to the colonists along the eastern North American seaboard as far away, nearly, and as difficult of approach as had
the problematical world itself beyond the western ocean to the times
prior to Columbus" (130).

Tradition, by definition, rests on repetition, and Williams' attempt
to create an American tradition rests upon a repetition of the inseminating moment of discovery. Boone's turning inland toward "the forbidden wealth of the Unknown" (131) not only reenacts Columbus'
discovery but is itself reenacted later in the book by Poe, whose "great-
ness," says Williams, "is in that he turned his back and faced inland, to
originality, with the identical gesture of a Boone" (226). It is the same
gesture with which Williams had planned to end his projected four-
book scheme for *Paterson*—a man emerges from the ocean, climbs the
shore and heads "inland" (P, 203). Boone is conceived by that gesture,

and quite literally so in *In the American Grain*, for Williams announces Boone's resolution at age thirty-six to enter the wilds of Kentucky as the true beginning of his life: "At this point Boone's life may be said really to begin" (133). Like other American heroes from Natty Bumppo to Huck Finn, Williams' Boone essentially gives birth to both himself and an American tradition by his fertilizing contact with the landscape.

Despite the weight of all Williams claims for him, Boone does seem thin compared to the voluptuous fleshiness of Rasles—but not just because Boone lacks Rasles's powerful voice and Williams has to shoulder the burden of Boone's role with his own language. The nature of *In the American Grain* shifts with "The Discovery of Kentucky." It becomes more difficult to make raw contact with the New World; the wilderness begins to vanish. Boone has to go in search of the naked spaces in which he might marry the New World, and his relationship to the land is as marked by dispossession and displacement as it is by rootedness. Even though Williams titles "The Discovery of Kentucky" to call attention to that particular passage of Boone's experience, and even though Williams identifies Boone's entry into Kentucky as the real start of his life, the structure of the chapter actually undermines the role Williams so plainly announces for Boone. Williams, in fact, gives Boone a biographical sweep from early childhood to old age—something that is generally withheld from other characters in the book—for the express purpose of structuring Boone's life as a series of forced removals.

"Three years the junior of George Washington," says Williams, "Boone was taken while still a child from his birthplace on the upper waters of the Schuykill River near Philadelphia to the then comparatively wild country of western Pennsylvania" (131). But that "comparatively wild country" where Boone grew up a hunter doesn't stay wild for long. Boone, "at eighteen, with his love of the woods marked for good, and his disposition for solitude, taciturnity and a hunter's life determined," must move once again, "this time from the rapidly settling country of Pennsylvania to the wild Yadkin, a river that takes its rise among the mountains that form the eastern boundary of North Carolina" (132). There were few places wilder than the Carolina backcountry on the eve of the Revolution, but even that is not enough for Boone.[9] He "at once traversed the Yadkin Valley at a point still more remote from the seaboard and nearer the mountain" in search of a spot to build his cabin. "But he was not to remain thus solitary!" Williams exclaims. "The lands along the Yadkin attracted the notice of other settlers, and Boone, at thirty, found the smoke of his cabin no longer the only one that floated in the air. . . . He soon became conscious that his time on the Yadkin was limited" (132).

Williams, however, tries to suggest that Boone is drawn to Kentucky rather than just pushed toward it by the ever-encroaching settlements. Boone senses that beyond the mountains "a new and unexplored country, invested with every beauty, every danger, every incident that could amuse the imagination or quicken action, lay before him, the indefinite world of the future" (132). But Boone's time in Kentucky proves just as limited as his time on the Yadkin. He is inevitably followed by others. Like Natty Bumppo at the end of *The Pioneers*, Boone opens a path for the very thing he would leave behind. Yet his departure from Kentucky is more crushing than his previous removals. In Kentucky he doesn't decide to leave for more open spaces, but is literally forced off the land—"by the chicanery of the law and in his old age," Boone has "every last acre of the then prosperous homestead he had at last won for himself after years of battle in the new country" stripped from him. He is left "homeless and ruined," wandering "through Tennessee for 'more elbowroom,' " and finally heading "for Spanish territory beyond the Mississippi where the Provincial Governor, having gotten wind of the old hunter's state of mind, was glad to offer him a large tract of land on which to settle. There he lived and died, past ninety, serving his traps as usual" (139).

Boone's cycle of westward removals evidences the rapid spread of settlement in America and marks a decisive change in the character of the book. Williams could have continued to penetrate inland, taking up Boone's removals where Boone himself left off, turning the geographic direction of *In the American Grain* firmly to the West to search out other spaces past the Mississippi, past the Rockies, even to the far edge of the continent, where yet other men continued to immerse themselves in the wilderness long after it had vanished in the eastern states. But marriage with the wilderness is merely a metaphorical ideal rather than a literal pursuit for Williams. And *In the American Grain* never really goes west of the Mississippi—it only gestures into that vague space with De Soto and Boone, and later with Sam Houston. Williams remains in the East in his book, just as he did in fact throughout most of his life.[10] The vast American West would always seem to him a penumbral realm, impossibly distant from his immediate world.

What had been witnessed as a restless spread of settlement to the West during Boone's life becomes by Sam Houston's time a progressive layering of civilization upon the land. The New World is not just superficially covered with a thin overlay of settlements—it is buried beneath the accreted strata of a nonindigenous culture. No longer can one simply turn inland. He must descend, like Houston. Williams, in fact, portrays Houston's westward movements in terms of descents rather than horizontal directions. And he marks the increasing difficulty of touching the body of the New World by voicing his own doubts about the possibility of getting beneath the plastered layers to perform the inseminating act:

> At fifteen years of age Samuel Houston, born 1793, Scotch-Irish, ran away from his brothers of whom he was a charge and joined the Cherokee Indians of Western Tennessee. He lived with them until eighteen, then reascended to the settlements for school. . . . The primitive destiny of the land is obscure, but it has been obscured further by a field of unrelated culture stuccoed upon it that has made that destiny more difficult than ever to determine. To this latter nearly all the aesthetic adhesions of the present day occur. Through that stratum of obscurity the acute but frail genius of the place must penetrate. The seed is tough but the chances are entirely against a growth. It is possible for every vestige of virtue from the New World to be lost, like the wood pigeon. (212)

Houston is the seed Williams would implant. His youth among the Cherokees had fertilized his character, making him "one of the few men of his time suited mentally, morally, physically for dominant achievement" (212). Houston seems especially suited to wield an influence upon his contemporaries that a solitary man like Boone could not, for Houston carries his raw beginnings into the political sphere, "reascending" from the Cherokees in western Tennessee to become Governor of Tennessee in 1827. As Williams sees it, Houston's life "has a plant in its purpose, in its lusts' eye, as gorgeous as Montezuma's garden of birds, wild beasts and albino natives in wooden cages" (213). But Houston, much more than Boone, fails to bear fruit. Rather than growing into prominence by virtue of his early descent among the Indians, Houston is branded for misfortune. And Williams reaches a despairing conclusion after his brief examination of Houston's life: "Those who come up from under will have a mark on them that invites scorn, like a farmer's filthy clodhoppers" (215).

Houston does indeed seem to have had that mark rule his destiny —he is pushed back down into obscurity by his society just as Boone had been pushed to the West. Williams recounts the somewhat mysterious circumstances surrounding Houston's sudden resignation of the governorship of Tennessee in 1829, citing the probable cause as his violent separation from Eliza Allen after only three months of marriage.

For Williams, "Surmise will suit the fancy" in explaining the "arresting character" of the incident, and he claims there was "a disproportion" between Houston and his wife—"a man of primitive vigors loosed upon her in private, she was overborne by him in some manner, or she refused to be overborne" (212–13). Houston's youth among the Cherokees, Williams suggests, made him too sexually powerful, endowing him with "primitive vigors" unsuited for society. In the wake of "the emotional recoil from the misfortune," says Williams, Houston "left everything behind him and took the descent once more, to the ground." Yet Houston, like Boone, is pushed even farther west to make his descent, for the Cherokees he goes to rejoin have been forced out of Tennessee and across the Mississippi to Arkansas. His turning back to the Indians, although "it is the saving gesture" for Williams, becomes at the same time "a gesture of despair" (213). Rather than purposefully embracing the wilderness, Houston seems to suffer banishment like an exile, vanishing into the obscurity of the western spaces.

And Houston does disappear from view. We glimpse him only briefly among the Cherokees as Williams mentions that "He was adopted into the tribe" and that "He took an Indian woman for a wife" (214). Otherwise, Williams quite literally loses sight of him in "Descent"—not because Houston has been regeneratively swallowed up like Rasles or Boone, but because he is submerged by Williams' own despair over an America "aesthetically satisfied by temporary fill-gaps." What "Descent" really concerns is the increasing impossibility of a reascent in America, the difficulty of any growth from the ground to succeed in breaking through a continually thickening surface of borrowed cultural values. Even though Williams argues that "All have to come from under and through a dead layer" in America (213), he cannot avoid the grim recognition that those who descend are likely to remain buried: "It is imperative that we *sink*. But from a low position it is impossible to answer those who know all the Latin and some of the Sanskrit names, much French and perhaps one or two other literatures. Their riposte is: Knownothingism. But we cannot climb every tree in that world of birds. But where foreign values are held to be a desideratum, he who is buried and speaks thickly—is lost" (214).[11]

Houston can hardly be said to provide an affirmation of the ground —or any verbal evidence of ever having been fertilized by his contact with it. He is even more silent than Boone. And although Williams claims that "he who is buried and speaks thickly—is lost," Houston is lost without speaking at all. Williams makes no attempt to search out the man's voice in the historical record, nor to dress the facts of

Houston's life in his own engendering language as he had done with Boone.[12] Houston is only a peripheral subject in "Descent." He resurfaces only one more time in the chapter, a fleeting glimpse at the end. Williams quickly lists the later successes of Houston's life in the West, but they offer no tokens of the kind of flowering he had found in earlier characters: "After many years with the Cherokees, having settled down thoroughly, this time, Houston rose again: defeated Santa Ana at San Jacinto and received the soubriquet 'Sam Jacinto,' Governor of Texas, U. S. Senator during a long term, several times mentioned for the presidency, married again, several children, when in deep thought whittled pine sticks, tigerskin vest, blanket, sombrero, joined Baptist Church, opposed secession of southern states, lived to have Lincoln recognize him by offer of a Major-Generalship, which he refused" (215).[13]

Williams' flat recitation of Houston's apparent rise to prominence collapses into the image of a man isolated and withdrawn. Houston sits "in deep thought," whittling "pine sticks" and wearing the "tigerskin vest, blanket, sombrero" that mark his wary rejection of Lincoln's proferred recognition. Denial is the final gesture of Houston's life. And denial, not affirmation, is Williams' final gesture in "Descent." The chapter ends with one of the most despairing statements in the book. "However hopeless it may seem," Williams concludes, "we have no other choice: we must go back to the beginning; it must all be done over; everything that is must be destroyed" (215).

Williams had planned to end *In the American Grain* with "Edgar Allan Poe."[14] The Poe chapter was to vindicate the very terms of Williams' book, both conceptually and structurally, by delivering a beginning at the end, bringing forth the birth of a truly American poet. Williams explicitly gathers together the regenerative gestures of his previous chapters to shape the character of Poe, pronouncing him "a new De Soto" (220) and calling him another Boone as well. " 'Rather the ice than their way' " (220)—Williams even quotes the opening line of his book in the Poe chapter to impress the *da capo* movement upon us. Poe overturns the despair of "Descent" by fulfilling the chapter's closing imperative—he takes us "back to the beginning" by destroying "everything that is," dismantling all the conceptual falsework erected upon the body of America, clearing the ground of all its layered European "aesthetic adhesions." The genius of the New World, Williams had warned, "is shy and wild and frail, the loveliest, to be cherished only by the most keen, courageous and sensitive. It may die" (214). But Poe releases the full savagery of the ground, an elemental chthonic power that cannot be subdued: "He was the first to realize that the hard, sardonic, truculent mass of the New World, hot, angry—was, in fact, not a thing to paint over, to smear, to destroy—for it WOULD not be destroyed, it was too powerful,—it smiled!" (225).

Williams' portrayal of Poe has often been thought more curious than accurate. Whitman, certainly, or Emerson or Thoreau would have seemed more logical choices if Williams needed someone to act the part that Larbaud saw Williams himself attempting to play—the St. George of America, the cultural liberator who would strike down the monstrous forms of Europe that had infested the land. But Williams gives us a Poe we have never seen before—and that accounts for a good deal of Poe's effectiveness in the book. Our very failure to have previously recognized Poe's uniquely American qualities seems to validate Williams' argument that "As with all else in America, the value of Poe's genius TO OURSELVES must be *uncovered* from our droppings, or at least uncovered from the 'protection' which it must have raised about itself to have survived in any form among us—where everything is quickly trampled." We have seen only the superficial Poe, Williams argues, the "surface of bizarre designs by which he's known and which are *not at all* the major point in question" (219). But it is not the surface alone that has kept Poe hidden from us, according to Williams—it is also because Poe is so thoroughly and originally American in his achievements:

> And for *that* reason he is unrecognized. Americans have never recognized themselves. How can they? It is impossible until someone invent the ORIGINAL terms. As long as we are content to be called by somebody's else [sic] terms, we are incapable of being anything but our own dupes.
> Thus Poe must suffer by his originality. Invent that which is new, even if it be made of pine from your own backyard, and there's none to know what you've done. It is because there's no *name*. This is the cause of Poe's lack of recognition. He was American. He was the astounding, inconceivable growth of his locality. Gape at him they did, and he at them in amazement. Afterward with mutual hatred; he in disgust, they in mistrust. It is only that which is under your nose which seems inexplicable.
> Here Poe emerges—in no sense the bizarre, isolate writer, the curious literary figure. On the contrary, in him American literature is anchored, in him alone, on solid ground. (226)

If Poe does succeed in carrying the weight of Williams' claims for him, it is in part because Poe brings to the book something that had been lacking in the immediately preceding chapters: a strong voice. Williams himself had had to carry the weight of a "taciturn" Boone and a "silent" Houston, explaining the men rather than letting them speak for themselves. But with Poe, Williams is able to deliver the man's own voice, quoting aptly and generously from Poe's numerous critical pieces.[15] The statements are strong. They do indeed speak what Williams claims for them: "a movement, first and last to clear the GROUND" (216). Poe chisels away the accretions of traditional literary practice, indicting contemporaries like Longfellow and Lowell as mere copiers and plagiarists of convention, announcing that American literature will have to stand by its compositional merits. Poe is quintessentially American not because he wrote of the New World in terms of Indians and wild spaces—indeed, these subjects "he counsels writers to AVOID," Williams points out—but because he devised a new way of seeing the world through language: "His whole insistence has been upon method, in opposition to a nameless rapture over nature" (227). Poe reconceptualized the way literature is put together. That, says Williams, is why the French had prized him—they saw Poe as "a new point from which to readjust the trigonometric measurements of literary form" (216). And that, of course, is why Williams seeds him so deeply in the ground of America. Poe germinates a center, forcing his immediate world into clarity around him. He reveals the ground for an American poetry by defining the local through the locus of self. "His attack," says Williams, "was *from the center out*" (219).[16]

Just here, however, Poe's role falls apart—or rather it truly reveals itself. Poe's marriage to the New World is a most tortured affair. Despite the deep roots Williams gives him, Poe doesn't really blossom. He suffers the same fate of displacement and dispossession as Boone and Houston. Even worse, in fact. He isn't forced into the West. He is swallowed up, consumed by the same "grotesque inappropriateness of the life about him" that had "forced itself in among his words" (220). Though Poe struggled "to get from sentiment to form, a backstroke from the swarming 'population,'" he couldn't escape: "darkening as he goes, losing the battle, as he feels himself going under—he emerges as the ghoulish, the driven back" (221, 223). Williams focuses on Poe's critical writings to make his inseminating gesture because the poetry —the very form that should most nakedly reveal the strength of Poe's rootedness in the soil—most plainly speaks Poe's defeat. "It is especially in the poetry," says Williams, "where 'death looked gigantically down' that the horror of the formless resistance which opposed, maddened, destroyed him has forced its character into the air, the wind, the blessed galleries of paradise, above a morose, dead world, peopled by shadows and silence, and despair—it is the compelling force of his isolation" (231).

Williams touches on Poe's poetry only briefly, and more to dismiss it than to lift it into expression. Poe "is known as a poet," Williams states, "yet there are but five poems, possibly three" (232). And other than merely mentioning that "To One in Paradise" is Poe's "best poem" (233), Williams doesn't even bother to specify which poems he has in mind, let alone to quote from any. Yet it is the poetry, nonetheless, that speaks the final word on Poe's role in *In the American Grain*, for it identifies Poe as the symbolic victim of an America whose sources of sustaining freshness have all gone dry. Though Williams claims it was the "truculent mass of the New World, hot, angry," that fed Poe's critical statements, the only thing to feed his poetry was his wife. Hardly a supplying female endowed with regenerative powers, she is but an ethereal ideal devoid of earthly passion. The imagery of Poe's poetry, says Williams, speaks "the desperate situation of his mind, thin as a flame to mount unsupported, successful for a moment in the love of—not so much his wife—but in the escape she filled for him with her frail person, herself afflicted as by 'ghouls' " (233).

Poe fails to flower because America offers him no fertilizing contacts. He could not break through to reach the naked body of the New World despite his attempts to clear the ground. So he imagined a world elsewhere—a woman elsewhere, that is—his own forever virginal Virginia. Not of this earth, she was "one in paradise" even before she died. Yet "When she died," says Williams, "there was nothing left. In his despair he had nowhere to turn. It is the very apotheosis of the place and the time" (232). Poe finally emerges not as "a new De Soto," but as one who shows the impossibility of becoming a new De Soto. Poe's gestures ultimately speak "a fury of impotence," the sound of his voice the tortured cries of a man "driven to be heard by the battering racket about him to a distant screaming—the pure essence of his locality" (233). In the end, it is Poe's defeat, not his success, that expresses the condition of his immediate world, a New World beaten down and destroyed.

In the American Grain fails to produce its implicit object—an American poet. Yet it is a purposeful rather than an unintentional failure. Though Williams attempts to cultivate the ground of an indigenous American tradition, his book ultimately depicts American history as the destruction of the native female element necessary to that tradition. In the first half of *In the American Grain*, the New World is a woman who aggressively strives to possess the newcomers from Europe. The Puritans have to struggle to fence out the untamed wilderness, to resist the transformative power of the land, stringing a line of defense with their taut rhetoric: "The jargon of God, which they used, was their dialect by which they kept themselves surrounded as with a palisade" (64). The New World repeatedly manifests itself, as Williams says at the end of the Champlain chapter, as "a force to leap up and wrench you from your hold and force you to be part of it; the place, the absolute new without law but the basic blood where the savage becomes brother. That is generous. Open. A break through." That force had indeed leapt up and seized Columbus, De Soto, and Ponce. And even though Champlain "couldn't" make that break through— "He with his maps, for France, for science, for civilization—his gentleness, his swoons"—he wasn't insulated from the violent shock of that power. Champlain's own men rebelled against him, striking "at him as an impertinence," says Williams, for "The place (that more vulgar men sensed as the strength in their arms) was outraged" (74).

But in the second half of *In the American Grain*, the New World changes from a naked body potent with regenerative violence to a progressively "stuccoed" continent, languishing beneath layers of borrowed culture. Envisionings of American history as the destruction of a female landscape are, of course, endemic in early twentieth-century American writing. Fitzgerald's *The Great Gatsby*, published the same year as Williams' book, offers the period's most well-known example of that vision: the "fresh, green breast of the new world" transformed into "a valley of ashes." But Williams' history doesn't engage this vision in the terms that most frequently typify the work of his contemporaries—the loss of nineteenth-century pastoral ideals, or images of the machine-in-the-garden. What accounts for the waning power of the ground in the latter chapters of *In the American Grain* is not so much the conquest of America's physical landscape, but the settlement of America's human landscape, the determining of a single, monolithic character for the inhabitants of the continent.

Such a settlement wasn't possible as long as heterogeneous European cultural groups were vying with each other for territorial possession of the New World. French to the north and west, English along the seaboard, Spaniards to the south, and Indians everywhere —the human landscape was too much in flux, the cultural groups too diverse for any one to assert authorship of the American character. Williams celebrates this diversity in the early chapters of his book, organizing them much like a debate between contending cultural conceptions of what shape life in the New World should take.[17] But in the second half of *In the American Grain* the human landscape becomes decidedly uniform. Debate gives way to consensus after the French, the Spanish, and the English vanish from the book. And cultural diversity gives way to cultural homogeneity as America becomes the sole possession of one group, perhaps the only real group in the book, the Puritans: "By their very emptiness they were the fiercest element in the battle to establish a European life on the New World. The first to come as a group, of a desire sprung within themselves, they were the first American democracy—and it was they, in the end, who would succeed in making everything like themselves" (63).

The Puritans do indeed "succeed in making everything like themselves" in *In the American Grain*. Of all the cultural elements in the book, the Puritans are the one that never gets swallowed up by the land and the Indians. They remain on top, in a position of mastery, thriving not just by the very force of their resistance to the ground but by their unified and dogmatic opposition to any conceptualization of America other than their own. Separatists in more than just a religious sense, the Puritans rigorously enforce a separation from sexual instincts upon the character of the New World's human landscape. When Thomas Morton comes to perform his Priapic ceremonies on the borders of their colony in "The May-Pole at Merry Mount," the Puritans arrest him and ship him back to England. The "official" charge against Morton was "selling liquor and firearms to the savages." But the real reason why the Puritans "chose finally to attack him," according to Williams, "was the moral one of his consorting with the Indian girls" (76). Morton dared to plant his seed in the soil. That the Puritans couldn't tolerate. They had to uproot him, to separate his dangerous sexual vigors from the character of their community.

Yet the Puritans' fierce determination to regulate America's human landscape inevitably leads to their domination of the physical landscape. Williams cites the "duplicity" of their military assault on Merry Mount, pointing out that the Puritans also had "the trade in beaver skins in view" (80). In England the Puritans' separatism cost them a loss of territory: they were forced into exile in Leyden. But in America, their separatism inevitably bred an expansionism more certain and deadly than anything the Spanish could have ever conceived. Just as they usurp Morton's lands under pretense of morality, they later kill Rasles at his Abnaki village and push their way farther north into Maine. The Puritans' removal of "immoral" elements from the vicinity of their colony inevitably results in the acquisition of new territories. Indeed, it is the Puritans' moral imperative to make "everything like themselves" that subverts the native energies behind the boldest territorial appropriation in American history—the American Revolution. Rather than a liberation of the native impulse, the Revolution merely removes the primary foreign political obstacle to a domestically authored control and homogenization of America. It is " 'those damned

Yankees'" who strip from Boone the Kentucky lands he had acquired just prior to the Revolution. And Boone heads for Spanish territory not just to find spaces still yet unsettled, but "to leave the young nation which he had helped to establish, definitely behind him" (139).

Williams, however, doesn't explicitly present the Revolution as the stepping-stone to a Puritan takeover. As an identifiable group, the Puritans cease to exist after the Rasles chapter. And as a historical event, in the conventional sense, the Revolution is not even visible in *In the American Grain*. But in his chapters on Washington and Franklin, Williams uses the character of the nation's founding fathers to reveal the founding of a national character. Indeed, Williams pointedly introduces Washington in terms of this symbolic capacity, presenting him as the key to understanding both the Revolution and the emerging nation: "Washington was, I think, the typically good man: take it as you please. But, of course, a remarkable one. No doubt at all he personally, was ninety percent of the force which made of the American Revolution a successful issue. Know of what that force consisted, that is, the intimate character of its makeup, that is, Washington himself, and you will know practically all there is to understand about the beginnings of the American Republic" (140).

Williams' choice of Washington to play this symbolic role is hardly surprising. Washington has been repeatedly treated as a symbol of national identity in American literature.[18] Yet Williams' estimate of him is anything but conventional. Washington emerges "in a great many ways thoroughly disappointing" (143), a man in whom native impulses and sexual vigors are repressed rather than released. He forms a marked contrast to Boone, the figure who immediately precedes him in the book, and Williams openly invokes comparison of the two men, remarking in "The Discovery of Kentucky" that Boone was but "three years the junior of George Washington" (131). Washington, in fact, entered the wilderness in his youth, just as Boone did. He had a "surveying contract which took him to Duquesne and the wilderness thereabouts," Williams points out, conjecturing that there, in those wild spaces, Washington "must have breathed a more serious air which cannot but have penetrated to the deepest parts of his nature." Yet Washington is no Boone. He returns to safe ground—"in his case it did not, as it might have done, win him permanently to that kind of an existence. There was in his nature a profound spirit of resignation before life's rich proposals which disarmed him" (140–41). Washington holds himself back from the bounty of the New World. Boone had released his ardors, freely coupling with the ground, but

Washington attempts to keep his generative vitality submerged beneath the surface. "Resistance was, I believe, his code," says Williams, and he delivers Washington in a word: "Encitadeled" (141).

Washington, nonetheless, is no Puritan, nor does Williams try to make him one. There is nothing "hard and little" (63) about him: "Here was a man of tremendous vitality buried in a massive frame and under a rather stolid and untractable exterior which the ladies somewhat feared, I fancy. He must have looked well to them, from a distance, or say on horseback—but later it proved a little too powerful for comfort. And he wanted them too; violently. One can imagine him curiously alive to the need of dainty waistcoats, lace and kid gloves, in which to cover that dangerous rudeness which he must have felt about himself. His interest in dress at a certain period of his career is notorious" (140).[19]

For Williams, the important fact about Washington is that he was endowed with a "tremendous vitality" and a "dangerous rudeness." He desired women "violently." But the only time he fully released himself, says Williams, was to General Lee during the war. Lee had disobeyed Washington's orders, losing the chance for an important victory at Monmouth, and Washington let himself loose upon him: "To Lee then in a fury, he opened the gates of his soul and Lee saw such hell fire that it was the end of him—retired muttering and half silly to his farm in Virginia where he stayed" (143). The event is proof of Washington's terrible potency—and of the powerful resistance Washington had to exercise to contain that potency. Indeed, it is this peculiar dynamic of resistance to his own volcanic energy that explains why Williams calls Washington "ninety percent of the force that made of the American Revolution a successful issue": "He couldn't give in. He couldn't give in without such a ruffling within himself that he had no choice but to continue. That's the secret of Valley Forge and the valor and patience of his battle, as great as the other, against an aimless, wavering Congress at Philadelphia. He couldn't give in. I believe he would have battled it alone if he had felt his army wasted from under him or even left the country" (141).

Yet Washington is a disappointment for Williams. But not just because Washington held back his native ardors—the real cause for disappointment is what happened to him because he had such powerful desires. Despite all his efforts to cover his "dangerous rudeness" with "lace and kid gloves" the mark of the ground was still on him. He had spent his early years in the wilderness, and though he returned to the settled spaces, he carried with him the inseminating instinct, which Williams finds manifest, characteristically, in Washington's sexual appetite. "Some girl at Princeton, was it? had some joke with him about a slipper at a dance. He was full of it" (142). So full of "it," in fact, that his society turned on him. That is the key to Washington's symbolic role in *In the American Grain*—not that he reflects the Puritan morality in himself, but that he was attacked because he didn't:

> America has a special destiny for such men, I suppose, great wench lovers—there is the letter from Jefferson attesting it in the case of Washington, if that were needed—terrible leaders they might make if one could release them. It seems a loss not compensated for by the tawdry stuff bred after them—in place of a splendor, too rare. They are a kind of American swan song, each one.
> The whole crawling mass gnaws on them—hates them. He was hated, don't imagine he was not. The minute he had secured their dung heap for them—he had to take their dirt in the face. (143)

Washington reveals the emerging national character by showing what elements are being extirpated from it. He does not symbolize the new man, the American, but a vanishing species, those "great wench lovers" who are "a kind of American swan song, each one." Such men, for Williams, are animated by a deep sexual tie to the ground, and they would provide just the native force to direct the course of the young nation—"terrible leaders they might make if one could release them." Release Washington is exactly what Williams does in his later and more affirmative treatment of him in *The First President*, projecting him "across the panorama of American History" to "galvanize us into a realization of what we are today."[20] Washington brings us into consciousness of ourselves in *In the American Grain*, too, but a consciousness of the loss of such leaders, "a loss not compensated for by the tawdry stuff bred after them." That "tawdry stuff" swarms over the landscape in the second half of the book, filling America with "a formless 'population'—drifting and feeding" (233), a "crawling mass" that attacks anyone who manifests native sexual powers. They tapped Washington's energies just long enough to wrest a nominal freedom from England, and then they turned upon the man: "The minute he had secured their dung heap for them—he had to take their dirt in the face." The American Revolution becomes, paradoxically, a betrayal of the native element, and our first president symbolizes, dismayingly, "the typical sacrifice to the mob" (143).

Williams directly forces our awareness of the settlement of America's human landscape by following the Washington chapter with the full text of Benjamin Franklin's *Information to Those Who Would Remove to America*. Written in 1782 while Franklin was serving as am-

bassador to France, *Information* was ostensibly intended to inform prospective immigrants about conditions in the young nation. Translated
into over twenty languages and widely circulated throughout Europe,
the document is also Franklin's effort to set the conceptual parameters
by which prospective Americans would function in the new country.
He clearly delineates the kinds of persons "proper" and "improper"
for America, and explicitly lays out an orderly scheme by which one
may become a "useful" citizen. Yet Franklin's efforts to standardize
the character of America's human landscape were only secondarily directed at prospective immigrants. Under the guise of "Poor Richard"
—Williams' title for the chapter—Franklin devised the axioms to regulate the attitudes and opinions of the domestic mass. "Poor Richard's
Almanac," says Williams, "was as important in founding the nation as
Paine's *Age of Reason*," and he pronounces Franklin "the balancer full
of motion without direction, the gyroscope which by its large spinning
kept us, at that early period of our fate, upon an even keel" (154, 153).

But Williams actually says very little about either *Information*,
which he quotes in full, or *Poor Richard's Almanac*, which he quotes
not at all. In his "Notes for a Commentary on Franklin," which he
appends to the text of *Information*, Williams instead concentrates on
revealing the unmistakable historical origins of Franklin's own character—and hence, by extension, of the character Franklin recommended
to the American people—in the Puritans' terror of naked contact with
the New World:

> It is necessary in appraising our history to realize that the nation
> was the offspring of the desire to huddle, to protect—of terror—
> superadded to a new world of great beauty and ripest blossom that
> well-nigh no man of distinction saw save Boone.
> Franklin is the full development of the timidity, the strength that
> denies itself. (155)

The instinct of the frightened herd, "the desire to huddle," reaches
its "full development" in Franklin—and in the formation of the nation.
Both the man and the population he strove to shape are the "offspring"
of the Puritan denial of touch. "His mighty answer to the New World's
offer of a great embrace was THRIFT," remarks Williams. "Work night
and day, build up, penny by penny, a wall against that which is threatening, the terror of life, poverty. Make a fort to be secure in" (156). Yet
Franklin is more than just the conduit for disseminating a secularized
Puritanism to the nation. He perfected the avoidance of direct contact
as a science—indeed, perfected it through science, in Williams' view,
using scientific inquiry as a way to touch, safely, that which Boone

so boldly embraced: "the forbidden wealth of the Unknown" (131). Franklin's "itch to serve science" (155) was born of a need to insulate himself from the shock of direct contact with the elemental powers of the New World, from the raw force of the lightning that so fascinated him: "Sure enough, he didn't dare let it go in at the top of his head and out at his toes, that's it; he *had* to fool with it. He sensed the power and knew only enough to want to run an engine with it. His fingers itched to be meddling, to do the little concrete thing—the barrier against a flood of lightning that would inundate him" (155).

Franklin's ceaseless industry, his technical innovations, his constant striving for efficiency—the marks by which we commonly know the man—all become evidence of a nervous vigilance against the wild power of native things. "He was the dike keeper, keeping out the wilderness with his wits," says Williams. "Fear drove his curiosity" (155). And even though Williams describes his purpose in "Poor Richard" as "not to mark Franklin, but to attempt to appraise the nature of the difficulties that molded him" (157), Franklin is definitely marked as a symbol of "the new breed" (156). His "scientific" mode of touch is what Williams uses to define the character of the leaders of the new nation:

> To want to touch, not to wish anything to remain clean, aloof—comes always of a kind of timidity, from fear.
>
> The character they had (our pioneer statesmen, etc.) was that of giving their fine energy, as they must have done, to the smaller, narrower, protective thing and not to the great, New World. Yet they cannot quite leave hands off it but must TOUCH it, in a "practical" way, that is a joking, shy, nasty way, using "science" etc., not with the generosity of the savage or the scientist but in a shameful manner. The sweep of the force was too horrible to them; it would have swept them into chaos. (157)

Franklin knew that chaos. And he knew its power was centered in the sexual instincts. "As a boy," remarks Williams, "he had tentatively loosed himself once to love, to curiosity perhaps, which was the birth of his first son. But the terror of that dare must have frightened the soul out of him" (156). Franklin's early sexual encounter, Williams suggests, had impressed upon him a frightening truth: "The terrible beauty of the New World attracts men to their ruin." And Franklin, Williams observes, "did not care to be ruined—he only wanted to touch" (155). His desire to touch might have made him, like Washington, another "sacrifice to the mob," for he, too, seemed made of the stuff of America's "great wench lovers." "But shh!" Williams cautions.

"Benjamin Franklin, who started black with an illegitimate son, was forced to turn white, Poor Richard, to save himself later. He saw the hell and warned us, warned us to save our pennies" (179). Franklin's life marks a decisive misdirectioning at a critical moment in our history, a crippling misplacement of the native sexual energies necessary to American cultural vitality.

Williams' view of the American Revolution and the seminal period of our national existence in *In the American Grain* not only defies our conventional notions, but also stands at odds with his own later treatments of the subject in "The American Background" and "The Writers of the American Revolution." In these essays from the 1930s Williams attempts to reveal the native impetus behind the establishment of the Republic, to search out evidence of "a real revolution in thought, hereditary to America," and of "a new world reconstituted on an abler pattern than had been known theretofore" on the political scene (SE, 39). But in *In the American Grain* Williams insistently focuses on what was lost rather than on what was gained during that critical juncture of our history. "The sense of the individual, the basis on which the war was fought, instantly the war was over began to be debauched" (194), Williams says in "The Virtue of History." And he presents that loss as something we have yet to recognize. "We are deceived by history," he claims. "America had a great spirit given to freedom but it was a mean, narrow, provincial place, it was NOT the great liberty-loving country, not at all. Its choice spirits died" (197).

Williams dismisses the idea that the essential matter of the American Revolution was political separation from England—"such uprisings are for old states where senility has become engrained," he comments. But America was "a half-wild colony, young, shooting out green wood," a place where people like Boone were only beginning to learn how to live. "England?" Williams asks. "A dry skin to be cast off, an itch, that's all. There was a deeper matter, a yeast in the sap, an untracked force that might lead anywhere; it was springtime in a new world when all things were possible." What the Revolution should have brought to flower was a cultural awakening to the possibilities of place, "a reawakened sense of life in the spirit of the New World." A reckoning with that nascent native urge was something the young country could not avoid: "Sooner or later it must have been the same awakening without the Revolution. The war was nothing." It just so happened, says Williams, that "England, by chance, stood in the way. But the defeat of England was the obvious false end" (193).

The only man who saw the true end was—Aaron Burr. Williams

surprises us, as he often does in the book. Burr would hardly seem readymade to play the role of the true son of liberty that Williams accords him.[21] Yet that is exactly part of Williams' point in choosing Burr. Williams implicitly attempts to convince us that we have failed to recognize Burr precisely because he is so quintessentially of the ground. And Williams explicitly attributes that failed recognition to the writing of history. The life of the past, Williams argues, has been falsified by a history that

> follows governments and never men. It portrays us in generic patterns, like effigies or the carvings on sarcophagi, which say nothing save, of such and such a man, that he is dead. That's history. It is concerned only with the one thing: to say everything is dead. Then it fixes up the effigy: there that's finished. Not at all. History must stay open, it is all humanity. Are lives to be twisted forcibly about events, the mere accidents of geography and climate?
>
> It is an obscenity which few escape—save at the hands of the stylist, literature, in which alone humanity is protected against tyrannous designs.
>
> But how small is the sum of good writing against the mass of poisonous stuff that finds its way into the history books; for the dead can be stifled like the living. (188–89)

Williams' plea for an "open history" forms the preface to his creation of an "open" Burr. Burr's life, Williams contends, has been "twisted" to fit the "tyrannous designs" of history, the man "stifled," the true marks of his character purged from memory. And Williams proclaims that "A country is not free, is not what it pretends to be, unless it leave a vantage open (in tradition) for that which Burr possessed in such remarkable degree. This is my theme" (197). Indeed, the virtue of history for Williams is that the past can become, in "the hands of the stylist," a tool by which "humanity is protected against tyrannous designs" (189). And he boldly presents Burr as the man who sought to protect us from the "tyrannous designs" of the newly established American government. He was the only one who took the Revolution seriously—that is, as a battle against all forces that would prevent the growth of America upon purely native grounds, and he didn't quit fighting even after everyone else thought the war had been won: "Either they had what they were fighting for or they did not have it. England or the mob, it made small difference to him. He WAS serious, they were triflers—their own dupes" (204).

Williams endeavors to show us a Burr who tried to bring to the new government a political vision beyond the merely political, one that was founded on creating new men for a New World: "Burr knew what a democracy must liberate. . . . Men intact—with all their senses waking" (206). His rebellion had begun even before the Revolution, Williams suggests. During his university years Burr repudiated "the whole mass of religious dogma" he had inherited from his forefathers —his literal forefathers, for "Jonathan Edwards," notes Williams, "was his grandfather on the mother's side" (198). Burr's rebellion against Puritanism, however, merely equips him for his rebellion against what Williams identifies, in his discourse on Puritanism to Larbaud, as the inevitable outcome of Puritanism's prohibition of touch—the Federal government: "From lack of touch, lack of belief. Steadily the individual loses caste, then the local government loses its authority; the head is more and more removed. Finally the center is reached—totally dehumanized, like a Protestant heaven. Everything is Federalized and all laws become prohibitive in essence" (128).

The American Revolution does indeed become, in an essential way, a Puritan takeover, for it removes the foreign impediment— England—to the transformation of America into an image of "a Protestant heaven," a place where cultural homogeneity is enforced by a centralized authority, where native diversity on a local level is subordinated to the control of a Federal government. Burr saw the danger, and he recognized the man in whom it was concentrated: Alexander Hamilton, author of the Federal system, the man perhaps most pertinent to our present-day form of government, the face on our ten-dollar bill. Someone needed to step in and defend the primacy of the individual and the local once England was removed from the picture. It could have been Washington but he just wanted to be left alone, to return to his private world at Mount Vernon, and "Alexander Hamilton, a type that needed power, found all this quite to his liking. Washington let him do" (143). It might have been Jefferson, but Williams doesn't deal with Jefferson's profound sense of the local in the book, nor his opposition to Hamilton.[22] The role falls entirely on the shoulders of Burr—not because Burr actually embodied the native spirit of liberty that Williams says he did, but primarily because Burr happened to perform a great symbolic act in Williams' vision of American history: he shot and killed Hamilton.

Hamilton was, in many ways, the villain Williams makes him. Secretary of the treasury from 1789 until his death in 1804, Hamilton had a deep distrust of democracy. He would have reinstituted a monarchy if he could have, believing that the inevitable outcome of the American experiment would be anarchy unless power was concentrated in a central authority, a strong federal government with close ties to the monied and aristocratic interests in the country. He fused those ties himself, establishing a national banking system that could exert monopolistic control over economic development in the country. That fact alone was enough to make Hamilton a particular object of enmity for Williams, and for Ezra Pound as well, both of whom vociferously denounce Hamilton and a monetary system based upon usury.[23] "The Federal Government was slipping in its fangs. The banks were being organized," Williams remarks in the Burr chapter. But the essential factor for Hamilton's role as tyrant, and Burr's role as hero, in *In the American Grain* is Hamilton's befouling of the New World's body with his plan for setting up a national manufactory in the Passaic River valley, Williams' own backyard: "Paterson he wished to make capital of the country because there was waterpower there which to his time and mind seemed colossal. And so he organized a company to hold the land thereabouts, with dams and sluices, the origin today of the vilest swillhole in christendom, the Passaic River; impossible to remove the nuisance so tight had he, Hamilton, sewed up his privileges unto kingdomcome, through his holding company, in the State legislature. *His* company. *His* United States: Hamiltonia—the land of the company" (195).

Hamilton raped and pillaged the very place that would become the site of Williams' attempts to marry the ground. Burr had killed Hamilton. And Williams reaches out to Burr as the passionate defender not just of liberty, but of the New World as a woman. It matters little to Williams that Burr had killed Hamilton for other reasons—that Hamilton disliked Burr not because of any substantial political incompatibility between them but because he saw Burr as someone who wanted absolute power for himself and who was therefore a potential interloper on Hamilton's own schemes. Williams makes no effort to discuss the specifics of Burr's political positions and deeds, of his having sided with the Federalists in an attempt to win the governorship of New York after Jefferson had dropped him as vice president, of his bizarre attempt to conquer Mexico with an army of mercenaries and declare himself emperor, which resulted in a trial for treason and exile in Europe. Instead Williams concentrates on Burr's relationship to the female sex—and Burr certainly does qualify, much more than Washington, as one of America's "great wench lovers." His alleged sexual freedom was the primary point upon which his detractors dwelt—plentiful proof for Williams of Burr's native powers. Burr had openly dared to touch the forbidden female body, and for that he was attacked, just as the Puritans had attacked Morton. Burr did pursue women, yet Burr is no profligate demon in Williams' view, and to the charge that Burr was immoral, Williams replies, "He was, safely so, by the flesh. He found safety in that flesh and among its sturdy guardians—women. Were they too idle in recognizing him? They loved him. Frivolous? He was perhaps the only one of the time who saw women, in the flesh, as serious, and they hailed and welcomed with deep gratitude and profound joy his serious knowledge and regard and liberating force—for them. Freedom? Then for women also—but such a freedom that the one defense must be—immoral. He laughed at that and dug in deeper" (204–5).

Burr is immoral, but "safely so, by the flesh." And Williams has schooled us to know exactly what this kind of "immorality" signifies in an America where "morals have but one character, and that,—SEX: while morals are deformed in the name of PURITY" (157). Burr recognizes the essential bond between the native powers of the New World and the native powers of the body—the female body. Women are the "sturdy guardians" of "that flesh" in which Williams locates the generative source of American cultural vitality. Burr was branded as "immoral" simply because he sought to release those powers "in the flesh." Yet women loved him, asserts Williams. Burr enabled women to express their native sexuality in a society which had officially prohibited it. He was a "liberating force—for them." The other men of his time, says Williams, didn't take women seriously enough to cultivate their feminine strength:

> The rest were frivolous with women. The rest denied them, condoned the female flesh, found them helpmates at the best and at the worst, horses, cattle, provincial accessories, useful workers to make coffee and doughnuts—and to be left to go crazy on the farms for five generations after—that's New England, or they'd hide the bull behind the barn, so that the women would not think it knew where the cows were—Bah, feudal dolls gone wrong, that's Virginia. Women? necessary but not noble, not the highest, not deliciously a free thing, apart, *feminine*, a heaven;—afraid to delve in it save like so much dough. Burr found the spirit living there, free and equal, independent, springing with life. Or did he? I say if he did he was before his time. Surely they drank of him like water. (205)

Burr produced an awakening of the female element, an element which in the flesh, just as in the soil, was denied cultivation in the making of modern America. Violated and destroyed, never lovingly touched—the fate of both the land and womanhood in *In the American Grain*. Both are harnessed to "practical" purposes—the land to Hamilton's manufactory, women to domestic slavery as "helpmates at the best, and at the worst, horses, cattle, provincial accessories, useful workers to make coffee and doughnuts." But Burr's role in the book shifts the focus from the relationship of men and the land to the relationship of men and women in America. Williams makes Burr a Boone who marries the human female in the landscape of his world rather than the female landscape itself. And in the struggle to create a new nation, Burr fights the revolution on the sexual front more than anywhere else, waging a battle to revitalize the female principle in America, to cultivate its essential qualities through the flesh and to find "the spirit living there, free and equal, independent, springing with life."

Burr's role as liberator of the female principle is certainly one of Williams' most audacious bits of Machiavellian playacting in the book. Burr, says Williams, is "in myself and so I dig through lies to resurrect him" (197). And Burr would indeed seem to be born out of Williams himself, for Williams peremptorily dismisses any basis for the man in the facts of the historical record: "No opinion can be trusted; even the facts may be nothing but a printer's error" (190). Yet Burr, if we are to believe Williams' later disclosures about his genesis, actually springs less from Williams himself than from his wife, who played the role of the "supplying female" for "The Virtue of History," fertilizing the poet who wrote the chapter. In 1939, Williams told Horace Gregory that "Mrs. Williams helped me a lot with my reading" for *In the American Grain*, indeed that "she did all the reading for the Aaron Burr chapter and it was, besides, her enthusiasm which fired it and which I took over complete, my part being merely to decide on the form of the make-up and go ahead" (SL, 186–87). And some years later, Williams gave his wife an even more seminal part in Burr's creation, telling Edith Heal that Floss was "solely responsible for Aaron Burr; she told me what she had read, told it so graphically and vividly I sat down and wrote the whole thing in one sitting," adding that "I should confess right here that I never read a single book on him!" (IW, 43).

To what extent these disclosures are mere posturing, and to what extent they contain a quantum of truth is difficult to say. Certain it is, however, that Burr's character shows too many marks of the sexual imperatives of Williams' own poetics for us to accept the chapter as "solely" Floss's responsibility—or for us to regard the disclosures about Floss's involvement in the chapter, as one critic has done, as Williams' "attempt to disown the work."[24] It may well be that Williams' comments to Gregory and Heal on the Burr chapter suggest the extent to which Williams came to associate "The Virtue of History" not just with his appropriation of Floss's "enthusiasm," which he "took over complete," but with his larger appropriation of the female role in the book as a whole. The apparent contradiction between Williams' claim that Burr is "in myself" and that Burr is wholly got out of Floss perhaps points to Williams' arrogation of the very thing Burr is ostensibly intended to release in *In the American Grain*, the fertilizing power of the female—a supposition that is reinforced by the symbolic genealogy Williams creates for Burr in the text.

Our first glimpse of Burr in the book comes at the end of "Jacataqua," the chapter that immediately precedes "The Virtue of History," as he marches through the forests of Maine to join Arnold's army for the attack on the British at Quebec in 1776. Standing in the woods and watching the assembling troops is a group of "twenty or more Abenaki braves," remnants of Rasles's beloved tribe, presided over by their "Sachem, Jacataqua, a girl scarce eighteen, in whom showed the best traits of her mixed French and Indian blood" (186). The symbolic offspring of Rasles's marriage with the ground, Jacataqua becomes Burr's "supplying female," the woman who fertilizes him for his role as liberator of the female principle. Their attraction to each other is immediate and sexual—"her black eyes met a pair as dark and flashing as her own, met and were held." Burr approaches, but it is Jacataqua who speaks the archetypal power of the female:

> In a moment, Burr was standing before the Indian princess, for the first and last time at a loss before a woman. Primitive and direct, it was she who opened the conversation and opened it with a challenge:
> "These," with a wave of her brown hand toward Howard and the group of officers, "these want meat. You hunt with me? I win." (187)

"Primitive and direct," Jacataqua embodies the potent sexuality of the New World as a woman every bit as much as the She of "De Soto and the New World." Like She, Jacataqua is a huntress—a huntress of men. Just as She had conquered De Soto, Jacataqua conquers Burr, who stands "for the first and last time at a loss before a woman." Presiding over her "twenty or more Abenaki braves," Jacataqua represents the native matriarchal essence of the New World, the primacy of the female. And like She, in fact, Jacataqua is entirely Williams' own invention. Both women are conjured out of Williams himself—except that in this case, Williams disguises Jacataqua's origins in his imagination by giving her an apparent origin in fact. Unlike She, Jacataqua is historically plausible in both name and details.[25] Williams supplies his own supplying female for the scheme of the Burr chapter as surely as he had done so for the De Soto chapter, yet with Jacataqua he slyly conceals the fabrication in order to mask an essential point of his sexual poetics in the book: Williams demands of the female a role that can only be fulfilled by the products of his own imagination, rather than actual women of historical record. His ostensibly matriarchal structure for *In the American Grain* is actually a pseudomatriarchy. Though Williams declares the primacy of the female, his reigning women are all got out of Williams himself, a repetition of the founding myth of patriarchy—Eve got out of Adam's rib.

"Jacataqua" is the only chapter of *In the American Grain* to name a woman as its subject. Yet significantly, Jacataqua herself is noticeably absent for most of the chapter. She appears only briefly in the closing paragraphs. Jacataqua becomes that which is missing in "Jacataqua"—and quite literally so, for Williams introduces her at the end of the chapter in terms of her filling an absence, of giving "to womanhood in her time, the form which bitterness of pioneer character had denied it" (186). Jacataqua is invented to fill an absence that is the actual subject of "Jacataqua"—the absence of a female flowering in America.

As a recent special issue of the *William Carlos Williams Review* devoted to Williams, women, and feminist criticism attests, scholars have begun to explore the ways in which Williams shapes and controls women in his writing.[26] Much interest has focused on Williams' appropriation of Marcia Nardi's letters in the writing of *Paterson*. Sandra M. Gilbert has spoken of that appropriation in terms of Williams' desire to subjugate a threatening female presence, which he attempts by a theft that he conceals as deftly as the Minister D——conceals his theft in Poe's "The Purloined Letter."[27] Williams hides his appropriation by displaying it in the open where no one would think to look. And in some ways, Williams has done the same with his appropriation of the female presence in *In the American Grain* by writing a chapter that explicitly proclaims "there have never been women" of significance in American history, that there has never been a woman of sufficient clarity or genius to serve his historical scheme—"Never a character to raise into story" (178, 186).

If it were Williams' desire to conceal the absence of actual women in his book by an all-too-plain revelation of it, he has succeeded quite well. No one has directly brought up the issue with regard to *In the American Grain*, and "Jacataqua" remains one of the virtually ignored chapters of the book. The only person to touch on the matter is, not surprisingly, a woman. Lola Ridge, in her 1926 review of the book, briefly alluded to signs of "sex-antagonism" in "Jacataqua."[28] And there are indeed such signs in abundance. Even though Williams castigates historians in "The Virtue of History" for portraying the individual life "in generic patterns, like effigies or the carvings on sarcophagi" (188), he portrays American women as generic types in "Jacataqua," calling them nothing but "pioneer Katies" and "good, firm Janes" (178, 179). Yet Williams, of course, doesn't present this twisting of American women into generic shapes as his own work— he attributes it to history itself, to "the great American tide inimical to women" (184).

American history, for Williams, is largely the story of the de- struction of the female body—and not just as metaphor, but also as literal fact. From Cotton Mather's *Wonders of the Invisible World*, Wil- liams selectively excerpts the trials of women, providing transcrip- tions of Mather's witchcraft trial testimonies for only Bridget Bishop and Susanna Martin.[29] Williams unmistakably points to the link be- tween the dark, demonic forces that the Puritans imagined massed against them and the reproductive powers of the female body. And in "Jacataqua," Williams suggests a horrible irony in the fact that the early New England Puritans conquered the frightening force of the wilder- ness by sapping the reproductive powers of women: "Do you know that the old town-records in Massachussetts show few men without two and many with as many as seven wives? Not at all uncommon to have had five. How? The first ones died shooting children against the wilderness like cannon balls" (179).

"Jacataqua," however, doesn't focus exclusively on women—it more largely addresses sexuality in American culture. And the chapter is less concerned with the past than with Williams' immediate present. Even though "Jacataqua" occurs within the historical chronology of the book at the close of the eighteenth century, Williams primarily directs his attention to his own twentieth-century America, making the chapter a cultural critique somewhat in the style popularized by Mencken and used by the various contributors to Stearns's *Civilization in the United States*. Indeed, Williams shows himself very much in the vogue of contemporary currents—he cites Freud's then recently pub- lished *Beyond the Pleasure Principle* and loosely uses Freud's notion of a polar opposition between the death instinct and the erotic instinct to frame his analysis in terms of the repression of eros and the starvation of sensual passions.[30] "The characteristic of American life," Williams proclaims, "is that it holds off from embraces, from impacts, gaining, by fear, safety and time in which to fortify its prolific carcass—while the spirit, with tongue hanging out, bites at its bars—its object just out of reach" (175).

Williams creates a grim picture of a sexually crippled America, a ghastly landscape of desperate people "bursting for lack of sexual satisfaction" (182). Sexual energies are sublimated in a frenzy for money-making, a manic excitement over natural disaster and catastrophe, a thrilling to the crude violence of football. "Our life drives us apart and forces us upon science and invention—away from touch" (179), says Williams, and he points to mechanisms of sublimation that clearly evidence the legacy of Franklin's science of avoidance and the Puritans' fear of an infiltrating Other: "The impact of the bare soul upon the very twist of the fact which is our world about us, is un-American. *That* we shun and rush off to the laboratory, the wheatfield (hiding our indecent passion in meddling, playing)" (178). Our passions are reduced "to the straining of a telescope" (175) in a world where desire is invoked only in the realm of the gaze, where "a kind of celluloid of gayety (I am speaking of the theaters), a numbing coat . . . cuts us off from touch" (180). And the female body—for Williams, the ultimate object of desire—becomes a mere visual image, a two-dimensional body without organs, "fit only to be seen in shows, or, in the train of a launch, on aquaplanes, six at a time, the swift motion only serving to give the authentic sense of slipperiness, pseudo-naiads without the necessary wildness and the chill—fit only to be seen by the box, like Oregon apples, bright and round but tasteless—wineless, wholesale" (183–84).

Williams, like his Burr, would restore "the necessary wildness" to American women—and the wildness necessary to his own poetics, the power of the "supplying female." Without that fertile source, there can be no poet. And Williams, in fact, presents the matter in just such rigidly axiomatic terms, stating "Never a woman: never a poet. That's an axiom. Never a poet saw sun here" (179). Yet just as Williams' failure to deliver a poet within the scheme of *In the American Grain* is a purposeful failure, so is his failure to find "a true woman in flower" (179). It becomes necessary for Williams to deny the presence of that which is necessary, according to his poetics, for American poetry. And rather than deducing the failure of American art from the failure of a female flowering in America, Williams actually induces his premise by examining its supposed effects, offering the emptiness of American art as proof of the emptiness of American women:

> Women—givers (but they have been, as reservoirs, empty) perhaps they are being filled now. Hard to deal with in business, more conservative, closer to the earth—the only earth. They are our cattle, cattle of the spirit—not yet come in. None yet has raised benevolence to distinction. Not one to "wield her beauty as a scepter." It is a brilliant opportunity.—But the aesthetic shown by American artists (the test of the women) is discouraging: the New England eunuchs,

—"no more sex than a tapeworm"—faint echoes of England, perhaps of France, of Rousseau, as Valéry Larbaud insists,—Ryder: no
detail in his foregrounds just remote lusts, fiery but "gone,"—Poe:
moonlight. It is the annunciation of the spiritual barrenness of the
American woman. (181)

Williams positions the male artist as the measure of a woman.
His "aesthetic" is her "test," the sounding of her depth. But American
artists have had nothing to measure but a spent quality, "reservoirs"
gone dry. Williams, however, seems to betray his own argument for
"the spiritual barrenness of the American woman" with the less than
convincing nature of his evidence. Exactly who "the New England
eunuchs" are he doesn't make clear—nor is it clear how Larbaud's
alleged comment on Rousseau applies to these "eunuchs" with " 'no
more sex than a tapeworm.' " Furthermore, Williams' judgment on
Albert Ryder's paintings—"no detail in his foregrounds just remote
lusts"—seems to be cribbed from Rosenfeld's chapter on Ryder in *Port
of New York.* [31] And the testimony of Poe's poetry is dispensed with in a
word—"moonlight." But what of the testimony of Williams' own art,
of the very book in which he passes these judgments? No real women,
just imaginary females. "Of course, our history has been short and
comparatively obscure, for the most part," Williams confesses. "There
must be character in out of the way places, naturally, but none has
raised the point of which I speak, to distinction" (185). None—including Williams himself. He has found it more expedient to supply
his own "supplying females" than to search for women of historical
record who might reveal something other than the "barrenness" of
the American female.[32]

Which is not to say there are absolutely no actual women in *In the
American Grain.* There are—but Williams makes no attempt to explore
their characters. They function only as symbolic devices, like Bridget
Bishop and Susanna Martin in the Mather chapter, who are but mere
signifiers of female victimization by the tide of American culture. So,
too, Emily Dickinson. Williams says she is "about the only woman
one can respect for her clarity" (180), pronouncing her "the very near-
est we have ever been" to producing "a true woman in flower." But
Williams looks no deeper into Dickinson's life or poetry other than to
point to her "starving of passion in her father's garden" as evidence
of a woman's fate in America (179). Even though Williams declares
Dickinson to possess qualities he would want to investigate, he uses
her simply as an emblem of the difficulty of living "against the stream"
(180)—and one wonders whether Williams could, within his sense of

the male artist as the measure of a woman, and within his conception of the New World as the necessary bride of an American poet, give serious consideration to Dickinson, a woman, as a poet.[33]

But not all the women in *In the American Grain* are symbols of victimization. They are just as often objects of idealization. Williams praises Burr for having envisioned women as "deliciously a free thing, apart, *feminine*, a heaven," a vision that Williams locates in Burr's obsessive devotion to his daughter Theodosia as an idealized image of femininity. Burr, says Williams, "had created her into his free world where he lived in unconstraint. She was as far above the women of her time as he would have had himself above the men" (203). Williams gives similar treatment to Raleigh's Platonic idealization of Elizabeth. She, too, becomes a woman "apart, *feminine*, a heaven" through Williams' depiction of Raleigh's sweeping imaginative search of the New World as "a voyage on the body of his Queen: England, Elizabeth—Virginia!" (60). Burr's Theodosia and Raleigh's Elizabeth, like Poe's Virginia, might well reflect Williams' own fascination with an idealized feminine form. "The one earthly island he found where he might live in something akin to the state he imagined," Williams says of Poe, "the love of his wife, had to be single and inviolate" (231). But Williams also makes clear Virginia's inadequacy for Poe, pointing to the cold sterility of the poetry she inspired. Like "the white daisy" at the end of *Spring and All*, Virginia "is / not enough." She lacks the "rich orange / round the purple core," the fertile hues of the "Black eyed Susan" that is "rich / in savagery." Williams' own idealized feminine forms are anything but "inviolate" virginal women—they are almost always images of a more sensuous flowering, images of the "Arab / Indian / dark woman" (SA, 151).

The "white" wife supplanted by the "dark" bride—Williams twists the conventional nineteenth-century topos of "light" and "dark" women for his own purposes in *In the American Grain*.[34] De Soto's Doña Ysobel is symbolically exchanged for Macanoche and Mochila, the daughters of the chief of Pacaha. Houston's Eliza Allen is replaced by a Cherokee wife. Williams insistently equates dark women with the regenerative power of the female earth. In "Advent of the Slaves," Williams points to this quality in both "colored men and women whom I have known intimately" (208). Yet Williams makes no attempt to express the lives of these women as he would later do in "The Colored Girls of Passenack—Old and New"—he merely gestures to the black female as a symbol of fertile womanhood.[35] Williams, in fact, uses a fictional character as his primary symbol of the dark woman's primal powers, citing the "thrilling pleasure and deep satisfaction" he de-

rived from "E. K. Means' tale, *Diada Daughter of Discord*, an outstand-
ing story of a wild nigger wench, billeted upon a friend's family by her
owner while he went for a short boat trip without her," admonishing
us, "Read *Diada*—cutting cane stalks, sharpening them with lightning
speed and driving them through the attacking hounds" (210).[36]

"Read *Diada*," says Williams—and if we do, the underlying qualities of Williams' dark women become all the more apparent. In E. K.
Means's vernacular southern folktale, Diada Daughter of Discord
strikes terror into the entire countryside. Polynesian rather than Afri-
can—an enormous Amazon of a Pacific Islander so hideous to behold
that "Every feature of that face was a horror"—Diada is ransomed
from captivity among hostile cannibals of another island tribe by a
seafaring Louisianan, then brought to a friend's plantation in the deep
south where she is left for two week's while her master goes on business to St. Louis. Like some female caricature of a Queequeg run amok
in civilization, Diada rapaciously gobbles raw meat, steals whatever
she can get her hands on, including a large butcher's knife, and stares
longingly at the Mississippi bayous, to which she soon escapes, sending a general panic through the population, white and black, before
she is finally brought to bay by a party of four hundred men and a
pack of dogs, only to drive back her captors by rapidly hacking spears
out of cypress saplings with the butcher's knife and hurling them with
deadly accuracy at the pursuing dogs.

Arab, Indian, dark woman—the uncontrollable savage female.
Williams found her in Diada, and he put her in She, his own female
embodiment of regenerative discord, coursing through the middle of
the American landscape. Yet it had been Diada rather than She who
first met De Soto at the Mississippi, Diada who had thrust herself into
Williams' mind as an image of the Great River when he originally envisioned De Soto's demise in *The Great American Novel*: "In armor De
Soto wandering haphazard over Alabama. The Seminoles for guides.
Buried him in the Mississippi. It is my river, he said. Roll Jordan roll.
It is *my* river for I discovered it and into it let my body, in full armor,
be put to rest. The cat-fish ate it. So roll Jordan roll. Diada Daughter
of Discord: read it" (192).

The only "real" woman in *In the American Grain* who perfectly
fits the symbolic demands of Williams' poetics is Freydis in "Red
Eric." Williams encountered two different versions of Freydis' story
in the Vinland sections of the Icelandic sagas he read for the Red
Eric chapter. "The Saga of Eric Red" identifies Freydis as "Eric's natural daughter," telling how she single-handedly drove off a band of

attacking "Skrellings" (Eskimos) after her warriors had fled in fear. Pregnant, unable to keep up with the retreat, Freydis seized the sword of a slain comrade and turning to face her pursuers, "stripped down her shift, and slapped her breast with the naked sword," at which the Skrellings fled in terror.[37] "The Vinland History of the Flat Island Book" gives Freydis a more darkly prominent role. She cruelly conspires against Helgi and Finnbogi, the two brothers who accompany her and her husband, Thorvard, in a second ship to the coast of Vinland. Freydis contrives a grievance by which she forces her husband and his crew to murder not only the brothers but their entire crew as well. The only ones spared in this bloodbath are the women, "and these no man would kill," states the saga. "At this Freydis exclaimed: 'Hand me an axe!' This was done, and she fell upon the five women, and left them dead."[38]

Williams was obviously captivated by the details of both versions, for he joins them together in a single composite version, making Freydis the central figure of the latter sections of "Red Eric." Otherwise, he alters his source material very little, narrating Freydis' exploits almost verbatim from the sagas themselves. Yet Williams didn't need to mythologize Freydis for his chapter, for the sagas—products of an oral folk tradition—had already performed that task. Freydis, whose name derives from Freya, the Norse goddess of love and fertility, is archetypally portrayed as a savagely violent matriarch, a woman who ruthlessly enforces her power through terror and bloodshed. What is remarkable about Williams' handling of that already inscribed role is the way he emplots it within *In the American Grain*. The truculent Freydis becomes the defender of the New World's matriarchal essence. Her bloody deeds are what drives the tide of history from the shores of America, restoring the New World to that state of "immaculate fulfillment" that continues inviolate until Columbus' symbolic rape.

Freydis, like Diada, reveals what Julia Kristeva terms "abjection," the powers of horror associated with the generative violence of the female body.[39] Williams fully releases those powers but once, within the distant space of a kind of prehistory in the book's opening chapter. They flare again in She, in her symbolic castration of De Soto as he plunges back to primal origins—but Williams seeks to contain that frightening female power rather than to release it in his book. Though it is a power that can fertilize the poet, immersing him in the rich chaos of the unknown, it can also destroy him, consuming him in the primordial darkness of mother night.[40] *In the American Grain* is Williams' symbolic struggle to appropriate that power for his art—a struggle that gains literal verity in his treatment of the Baroness, perhaps the most significant actual woman to appear in the book. "I don't suppose," writes Williams in "Jacataqua," that "there has ever been an American woman like Kiki or that delightful Baroness who paraded Fifth Avenue one day with a coal-scuttle for a chapeau. Naturally they arrested her. Naturally. She would have been arrested in any city, but not, I imagine, with quite such a sense of duty as in America. To permit such a thing would cast a very awkward light on us all" (178).[41]

The Baroness is not an exemplar of "spiritual barrenness." Her unorthodox behavior speaks the release of chthonic female powers, and Williams points to her arrest as emblematic of his culture's fear of the unrestricted female. But Williams doesn't mention the "very awkward light" the Baroness cast on him—nor that he himself had the Baroness arrested and jailed in New York. Williams' own relationship with Else von Freytag-Loringhoven, a German woman of title prominent in the avant-garde circles of Paris and New York, is quite different from what he suggests in "Jacataqua." Williams refers to her as "*that* delightful Baroness," as if she were not of his direct acquaintance, but his own encounters with her were intensely intimate and, in the end, intensely violent. Yet his need to distance her as *that* Baroness was no doubt acutely felt, for she continued to haunt his consciousness while he was writing "Jacataqua." He had tried to rid himself of her—indeed, he had even paid to have her sent back to Paris just before he began work on *In the American Grain*. "The Baroness, though," as Williams wryly remarks in his *Autobiography*, "didn't leave me so easily" (A, 166). But the Baroness was long dead at the time he wrote the *Autobiography*, and he could afford to jest. During the composition of *In the American Grain* she was still very much alive—threateningly so, to Williams' mind.

The Baroness was certainly not the only woman to fascinate Williams during that period—there were others, such as Evelyn Scott, who also seemed to offer Williams what he so eagerly sought: the power of a woman, reckless and flamboyant, living against the grain.[42] Yet the Baroness appeared to be that very power incarnate, a kind of Diada of Dada, a female creature of wild and exotic plumage who might be seen parading Fifth Avenue with a coal-scuttle on her head or walking the rank streets of the Village, her head shaved, face painted, and tea balls hanging from her breasts. Williams was in his mid-thirties when he met her in 1919—she some ten years older than he. He admired her radical spirit, her inconoclastic poems in *The Little Review*, her outré costumes, her sexual abandon and appetite. He made the initial gesture of wanting to ravish her, but when the Baroness responded with the full force of her passion, Williams fled in horror. She wanted to regenerate him with her body, to suck him into her vortex much as She does with De Soto. She did, in fact, bite his lips, drawing blood when he kissed her once. And she demanded that he make love to her so that he would contract her venereal disease and thus rid himself of his bourgeois tendencies and become a true artist. She hunted him, and he found her pursuit intolerable. She proved a true "daughter of discord" who could destroy the structure of his world. She invaded his domestic life, physically assaulting him at his home in Rutherford where he thought he was safe from her, and he bought a punching bag to vent his frustrations. Or was he honing his skills for a counterattack? The next time he encountered her on the street in New York, he "flattened her with a stiff punch to the mouth" (A, 169). Then he had her arrested for assault.

But the Baroness responded with something even more threatening than physical violence. She turned to art. Under the guise of reviewing his *Kora in Hell*, which had been appearing serially in *The Little Review*, the Baroness accused Williams of "male-bluff" posturing, of trying to hide his bourgeois nature under the cloak of art.[43] She had to be silenced. And Williams turned to the most effective tool he had for finally controlling her—his writing. In his own magazine, *Contact*, Williams published "The Three Letters," a piece that plays on the Baroness' charging him with posturing by plainly exposing the bluffing disguises of his own art. The apparently fictional masks he employs are designed to reveal rather than conceal the actual identities of the protagonists. William Carlos Williams is Evan Dionysius Evans, the Baroness simply La Baronne.[44] Far from attempting to conceal the details of his involvement with the Baroness as he does in "Jacataqua," Williams makes them all too visible. If there is a deception here, it is, once again, done in the manner of "The Purloined Letter."

And there are indeed purloined letters of a sort in "The Three Letters," the very letters announced in the title, the letters that Evans sends to La Baronne and that she threatens to publish when he rejects her passions: "I want you, Evan Dionysius Evans, she had hissed. Well, you can't have me, he said, like that. Then I'll publish the letters, she whispered. Be sure you don't miss any, he rejoined."[45] The weapon with which La Baronne threatens Evans is perhaps the same one Williams feared the Baroness would use against him in the wake of her piece in *The Little Review*. He evidently realized that the letters were a weapon only if he tried to suppress them. Plainly exposed to view, they would be harmless—and they are, in fact, plainly exposed in the text of "The Three Letters." Evans so cheerfully dismisses the

threat of the letters, reminding La Baronne not to miss any, because
Williams has already published the contents of each during the course
of the narrative:

1. I love you.
2. *Quod licet Jovi non licet bovi.*
3. You damned stinking old woman . . . you dirty old bitch.[46]

Though Williams disperses the letters in his text, gathered together
they tell the essential story of his relationship with the Baroness.
Evans declares his love for La Baronne, but when she responds in
kind, unleashing passions that threaten to overwhelm him, he draws
the line. *Quod licet Jovi non licet bovi*—What is lawful for Jove isn't lawful for a cow. The Latin proverb had purportedly been sent by Evans
because La Baronne wanted to quote it in an article she was writing. But Williams' message is clear enough—men have privilege over
women, like Jove over a cow. As he says in "Jacataqua," women "are
our cattle, cattle of the spirit—not yet come in." Yet when they do
come in, not docilely, but with a vengeance, Williams recoils in horror.
Evans brands La Baronne a "damned stinking old woman," a "dirty
old bitch."

But "The Three Letters," one of Williams' last prose pieces before *In the American Grain*, is about much more than Williams and the
Baroness—it is also about his conception of the "supplying female"
and the New World as a woman. Evan Dionysius Evans is a man for
whom "America, since his boyhood, had stood . . . as a virginal young
woman—inclined, of course, to grant important favors to certain individuals of special distinction." Evans' America, however, doesn't
bestow herself upon him as a young virgin. She is an old woman
with a "reek" that "stood out purple from her body, separating her
forever from the clean muslin souls of Yankeedom." But this woman,
though sexually ravished, is nonetheless strangely virginal, "mystically dirty" like her "unspeakably filthy tenement." And for Evans,
she is "the fulfillment of a wish. . . . America personified in the filth of
its own imagination."[47] The Baroness incarnates the sexual dichotomy
that Williams later explicitly fuses in "The whore and the virgin, an
identity" in *Paterson* (P, 210). She is an inexhaustible Eden, an ever
virginal whore, the poet's idealized embodiment of America.[48]

Williams, furthermore, pointedly makes "The Three Letters" the
story of his own poetic genesis. "At age thirty five," Williams says as
he introduces La Baronne, "Evan Dionysius Evans met, in the flesh,
the Old Woman he had praised" in a "long love poem about the Pas-

saic River and an old woman, which Orick Johns, dear Orick, called great and Ezra Pound printed in his Catholic Anthology. The Wanderer, it can be found also in my book, Al Que Quiere." [49] Williams emerges from behind his thin mask, directing us to the very poem that records his birth as a poet. In "The Wanderer" he had created his archetype of the "supplying female," patterning it upon his own grandmother, Emily Wellcome, the " 'gypsy' " of the family (A, 166). [50] "Ominous, old, painted— / With bright lips and lewd Jew's eyes / Her might strapped in by a corset / To give her age youth, perfect / In her will to be young," she baptizes the poet in the ravished body of America, "the filthy Passaic" (CEP, 5, 11). The Baroness offered Williams a renewal of his origins, and he indeed verbally enacts it through Evans and La Baronne: "To her kind only could his mind go to be kindled," says Williams, and Evans professes his love for her "just as he had cried out, I love you, in the direction of his own unbelievable grandmother, the wolf of the family." [51]

But the Baroness is not used for a mere mythogenetic repetition of the earlier poem—her story significantly alters the narrative. In "The Wanderer," the poet is fertilized by submitting himself to the woman's power—in "The Three Letters," he is kindled by the struggle to subdue it, to control it by exercise of his art. Nor does Williams attempt to conceal that fact in his creation of the Baroness. He imagines Evans' triumph over her in terms of generating her "from his neck" in the same "way the Greek gods would sometimes get themselves created out of each other's thighs or shoulders. Eve, too, from Adam's brisket." [52] Williams ultimately generates himself as poet by generating the women who ostensibly generate him, giving birth to them in the body of his writing, fertilizing himself by the very struggle to contain their potentially destructive powers within the substance of the written word. [53]

"Determined women have governed my fate," Williams says in the introduction to *Yes, Mrs. Williams,* his "Personal Record" of his mother. Perhaps for that reason Williams was so determined to gain some control over the lives of women in his writing. *Yes, Mrs. Williams* is quite plainly Williams' attempt to contain his mother's life in writing, to create for himself the woman who created him—and it is more than mere coincidence that he began assembling his materials for the book at the same time he was writing "Jacataqua" and declaring that women in America "have been, as reservoirs, empty." Elena Rose Hoheb Williams is certainly not empty, for *Yes, Mrs. Williams* is a reservoir filled—filled with the raw stuff of a mother tongue. The book primarily consists of direct transcriptions of his mother's speech, the rich female language that is Williams' fertilizing food.

"It is the woman in us / That makes us write—"Williams proclaims in an early poem. "Let us acknowledge it— / Men would be silent" (CEP, 34). Yet what he really suggests is that it is the woman who gives the writer speech, because writing devoid of speech is, for Williams, a kind of deafening silence. Speech rather than writing—vernacular rather than literary language—is the ground of Williams' attempt to generate an American literature. Indeed, speech comes from the ground, while the written word imposes itself on the ground, as Williams' vision of Columbus' first moments on the shores of the New World in *The Great American Novel* suggests.[54] And Williams finds the key to an American language in the power of speech to disrupt the fixity of writing. Speech is the medium by which She conquers De Soto, by which Williams regeneratively disorders the inscriptions of the expedition's chroniclers. Speech is what Williams drew from his grandmother to create poems such as "Portrait of a Woman in Bed."[55] Speech is what Williams received from his wife to create the Burr chapter—a chapter that presents itself as speech, in the form of a dialogue between two opposing voices. Indeed, the whole of *In the American Grain* is structured as speech—both explicitly in chapters employing dialogue (like those centered on Rasles and Champlain) and implicitly in the dialogue of voices between chapters. Williams' book is a brilliant polyglossal display of voices created, imitated, simulated, appropriated, juxtaposed. And Williams' transcriptions of his mother's speech, first begun while working on the book, make *Yes, Mrs. Williams* in many ways an unacknowledged chapter of *In the American Grain*. At the end of Williams' chronology of the lives of men in the New World stands the life of the woman who truly gave birth to the poet.

Significantly, Williams initially perceived his mother as threatening to consume him, to deny his birth as a poet. "Her interest in art became my interest in art," Williams remarked when describing his mother's domination of his early development as a writer. "I was personifying her, her detachment from the world of Rutherford. She seemed an heroic figure, a poetic ideal. I didn't especially admire her; I was attached to her. I had not yet established any sort of independent spirit" (IW, 16). Williams' earliest poems can indeed be seen as influenced by his mother's insistence on traditional standards of artistic beauty, on shunning the vulgar, the sexual, the filthy. And Williams' fears over the consequences of "personifying her" are perhaps best revealed by his telling in the *Autobiography* of how he actually did impersonate her once in Paris when he was fourteen, putting on her dress and hat, carrying his masquerade into public. The disguise was good enough to make his aunt Alice think she was receiving a visit from Elena—but the little game turned ominous when his aunt "scared hell" out of Williams, telling him "it was strictly against the law to impersonate the opposite sex on the city streets." Williams says he "got back, all right, but it gave me a good scare," conjecturing that "I could have taken off the dress, I suppose, but probably didn't have much on under it" (A, 37). Williams' admission of nakedness beneath the adopted image of his mother points to his own naked dependence upon her identity.

Williams changed that identity, and he did so by his writing. That is precisely what *Yes, Mrs. Williams* performs. The book explicitly repudiates the image of his mother as a "defeated romantic" detached from the immediacy of life. That image, says Williams, is the surface only: "Under it lies the true life, undefeated if embittered, hard as nails, little loving, easily mistaken for animal selfishness. Unexcavated from her own consciousness, the good that is in her—crying for release, release from herself, a most difficult animal" (YMW, 33–34). Williams excavates his mother's darker, hidden qualities in the same way that he descends beneath the surface of his source documents for *In the American Grain*, excavating "the strange phosphorus of the life." Yet his excavation of his mother "from her own consciousness" is actually a revelation of his own unconscious, a release of himself as writer from the domination of his mother, "a most difficult animal."

He had, in fact, already begun that process in *Kora in Hell*, transforming his mother into the chthonic female who nurtures the poet. The rhythms of speech in Kora do indeed resemble the rhythms of his mother's speech recorded in *Yes, Mrs. Williams*.[56] And Williams speaks at length about his mother at the opening of the prologue, calling her "an impoverished, ravished Eden but one indestructible as the imagination itself" (KH, 7). Elena becomes Kora, the "supplying female," the virginal yet maternal body of Williams' America. She is not simply "as indestructible as the imagination," she is made indestructible by the imagination, created mystically inviolate by Williams' art so that the imagination may repeat the original conjugation again and again. In both *In the American Grain* and *Yes, Mrs. Williams*, Williams enacts that symbolic ravishment of the New World by appropriating the female reservoir of speech to fertilize his writing—an enactment that becomes literal fact in Williams' violation of his mother by the very writing of *Yes, Mrs. Williams*, for she expressly told him not to put her speech into writing, as Williams himself admits in his description of how he caught her words straight from her mouth:

> All sorts of things . . . would come out of her from time to time. I got in the habit of writing them down—on the back of an envelope, on any piece of scrap paper I could lay my hands on quickly—so as to preserve the flavor and the accurate detail.
>
> Often, though her eyes have been failing in recent years, she would detect me and ask what I was doing. I just want to remember some of these things, Mother—to tell the boys sometime—and for their own sakes. It's interesting.
>
> Don't you write about me, she would say—but I confess that I paid little attention to her. (YMW, 23–24)

Williams' violation of his mother's word by the very fact of writing gives a sharp irony to the title *Yes, Mrs. Williams*, for the book itself says "No, Mrs. Williams" to her desire to remain speech without inscription. Elena Williams didn't want to become historicized in writing any more than the immaculate flower of the New World wanted to be violated by history. And even though Williams presents his own writing of history as the marriage of word and place rather than the rape of place by word, Williams' poetics actually celebrate a ritualized violation of the woman in *In the American Grain* as well as *Yes, Mrs. Williams*, forcing an inscription upon the female, writing upon the body of the mother.

NOTES

1. William Carlos Williams, "Comment," *Contact* 4 (Summer 1921): 18.

2. Annette Kolodny, *The Lay of the Land: Metaphor as Experience and History in American Life and Letters* (Chapel Hill: University of North Carolina Press, 1975).

3. William Carlos Williams, "Letter to an Australian Editor," *Briarcliff Quarterly* 3 (Oct. 1946): 205.

4. T. S. Eliot, "Tradition and the Individual Talent" (1919), in *Selected Essays* (New York: Harcourt, Brace and Company, 1950); Harold Bloom, *The Anxiety of Influence, A Theory of Poetry* (New York: Oxford University Press, 1973).

5. Williams Carlos Williams, "Letter to an Australian Editor," 208.

6. Ibid., 206.

7. One is reminded, certainly, of Williams' relationship with his own father, an Englishman who not only remained singularly unattached to the America his son sought to embrace, but looked disapprovingly on the kind of poetry Williams was endeavoring to create. (See Williams' telling dream in A, 14).

8. Filson actually wrote his book less with an eye toward making an authentic history than a financial profit. He had acquired 12,000 acres of Kentucky land just after the Revolution and wanted to attract settlers to the region. Filson uses Boone as his mask for extolling the virtues of nature to combat the commonly held perception of Kentucky as a fearful and howling wilderness. Williams, furthermore, didn't even come at this highly colored portrayal of Boone directly through Filson's book, but found it attached as a brief appendix in Cecil Hartley's *Life and Times of Colonel Daniel Boone* (Philadelphia: G. G. Evans, 1860), the source volume from which Williams draws his biographical material for "The Discovery of Kentucky."

9. For others, such as Charles Woodmason, it was more than wild enough. See his *The Carolina Backcountry on the Eve of the Revolution*, ed. Richard J. Hooker (Chapel Hill: University of North Carolina Press, 1953) for a counterperspective to Boone's view of the "wilderness."

10. Though Williams had traveled extensively in Europe both prior to and during the writing of *In the American Grain*, he had been west of the Mississippi only once—significantly, on an errand of burial. While an intern at Child's Hospital in New York in 1908, he went as attending physician to a wealthy Mexican who wanted to go home to San Luis Potosi to die. It was less than two years before the outbreak of the Mexican Revolution, and Williams entered not just a landscape "which was entirely unfamiliar to me," but a precarious situation in which he felt his own life to be at stake. He had all he could do to keep the old Mexican alive with frequent injections of caffeine and sodium benzoate, fearing the possibility "of being lynched if I arrived at the border in a couple of days with a corpse" (A, 73). That experience might have provided the impetus for the Pancho Villa section that Williams wanted to include in his planned sequel to *In the American Grain*, "a second volume, taking up the skein at Jefferson and coming up, this time with a big jump to Grover Cleveland; and then, more slowly to the present day to end with Pancho Villa" (A, 237). Williams had, in fact, already sketched out the Villa material in *The Great American Novel*, which narrates the near death of an Englishman in a Villista raid on the town of Los Mochis (GAN, 183–85). Williams seems to have associated the immanence of death with those distant territories beyond the Mississippi, and his sections in *The Great American Novel* on the Mormon's trek "over the prairies and deserts—through Sioux country, in search of Zion" and the Mountain Meadow massacre of an entire wagon train of California-bound gold seekers (GAN, 186–87) perhaps indicate that Williams was planning another section for his sequel to *In the American Grain* that would treat the West as a shadowy and violent ground. Interestingly, in 1950, after a stroke had made Williams aware of his own impending end, he would once again encounter the West as a spectral realm of death. During his visit to Robert McAlmon in New Mexico, Williams was struck by the sight of an Indian, possibly dead, wedged in the girders beneath the International Bridge between El Paso and Juarez. That vision serves as the generating image for "The Desert Music," a poem in which Williams asserts his creative powers

as artist against the immanence of death. See Sherman Paul's excellent study, *The Music of Survival* (Urbana: University of Illinois Press, 1968).

11. Williams implicitly targets Pound and Eliot here as "those who know all the Latin and some of the Sanskrit names."

12. Houston's voice was, however, about as inaccessible in the record as Boone's was for Williams. The first substantial publication of Houston's writings—Amelia C. Williams and Eugene C. Barker, eds., *The Writings of San Houston*, 8 vols. (Austin: University of Texas Press, 1938–43)—was not available until sometime after the publication of *In the American Grain*. Williams did, nonetheless, have access to some of Houston's letters and speeches in his source volume for "Descent," Henry Bruce's *Life of General Houston* (New York: Dodd, Mead, 1891). But other than to quote Houston's remark that " 'Eliza stands acquitted by me' " (212; Bruce, 49), Williams makes no attempt to let Houston speak.

13. Williams' details for this portrait come primarily from personal recollections of Houston by Maggie Houston Williams, his daughter, and Oliver Dyer (Bruce, 209, 224).

14. The Lincoln chapter, according to Williams, was added at Charles Boni's request when Williams delivered the completed manuscript to him: "When he looked through the manuscript he said, 'Are you going to write a book about America without *Lincoln*?' So I wrote a short chapter and he accepted it" (IW, 43–44; Williams tells the same anecdote about Boni and the Lincoln chapter in A, 236). It is worth noting that Williams, with his book already finished and gone from him, makes Lincoln a *maternal* figure presiding over a loss, "a woman in an old shawl" holding together the rent pieces of America, "a woman, born somehow, aching over it, holding all fearfully together. It was the end of THAT period" (234).

15. Williams ranges widely over Poe's critical writings in the chapter, quoting from relatively obscure pieces, such as Poe's review of Captain Marryatt's *Joseph Rushbrook, or the Poacher*, as well as from Poe's more well-known judgments of Cooper, Longfellow, Bryant, Hawthorne, and Lowell. Williams' probable source edition was *The Complete Works of Edgar Allan Poe*, ed. James A. Harrison, 17 vols. (New York: Thomas Y. Crowell & Company, 1902; rpt. New York: AMS Press, 1965), the most complete edition of Poe's writings available to him. For a good discussion of how Williams shapes Poe to answer the loss of Pound and Eliot on the American literary scene see E. P. Bollier's "Against the American Grain: William Carlos Williams between Poe and Whitman," *Tulane Studies in English* 23 (1978): 123–42.

16. This positioning of the writing self in Williams' own poetics becomes the vital element of Charles Olson's approach to poetry as a "field of composition" generated by the kinetic sparks of the poet's own self in immediate contact with the world, "Projective Verse" (1950), in *Selected Writings of Charles Olson*, ed. Robert Creeley (New York: New Directions, 1966), 15–26. Williams recognized Olson as one of his tribe, quoting a lengthy portion of "Projective Verse" in his *Autobiography*, praising Olson for working to reorganize "the basis of our thinking" (A, 329).

17. Vera M. Kutzinski discusses *In the American Grain* in terms of Williams' inclusion of cultural elements generally marginalized by traditional assessments of the origins of American cultural identity in the opening chapter of her *Against the American Grain: Myth and History in William Carlos Williams, Jay Wright, and Nicolás Guillén* (Baltimore: Johns Hopkins University Press, 1987), 1–46.

18. See William Alfred Bryan, *George Washington in American Literature, 1775–1865* (New York: Columbia University Press, 1952).

19. Williams' main sources for the Washington chapter seem to have been Paul Leicester Ford's *The True George Washington* (Philadelphia: J. B. Lippincott, 1897) and George Washington Parke Custis' *Recollections and Private Memoirs of Washington* (New York: Derby & Jackson, 1860), the same works Williams cites as background reading for *The First President* (1939), his libretto for an opera on Washington, in *Many Loves and Other Plays, the Collected Plays of William Carlos Williams* (New York: New Directions, 1961), 317, 318. Ford speaks at length about Washington's wardrobe (186–91), and also has chapters titled "Physique" and "Relations with the Fair Sex" (39–59, 84–112), from which Williams gathers the other details by which he illuminates Washington's character.

20. Williams, *The First President*, 303.

21. For a study of other representations of Burr in American literature, see Charles F. Nolan, Jr., *Aaron Burr and the American Literary Imagination* (Westport, Conn.: Greenwood Press, 1980).

22. Williams, however, says that his planned sequel to *In the American Grain* was to begin with Jefferson (A, 237). And Williams' remarks on Jefferson in "The American Background" suggest that he was indeed to have played a vitally affirmative role in the continuation of the history. "In this inevitable conflict of interests," says Williams in reference to the struggle between native and foreign cultural impulses at the time of the Revolution, "Thomas Jefferson stands out as the sole individual who seems to have had a clear understanding of what was taking place" (SE, 138).

23. Williams renews his attack on Hamilton in *Paterson* 2, focusing on the economic issues underlying his plan for establishing The Society for Useful Manufactures on the Passaic, and denouncing the Federal Reserve banks, which Hamilton organized, as "a Legalized National Usury System, whose Customer No. 1 is our Government, the richest country in the world. Everyone of us is paying tribute to the money racketeers on every dollar we earn through hard work" (P, 67, 69, 73–74). Pound, an even more outspoken critic of "usury" who influenced Williams' views on the subject, offers the following on Hamilton in canto 62: "and as for Hamilton / we may take it (my authority, ego scriptor cantilenae) / that he was the Prime snot in ALL American history," *Selected Cantos of Ezra Pound* (New York: New Directions, 1966), 77.

24. Breslin, 118. Breslin—who identifies the source for "The Virtue of History" as James Parton's 1858 biography of Burr, *The Life and Times of Aaron Burr* (New York: Mason Brothers, 1858; rpt. New York: Johnson Reprint Corporation, 1967)—lodges strong reservations about both the document itself

and the way Williams used it. Parton's book, Breslin points out, is a second-ary rather than primary source. Although it reprints excerpts from much of Burr's correspondence as well as that of his contemporaries, it doesn't contain as many primary documents as M. L. Davis' *Memoirs of Aaron Burr*, 2 vols. (New York: Harper, 1836–37)—a work that Breslin conjectures Williams may have consulted, and that, Breslin implies, in any case he should have drawn upon more extensively. Breslin sees the process behind the Burr chapter as the inverse of that behind the "best" chapters in the book, i.e., the early chapters in which Williams made a symbolic descent into primary documents and "slowly absorbed his material so that it became an almost physical part of his life" (119). Indeed, Breslin points to the Burr chapter as representative of what is wrong with most of the later chapters of *In the American Grain*, terming Williams' handling of Parton's book "hotheaded" (238), and suggesting that Williams' statements about his wife's part in the chapter were an attempt to displace the responsibility for his poor performance. Yet Breslin essentially at-tributes his own displeasure with the chapter to Williams himself, and I think we could do better than to quarrel with *In the American Grain* for refusing to evince a unity it doesn't wish to yield.

25. The setting for Burr's meeting with Jacataqua is real enough. Burr did indeed join Arnold's troops in Maine for the march to Quebec (Parton, 69–70). And "Jacataqua" is plausible as a French and English corruption from one of several Indian languages of the Northeast, including Algonquian, Huron, and Abnaki. (A similar form occurs in the name of Chautauqua County in New York, of Huron origin.) But as an actual person, Jacataqua, to the best of my knowledge, occurs nowhere but in Williams' chapter. Williams, however, seems to have had both the form of the name and the basis of a connection with Burr roughly in mind as early as *The Great American Novel*. Mentioning, among many other swirling fragments of the American past, Burr's marriage to the elder widow Mrs. Prevost, Williams exclaims, "Jataqua!" (GAN, 190). There is some possibility that Williams may have received either the Jacata-qua legend or the inspiration for it from Wallace Gould, a one-quarter Abnaki from Maine. Gould, who wrote several books of poetry that incorporate ma-terial from Indian legends—but none of which mention Jacataqua—stayed at Williams' home in Rutherford for several months in 1921 (A, 164–65).

26. *William Carlos Williams Review* 11 (Fall 1985).

27. Sandra M. Gilbert, "Purloined Letters: William Carlos Williams and 'Cress,'" *William Carlos Williams Review* 11 (Fall 1985): 5–15.

28. Lola Ridge, "American Sagas," *New Republic* (24 Mar. 1926): 149.

29. Yet Williams' selection is hardly a distortion, for most of the victims of the witchcraft trials were women. Mather records five trial proceedings in *Wonders of the Invisible World* (London, 1693), four of which name women as the accused. Other than selectively excerpting portions of Mather's text, Williams faithfully reproduces Mather's words verbatim, making no use of the kinds of material—an editor's introduction or annotations—that can often identify exact editions of his sources. Yet given what seems to have been Williams'

preference for modern reprintings of older works, he probably used Samuel Gardner Drake's *The Witchcraft Delusion in New England* (Roxbury, Mass.: W. E. Woodward, 1866), vol. 1, which reprints the London edition of 1693.

30. Williams, in a characteristic bit of posturing, dismisses his own reference to Freud: "the dangerous ground of pleasure: *Jenseits des lust princip* [*sic*], Freud sees it, beyond the charmed circle. It is no matter, since it is unknown in the province I am discussing. Here, through terror, there is no direct touch; all is cold, little and discreet:—save just under the hide" (176). Despite the "no matter," Williams does indeed incorporate Freud's opposing of the death and life instincts, developed in the closing sections of *Beyond the Pleasure Principle*, in "Jacataqua" as well as earlier chapters of *In the American Grain*. An organism's motivation for self-preservation through hermetic closure to foreign contacts and external stimuli that would disrupt the organism's normal metabolic processes, Freud maintains, expresses the death instinct, the instinct to let life progress uninterruptedly toward its predestined end, i.e., toward death, the natural dissolution of the organism. Conversely, erotic desire, which causes an organism to seek out contact with external stimuli, violates an organism's hermetic closure. Eros expresses the life instincts, for it disrupts an organism's inevitable movement toward death. The repression of eros and preservation from contact with the unfamiliar are, of course, the very characteristics by which Williams defines the Puritans, whose attempt to shut out the New World patently expresses the death instinct. "Their religious zeal," says Williams, "mistaken for a thrust upward toward the sun, was a stroke in, in, in—not toward germination but the confinement of a tomb" (66). Indeed, the opening paragraph of "The Destruction of Tenochtitlan"—the first chapter of the book Williams successfully completed—pictures the Spaniards' desire to seize and destroy the New World as spurred by "the force of the pack whom the dead drive," suggesting a curious feeding of Eros through the impulse of Thanatos. Since much of Williams' book was already finished by the time the first English translation of *Beyond the Pleasure Principle* was published in America (New York: Boni and Liveright, 1924), Williams had possibly obtained a copy of the first English printing (London: International Psycho-Analytical Press, 1922), but there is also some possibility he might have obtained and read the work even earlier in the original (Vienna: Internationaler Psychoanalytischer Verlag, 1920), struggling through it with his passable reading knowledge of German. Williams does, after all, cite the work by its German title in *In the American Grain*—and this supposition might gain further credence in light of the posturing implied in Williams' fictionalization in *Voyage to Pagany* of his having seen a copy of Freud's work in a Vienna bookshop window in 1924 during his European sojourn: "*Jenseits des Lustüprinzips* and a list of Freud's pamphlets, an amazing list, and all perhaps soon to be refuted, he said to himself uninterestedly" (VP, 181). For a full treatment of Freud's impact upon Williams' literary milieu, see Frederick J. Hoffman, *Freudianism and the Literary Mind* (Baton Rouge: Louisiana State University Press, 1945), particularly 58–84.

31. Rosenfeld remarks of Ryder's painting that "Sexual fear in particular speaks from the forms. It was the sexual expression of the mechanism of resistance to the present moment that kept the foregrounds comparatively empty, and gave interest preponderantly to the middle and upper reaches of the canvas" (*Port of New York*, 14).

32. It is interesting to note that at approximately the same time Williams was writing "Jacataqua," Elizabeth Anthony Dexter published her pioneering study, *Colonial Women of Affairs, a Study of Women in Business and the Professions in America before 1776* (Boston: Houghton Mifflin Company, 1924). Dexter certainly manages to find "character in out of the way places" as well as in prominent places, belying Williams' claim.

33. In "The American Background," Williams praises "the authenticity of Emily Dickinson's unrhymes" (SE, 155). And in "The Somnambulists," a 1929 review of Kay Boyle's *Short Stories*, Williams identifies "first Emily Dickinson and then Kay Boyle" as the two most noteworthy women writers in America to waken from the narcotic sleep that isolates the individual from a sense of immediacy and contact (*Imaginations*, 340). Williams was acutely and sympathetically aware of the difficulties faced by women writers "in a world where men are expected to take a leading place"—see his letter to Mary Ellen Solt, *William Carlos Williams Review* 11 (Fall 1985): 3—and indeed outspokenly supportive of writers like Lola Ridge, Kay Boyle, Djuna Barnes, and Marianne Moore throughout his life. But in *In the American Grain*, Williams attempts to exploit rather than to alleviate the difficult position of women in American society to further his own scheme.

34. Note also the prominently symbolic character of Grace Black in *A Voyage to Pagany*, who represents the dark female power of America in a bitterly self-imposed exile. Williams has Evans give her a copy of none other than *In the American Grain* at parting: "He gave her for a keepsake a copy of a book he had once published upon some characters from the American History. She was delighted —Free from the collegiate taste, she wagered, pressing it with real pleasure" (VP, 214).

35. In "Advent of the Slaves" Williams merely mentions Georgie Anderson "as some female who walked upon air and light—in her wild girlhood" (211). In "The Colored Girls of Passenack—Old and New," he devotes several pages to her, *The Farmers' Daughters: The Collected Stories of William Carlos Williams* (New York: New Directions, 1961), 50–53. Interestingly, Anderson, who worked in the Williams' household as a maid during Williams' youth, was the first woman, besides his grandmother, Williams ever saw naked, and both women would become almost obsessive images of his desire for the female body. (See also A, 12.)

36. Williams' reference is to E. K. Means's "Diada, Daughter of Discord," the first piece in his collection of tales about black life in the South, *More E. K. Means* (1919; rpt. Freeport, N.Y.: Books for Libraries Press, 1972), 1–69.

37. "The Saga of Eric the Red," trans. Arthur Middleton Reeves, in Olson and Bourne, *The Northmen, Columbus, and Cabot, 985–1503*, 32, 38. This is the same volume from which Williams drew his Columbus material.

38. "The Vinland History of the Flat Island Book," trans. Arthur Middleton Reeves, in Olson and Bourne, 62–64. Williams habitually misrecalled this document as *The Long Island Book* (SL, 186; A, 178).

39. See Julia Kristeva, *Powers of Horror, an Essay on Abjection*, trans. Leon S. Roudiez (New York: Columbia University Press, 1982), particularly "Those Females Who Can Wreck the Infinite," 157–73.

40. See the "Night" chapter in Williams' *A Voyage to Pagany*. The poet is symbolically thrust back into the "nameless terror" of origins in Genoa, the city of Columbus' nativity, experiencing the primal dread of night, "the mother stuff," out of which all art is generated (VP, 90–94).

41. Kiki was Man Ray's mistress, who had visited America in 1924. Williams had previously made another fleeting reference to her in one of his *Spring and All* poems (SA, 113). Her life as one of the most celebrated personalities on the Parisian bohemian scene has recently been treated by Billy Klüver and Julie Martin in *Kiki's Paris: Artists and Lovers 1900–1930* (New York, Harry N. Abrams, 1989).

42. Like the Baroness, Evelyn Scott was a familiar figure on the avant-garde scene of New York throughout the early 1920s. Williams may have first met Scott at one of Lola Ridge's monthly gatherings at her apartment in the Village. Williams was a regular at these parties, and he undoubtedly saw the Baroness as well as Scott there with no little frequency. A writer of extraordinary talent whose remarkable life has recently been salvaged from obscurity by D. A. Callard in his *Pretty Good for a Woman: The Enigmas of Evelyn Scott* (London: Jonathan Cape, 1985), Scott also admired the Baroness, and in 1920 had defended her poems in *The Little Review*, later writing to Lola Ridge that "The Baroness now was the real stuff, the real lallypaloodle girl. She was the only one who dared to be a woman" (Callard, 88). Yet in the same letter Scott also expressed her disillusionment with Williams, who had refused to reciprocate her declaration of love for him. Speaking of *The Great American Novel*, Scott seemed to find an analogue for the way Williams had backed away from her in the way his prose failed to sustain the "suicidal radiance" with which it began: "Mr Buffalo Bill Williams, the great tamer of the vanities of America, has just become nothing at all, a kind of flatulent effigy of his own patent medicine" (Callard, 87–88). See Paul Mariani's review of Callard's book, *The William Carlos Williams Review* 12 (Spring 1986): 41–45, for further discussion of those sections pertinent to Williams' relationship with Scott.

43. Else von Freytag-Loringhoven, "Thee I call 'Hamlet of Wedding-Ring,'" *The Little Review* 7 (Jan.–Mar. 1921): 48. Von Freytag-Loringhoven's piece on Williams was so long that the editors, Jane Heap and Margaret Anderson, who had initially introduced Williams to the Baroness, had to print it in two separate parts, the second not appearing until after the "The Three Letters" had already come out. The delay in publication might be said to make the opening line of the second part a nicely anticipatory response to the *Contact* piece: "Put woman into book because cannot put her with good conscience—grace—right touch—anymore into bed!" *The Little Review* 8 (Autumn 1921): 108.

44. Williams' naming of Evan Dionysius Evans here points to the associations Williams had with his own Spanish middle name, and to the naming of his protagonist in *A Voyage to Pagany*.

45. William Carlos Williams, "The Three Letters," *Contact* 4 (Summer 1921): 13.

46. Ibid., 11, 12, 13.

47. Ibid., 10, 11.

48. This dichotomy is exactly the element that Williams claimed to find so compelling in Nancy Cunard, another woman who was very much on his mind while he was writing *In the American Grain*, particularly the "Jacataqua" chapter. Williams saw much of Cunard throughout his European travels during 1924—first in Paris, then at Villefranche and Rome, and again in Paris just before his return to America—and he was transfixed by the beautiful young British shipping heiress and poet who seemed to give herself so freely to life, defiantly open in her sexuality. Williams found "a depraved saintliness" in her sexual profligacy, remarking of Cunard and her friend Iris Tree in his *Autobiography* that "Depravity was their prayer, their ritual, their rhythmic exercises: they denied sin by making it hackneyed in their own bodies, shucking it away to come out not dirtied but pure" (A, 221–22). It was in Rome that Williams' passion for Cunard came to a head, bursting out in the libidinous verbal explosion of *Rome*, a violently sexual prose improvisation written in the heart of Pagany, a kind of uncensored *Kora in Hell* that he took time out from his ongoing work with the Boone chapter to write. A forty-six-page manuscript that Williams himself knew to be entirely "unprintable" (SL, 61)—it was not published until recently, in the *Iowa Review* 9 (Summer 1978): 1–65—*Rome* may have been the seed bed from which "Jacataqua" grew—or rather, failed to grow, for in "Jacataqua" Williams laments the absence of the regenerating sexual power he found in Cunard and the city of Rome itself, that great spawning center of civilization. (See also Williams' chapters on Rome in *A Voyage to Pagany*, 106–18.) Significantly, Williams sent "Jacataqua" back to Italy to be published in the Milan-based expatriate magazine *This Quarter* 1 (Autumn–Winter 1925–26): 182–94, where the chapter appeared about the same time *In the American Grain* was published in New York. It is tempting to speculate that Williams might even have written "Jacataqua" in Italy and given it to someone connected with *This Quarter*, which was also publishing work by McAlmon, Hemingway, Gertrude Stein, and Kay Boyle. But the piece printed in *This Quarter* is exactly the same as that in *In the American Grain*, differing not a word, and thus bearing none of the marks that might suggest it to be an early version of the chapter.

49. Ibid., 10. Williams refers to Orrick Johns, a poet who frequented the *Others* group (A, 135).

50. In his conversations with Edith Heal, Williams remarks of "The Wanderer" that "The old woman in it is my grandmother, raised to heroic proportions. I endowed her with magic qualities. She had seized me from my mother as her special possession, adopted me, and her purpose in life was

to make me her own. But my mother ended all that with a terrific slap in the puss" (IW, 26). Williams seems to conflate the symbolic drama of the poem with an event from his childhood in which his mother struck his grandmother for intruding upon her dominion over Williams. It is an event Williams fondly remembers in the *Autobiography* because it revealed the darker underside of his mother's character, the side he prizes in *Yes, Mrs. Williams*. That violent explosion, says Williams, "did her more good, in fact, than anything that had happened to her since her coming to the States from Santo Domingo to be married" (A, 5). Williams' grandmother—whose name, interestingly, was Emily Dickinson Wellcome—became his instrument for both rebelling against his mother and provoking from her the qualities Williams wanted to see. And significantly, in the chapter of the *Autobiography* that Williams devotes to laying the episode of the Baroness to rest, he also narrates the death of his grandmother, laying her to rest as well (A, 167–68).

51. Williams, "The Three Letters," 11.

52. Ibid., 13.

53. See again the "Night" chapter, in which Williams writes from that fertilizing terror, "Darkness and despair: These are my home. Here I have always retreated when I was beaten, to lie and breed with myself" (VP, 93).

54. Williams imagines Columbus' arrival in the New World in terms of a journey "through the changes of speech: Sanscrit, Greek, Latin growing crooked in the mouths of peasants who would rise and impose their speech on their masters, and on divisions in the state and savage colonial influences, words accurate to the country, Italian, French and Spanish itself not to speak of Portuguese. Words!" (GAN, 182).

55. Williams himself cites this poem, which seems to be an almost pure transcription of his grandmother's speech, in relation to his need "to be kindled" by women such as the Baroness and his grandmother ("The Three Letters," 11).

56. See Kerry Driscoll's *William Carlos Williams and the Maternal Muse* (Ann Arbor, Mich.: UMI Research Press, 1987), particularly "Mother Tongue, Mother Muse," 81–108.

5

The Books, the Records

> In these studies I have sought to re-name the things seen, now lost in chaos of borrowed titles, many of them inappropriate, under which the true character lies hid. In letters, in journals, reports of happenings I have recognized new contours suggested by old words so that new names were constituted. Thus, where I have found noteworthy stuff, bits of writing have been copied into the book for the taste of it. Everywhere I have tried to separate out from the original records some flavor of an actual peculiarity the character denoting shape which the unique force has given. Now it will be the configuration of a man like Washington, and now a report of the witchcraft trials verbatim, a story of a battle at sea—for the odd note there is in it, a letter by Franklin to prospective emigrants; it has been my wish to draw from every source one thing, the strange phosphorus of the life, nameless under an old misappellation. (v)

In the American Grain is a book of the library. To perform his task of revealing "the true character" of the American past, Williams spent many hours in the American History Room at the New York Public Library, reading the books and records of the early comers to the New World, and even writing sections of his own book right there in the reading room, smack in the heart of the archives.[1] The library, in fact, offered Williams a kind of structural model by which to shape his book, for he makes *In the American Grain* itself a library, a container of books, an encyclopedic work richly larded with excerpts from primary historical documents. But no single technique or methodology characterizes Williams' treatment of his documents. In some instances, such as in his creation of Red Eric's voice from his reading of the Vinland Sagas, Williams quite literally constitutes "new names" from "old words," freely transforming the language of his sources so that a new text is generated. In other instances, such as his discussion of Mather's books in "Père Sebastian Rasles" and Bradford's *Of Plymouth Plantation* in "Voyage of the Mayflower," Williams critically dissects the language of his source texts, analyzing the tropes and verbal configurations of early American writing. In yet other chapters, such as "The Discovery of the Indies" and "De Soto and the New World," Williams juxtaposes excerpts from his sources with interstitial material of his own, weaving the documents into a new pattern. Some of the book's most striking chapters, however, are those in which Williams makes the purely bibliographical thrust of his enterprise starkly apparent, copying entire documents verbatim into his book, reprinting substantial portions of the historical record in the manner of an anthologizer.

In "Cotton Mather's Wonders of the Invisible World," Williams cuts and pastes chunks from Mather's book on the evidence and occurrences of witchcraft without otherwise altering a single word. In "Poor Richard," he gives us the complete text of Franklin's *Information to Those Who Would Remove to America*—and in the subsequent chapter, "Battle between the Bon Homme Richard and the Serapis," Williams again reprints an entire document, Jones's letter to Franklin about the absurdly disastrous events that beset his naval operations off the English coast during the Revolutionary War. But Williams doesn't merely anthologize these documents—he also edits and editorializes about them. Nor is the kind of selective excerpting he employs in piecing together twenty pages of text from Mather's two-hundred-page *Wonders of the Invisible World* Williams' only means for mediating his anthologized material. In the Franklin chapter Williams supplements rather than shortens his source, appending his own "Notes for a Commentary on Franklin" to the text of Franklin's *Information to Those Who Would Remove to America*. And in the Jones chapter, Williams sets up a brilliant interplay between his documents—he selects a letter written to Franklin from Jones detailing the ill fortunes of the *Bon Homme Richard*, the unfortunate ship Jones named after Franklin's celebrated persona, Poor Richard. Williams directly invokes "Poor Richard" in his title for the Franklin chapter, pointing to a possible reading of Jones's narrative not simply as a letter to Franklin, but as a response to Franklin's own text about the happy stability of American life. Jones's report to Franklin of deceit and disorder on the high seas thus trenchantly undercuts the tidy and efficient order of Franklin's neatly uttered America in the *Information*.

Williams knits these documents into the scheme of *In the Ameri-*

can Grain in even more subtle ways. In the "Curiosities" section of his
Wonders, for example, Mather writes how "That Reverend and Excellent Person, Mr. *John Higginson,* in my Conversation with him, Once
invited me to this Reflection; that the Indians which came from far to
settle about *Mexico,* were in their Progress to that Settlement, under a
Conduct of the *Devil,* very strangely Emulating what the Blessed God
gave to Israel in the Wilderness" (101). Mather's view of the Aztecs as
the legions of Satan is implicitly undermined by Williams' treatment of
the ancient Aztec capital as the brightest flowering of civilization in the
New World. And in *Information,* Franklin's insistence that "America
is the land of labor, and by no means what the English call *Lubber-
land,* and the French *Pays de Cocagne,* where the streets are said to
be paved with half-peck loaves, the houses tiled with pancakes, and
where the fouls fly about ready to be roasted, crying, *Come eat me!"*
(147) is ironically subverted by Williams' metaphors and facts of food
in "Père Sebastian Rasles." Rasles learns to adjust to the difficulties
of the native diet, thereby finding an abundance that Franklin's parsi-
monious character could never perceive in the New World, save in an
immigrant's fanciful dream of a land of plenty.

Yet these are only a few of the possible readings we might give
of these verbatim documents—and Williams himself remarks none
of these potential verbal interplays for us. Other than establishing a
context in which the documents might take on particular resonances,
Williams offers virtually nothing in the way of explicit interpretive
comment or directive. In the Mather and Jones chapters, he gives us
nothing but the words of the documents themselves. And even though
he appends a commentary to Franklin's *Information,* Williams doesn't
deliver a reading of Franklin's text at all, but comments more largely
on Franklin's role in disseminating a secularized Puritanism to the
young nation. In these three chapters, the task of reading the documents—the act of making history *mean*—is left to us alone.[2] Williams
structures his library to initiate us as readers of early American texts,
asking us to begin our own studies in the verbal grain of America.

Williams does, however, provide us with a possible model for the
process of reading these documents. Through his reading of a passage from Champlain's *Voyages,* Williams gives a marvelously dynamic
enactment of the reader's mind at creative play, making "The Founding of Quebec" not simply a narrative of Champlain's adventures, but,
more insistently, an adventure in reading Champlain's narrative. Williams, in fact, narrates "The Founding of Quebec" as if he himself has
Champlain's text directly at hand, punctuating his progress through

the Frenchman's account of the treacheries that nearly thwarted the founding of the city by repeatedly asking "What's happened?" (70) and exhorting us to "imagine what comes next" (73). Williams invokes our imaginative involvement on the level of the plot, and there is indeed an engrossing plot to the section of Champlain's *Voyages* Williams chooses for his chapter—a plotted mutiny that Champlain has to unravel if he is to succeed in founding his colony at Quebec. Williams uses that plot to engage us more fully in the process of reading, but it is not the suspense of the attempted insurrection that makes Champlain's relation remarkable reading for Williams. After giving the background to Champlain's and Pont Gravé's joint voyage to New France in 1608, Williams brings Champlain to the harbor at Tadoussac, on the St. Lawrence, then endeavors to instruct us how to read the signs that more accurately constitute the man's character:

> But what has happened? Where is Pont Gravé and the other ship? The New World presses on us all; there seems no end to it—and no beginning. So too with him. They see a ship's boat coming. So Pont Gravé has gained the harbor. Good. But there's a stranger in the skiff. A Basque. There's been trouble.
> To me there is a world of pleasure in watching just that Frenchman, just Champlain, like no one else about him, watching, keeping the thing whole within him with almost a woman's tenderness—but such an energy for detail—a love of the exact detail—watching the little boat drawing nearer on that icy bay. This is the interest I see. It is this man. This—me; this American; a sort of radio distributor sending out sparks to us all.
> Well, here's the boat. What's happened? Ah, Pont Gravé is here, of course. Well? There was a Basque in the ship in the bay before him, they refused to stop their trade in furs at the King's order. A short battle. Pont Gravé wounded. This Basque with us has come to make a truce. Champlain was "greatly annoyed," his records say, at such a beginning. Greatly annoyed! Isn't that a treasure? (70–71)

Williams attempts to cultivate in us as readers the same quality he reads in Champlain as writer—"a love of the exact detail." Not just the details of the unexpected turn of events at the beginning, but the details of the whole with "no end" and "no beginning," the entire field of verbal action. He cites Champlain's attentiveness to "the little boat drawing nearer on that icy bay" as indicative of Champlain's acute focus on both the world and word at hand, momentarily isolating that fact from the plot in order to delight in watching Champlain himself in the act of "watching, keeping the thing whole within him." It is just such watchfulness over the whole scene of reading that enables

Williams to discover the character-revealing contours in Champlain's admission that he was " 'greatly annoyed' " at the news from the boat. "Greatly annoyed!" proclaims Williams. "Isn't that a treasure?" And he expresses the same delight in later noting that Champlain was busy preparing a garden when he received further intelligence of the plot against him. " 'I was in a garden that I was having prepared,' he writes. In a garden! that's wonderful to me" (72).

But Williams uses Champlain's account of the near mutiny for something more than a mere device to hook the reader's interest in detail. He also uses it to view Champlain's character through the qualities of his responses to the mutineers. Champlain proves not only a perceptive reader of situations but an adept author of events as well. Once he learns the names of the chief conspirators, he sends them two bottles of wine and an invitation to dinner, then arrests his unsuspecting foes when they arrive. "Can you beat it?" asks Williams. He revels in Champlain's artful foiling of the mutiny, relating with gusto how Champlain finally decided it was sufficient to kill the ringleader and put his head upon a pike as an example to the rest. "To me the whole thing's marvelous—all through," says Williams, and it is indeed the textures of the "whole thing" that he tries to impress upon us "all through" his reading of Champlain.

We can well imagine how Williams might give such a playfully attentive reading of yet another tale of treachery and mutiny—the one he leaves for us to read alone in "Battle between the Bon Homme Richard and the Serapis." At the opening of his letter, Jones asks his reader to pay strict attention to the details of his narrative. He states the conditions upon which he set sail with the apparent support of a French squadron, then remarks, "Whether I was or was not deceived will best appear by a relation of circumstances" (158). What follows is an astounding account of disguised intentions and deceptive twists as Jones's subordinate captains show themselves insubordinate traitors. But though Williams leaves us to tackle Jones's relation on our own, he has schooled us in reading such narratives—and he has also cautioned us with a startling demonstration of the instability of any one interpretation. At the end of "The Founding of Quebec," Williams seemingly subverts everything he has just said about Champlain, expressing his fascination with that same unpredictable and mutinous spirit that nearly reduces everything to chaos in both Champlain's narrative and Jones's letter to Franklin.

In the American Grain is an act of digging, an archaeology of knowledge, as Olson would see it.[3] Pound and Eliot, in the *Cantos* and *The*

Waste Land, had also sought such an archaeology, but Williams is less interested in penetrating distant origins in ancient Greek and Sanskrit texts than in peeling encrusted layers of writing from American texts more directly at hand. He dedicates his book to the task of rescuing America's history from a "chaos of borrowed titles." And in "The May-Pole at Merry Mount," Williams pursues that task with literal verity, endeavoring to release Thomas Morton's *New English Canaan* from the obscuring patina of Charles Francis Adams' lengthy introductory essay to the text. Williams admits that Morton's book "was no great literary feat," but he contends that "as a piece from American History it has a savor which Adams dulls rather than heightens—which is too bad" (80).

Williams makes Adams the living symbol of what is wrong with academic historians, claiming that "He has seen the time too near." Adams perpetuates the distorting myopia that characterizes much American historical writing for Williams. "A most confusing thing in American History, as we read it, is the nearly universal lack of scale," states Williams, and he attacks Adams for his "parochialism" in viewing Morton as a licentious drunkard among the Puritans: "The description, 'a vulgar libertine, thrown by accident into the midst of a Puritan Community, an extremely reckless but highly amusing old debauchee and tippler,' is not adequate to describe a man living under the circumstances that surrounded Morton; its tone might do for a London clubman but not a New World pioneer taking his chances in the wilderness. It lacks scale" (75).[4]

Williams devotes more of "The May-Pole at Merry Mount" to disputing Adams than he does to quoting or discussing Morton's text, mangling the well-known historian's name with flagrant carelessness by calling him "A. C. Adams." He charges Adams with failing the office of historian, which should have been to give "a simple exposition of the facts relating to" Morton's book: "Thomas Morton was unique in our history and since Adams does attempt an evaluation of his book it is a pity he did not realize that, in history, to preserve things of 'little importance' may be more valuable—as it is more difficult and more the business of a writer—than to champion a winner" (76). In Williams' view, Adams, not unlike his New England forbears, couldn't really see Morton's qualities, because he let the question of Morton's sexual relations with the Indians overshadow all other concerns. In one of the verses he composed to be sung around the infamous may-pole, Morton had beckoned, "Lasses in beaver coats comes away / Ye shall be welcome with us night and day." Adams, in his introduction, cites those lines as his primary proof of Morton's profligacy, and Wil-

liams quotes Adams on that point to fault him for his handling of the
evidence: "Some of the earlier writers on the New England Indians
have spoken of the modesty of the women; Wood, in his *Prospect*, for
instance, and Josselyn, in the second of his Two Voyages. 'Morton
however is significantly silent on this point, and the idea of female
chastity in the Indian mind, in the rare cases where it existed at all,
seems to have been of the vaguest possible description. Morton was
not a man likely to be fastidious, and his reference to the "lasses in
beaver coats," is suggestive.' This is as near as Adams ever gets to a
full statement of the facts" (77).[5]

Williams goes on to give us a much more "full statement of the
facts," delivering an impressive display of scholarship. From Parkman's *Jesuits in North America* he quotes the Jesuit missionary Le
Jeune's comments on Algonquian attitudes toward sexuality, then
quotes Parkman himself before delivering passages concerning Indian
sexual mores from Roger Williams' *A Key into the Language of America*
and Morton's own *New English Canaan*. And last but not least, Williams provides a substantial excerpt from William Strachey's *Historie
of Travaile into Virginia Britannia,* quoting the passage on "Pocahuntas,
a well featured, but wanton yong girle, Powhatan's daughter" that
Hart Crane would incorporate into *The Bridge*.[6] Yet none of the evidence points decisively one way or another on the issue of female
chastity among the Indians, and Williams concludes—against Adams'
contention that Morton's failure to speak of Indian modesty suggests
a meaningful omission—that using the issue of female chastity among
Indians as grounds to judge Morton is untenable because "From conflicting reports from many sources the truth seems to be that the state
of affairs with respect to this trait of female chastity was a matter
largely of individual inclination" (78).

Williams marshals his evidence with precision. He even provides
the kind of bibliographical references he generally omits from *In the
American Grain*, citing not only authors' names and titles of books,
but even chapter and page numbers. With Parkman's *Jesuits in North
America*, Williams documents his material as "(ch. iv)," and with Strachey he directs us to "(Historie p. 65)." Yet such assiduity with bibiliographical details seems somewhat out of character for Williams' handling of documents. And indeed it is. Both the bibiliographical data
and all the conflicting reports on Indian sexuality are pirated directly
from Adams, taken straight out of the footnotes to both his introductory essay and Morton's own text.[7] Such appropriations are, of course,
very much in the character of *In the American Grain*. But of all Williams'
borrowings in the book, his lifting of Adams' footnotes is the most

brazen theft. Williams not only nakedly plagiarizes this material, he turns it against its author, using Adams' own scholarship to dismiss Adams as scholar.

Williams' treatment of Adams points to Williams' own paradoxical relationship with history and historians. Though he aggressively wages a dispute with historians throughout *In the American Grain*, Williams actually relies quite heavily on the work of historians—and not on just their factual researches, like Adams' extensive notes on conflicting reports of Indian sexuality, or Bourne's copious supplementary notes to Columbus' journal. In several chapters of his book, Williams relies solely on a single historian's account of the figure in question. Williams' claim to have studied only autobiographical documents— "The plan was to try to get inside the heads of some of the American founders or 'heroes,' if you will, by examining their original records. I wanted nothing to get between me and what they themselves had recorded" (A, 178)—is not entirely consistent with his practice. And in his chapters on Washington, Houston, and Burr, Williams seems to have actually preferred viewing his subject from the outside, at a distance, through the lenses of the historian's vision.

Yet Williams is even more profoundly dependent upon historians. They are the ones who made available to Williams the very books and records so vital to his studies in *In the American Grain*. Williams' book is an archaeology of knowledge—but Williams didn't do his digging in an untouched field. When Williams went to the New York Public Library, he found not just a field already laid out by the structure of the library itself—an American history reading room with books catalogued and arranged by topic on shelves—but a field made rich by the historians who had preceded Williams in his task. *In the American Grain* profits immensely from that era in our national history, from the late nineteenth to the early twentieth century, when many American historians dedicated themselves to making available modern, annotated editions of early American historical records. Projects like J. Franklin Jameson's multivolumed "Original Narratives of Early American History" series and the Prince Society's reprint series of early American documents provided Williams with both reliable texts and scholarly insight.

Indeed, Williams' whole book seems to be structurally patterned upon one such reprint series—the *Old South Leaflets* issued from 1895 to 1922 by the directors of the Old South Studies in History at the Old South Meeting House in Boston. Williams most probably encountered these leaflets at an early point in his investigation of the library's resources.[8] Collected in bound volumes, the *Old South Leaflets* not only became Williams' basic American history primer, they also determined to a great extent his apprehension of early American history. Like the leaflets, *In the American Grain* conceptualizes history episodically, devoting ten- to twenty-page sections to some particular figure or event in American history. And in more than one case Williams let the leaflets decide not only which passages of a given historical record he would select, but how he would title his chapter as well. In "Voyage of the Mayflower" Williams discusses only those portions of Bradford's voluminous *Of Plymouth Plantation* that are reprinted in the leaflets under the title "Voyage of the Mayflower,"[9] while in "The Founding of Quebec," Williams' reading of Champlain is based entirely upon the passage from his lengthy relations that the leaflets print under the title "The Founding of Quebec."[10] And in "Battle Between the Bon Homme Richard and the Serapis," Williams essentially reproduces *Old South Leaflet* no. 152, title and all.[11]

The *Old South Leaflets* also provided Williams with the text of Franklin's *Information* that he reprints in "Poor Richard."[12] But in several instances Williams relied upon the leaflets to introduce him to particular texts and figures which he later went on to investigate more deeply. In leaflet no. 35, Williams found the genesis of "The Destruction of Tenochtitlan" by reading "Cortes's Account of the City of Mexico," an excerpting of Cortez's amazed attempt to comprehend Tenochtitlan's splendor from Folsom's *Despatches of Hernando Cortes*.[13] And in leaflet no. 36, Williams discovered the materials for "De Soto and the New World" by reading "The Death of De Soto," which reprints passages from the narrative of the anonymous Fidalgo of Elvas concerning De Soto's demise on the banks of the Mississippi.[14] "Red Eric," too, may have been suggested to Williams by reading "The Voyages to Vinland, from the Saga of Eric the Red" in leaflet no. 31—which delivers the Arthur Middleton Reeves translation of the Vinland portions of the *Flat Island Book* that Williams later met again in Olson and Bourne's *The Northmen, Columbus and Cabot 985–1503*—while Williams' lyrical performance in "Sir Walter Raleigh" was spurred by his reading of "The First Voyage to Roanoke" in leaflet no. 92 and "The Invention of Ships, by Sir Walter Raleigh" in leaflet no. 166.[15] And Williams most probably had his first contact with *New English Canaan* through leaflet no. 87, which reprints sections of Morton's text as "Manners and Customs of the Indians" from Charles Frances Adams' Prince Society edition of the work.[16]

In the American Grain is not just a study of early American writing —it is the work of a student. Williams had no extensive knowledge of American historical documents prior to writing his book. Indeed, Williams undertook the creation of *In the American Grain* to gain such knowledge, to educate himself about the writers and texts of early America. But Williams also needed to play an educated part for his own students, the readers of *In the American Grain*, and at times he found himself juggling the roles of student and teacher, a process he dramatically enacts in his discussion with Valery Larbaud, posing himself alternately as a crude, untutored block and a knowing teacher of things American. Williams manages to play this dual role by appropriating the material of scholars whenever possible. It may very well have been Larbaud, rather than Williams, who spoke of both Mather and Rasles that day in Paris. And just as Williams would steal Charles Francis Adams' words, turning them against their own speaker, so he perhaps lifted what Larbaud had been able to teach him about the books and records of early America.

Old South Leaflets offered Williams just what he needed—expedient access to materials. A kind of library within the library, the leaflets give excerpts from some two hundred primary documents, many of them accompanied by bibliographical and biographical source citations. They provide an excellent representation not only of documents, but of the work historians had done since the mid-nineteenth century to make such documents available. *Old South Leaflets* was dedicated to publicizing that work by reprinting portions of it. The leaflets were printed in massive numbers and sold cheaply to the public, the directors of the project announcing it as their purpose "to bring important original documents within easy reach of everybody."[17] Williams was sympathetic to that populist effort, and his own reprinting of selections from the Old South reprints adds another disseminating thrust to the process, continuing the Old South directors' campaign to acquaint Americans with the basic original texts of early American history.

Yet unlike the Old South Studies, Williams' studies didn't entail his leaving clear tracks to mark his passage through the library. Williams, in fact, claimed not to be able to remember his sources for *In the American Grain*, telling Gregory in 1939 that "I am sorry I didn't keep a record of all the things I read" (SL, 186). Williams most probably hadn't forgotten the *Old South Leaflets*, which essentially are a record of much that he had read for his book. And Williams' apparent desire to keep the bibiliographical origins of his work cloaked in obscurity underscores the importance he placed on letting *In the American Grain* stand as his answer to the European tradition of scholarly attainment. Williams was acutely aware that in the eyes of that tradition—particularly as it was symbolized for him by Pound and Eliot, those Americans who had gone to Europe to steep themselves in it —he was no intellectual. At times he sought to play up the image of himself as the crude and unrefined American, "a beginner . . . United Stateser," as he had put it in *The Great American Novel* (GAN, 175)— "the brutal thing itself," as he says of himself in Larbaud's presence (107). Yet Williams explicitly acknowledged in "Descent" that "from a low position it is impossible to answer those who know all the Latin and some of the Sanskrit names, much French and perhaps one or two other literatures" (214). And he attempted to achieve his own "high" position by a kind of scholarly posturing much like that which he had mocked in Pound. In the prologue to *Kora in Hell*, Williams mentions how Pound was once "glancing through some book of my father's. 'It is not necessary,' he said, 'to read everything in a book in order to speak intelligently of it. Don't tell everybody I said so,' he added" (KH, 10). Williams defied Pound by publishing his remark, but he also followed Pound's advice. He knew that *In the American Grain* would serve him best if the book could create the impression that he had a more extensive command of the archives than he actually did, and he never let on just how he came by his materials.

Unfortunately, *In the American Grain* itself has languished in general obscurity. Though he might not have had the grand visions of a Whitman, who desired to see all his fellow citizens walking about with copies of his work stuffed in their back pockets, Williams certainly had high hopes for his book's success. It was his first shot with the strength of a commercial publishing house behind him, and he wrote *In the American Grain* at a critical moment in his career, when he felt the need to refigure the enigma of America from the moments of its earliest inception, to know for himself, as he told Horace Gregory, "the locality which by birthright had become my own" (SL, 185). Yet the book never has gained the hearing Williams wanted for it. *In the American Grain* remains too little read today, despite its wide availability. And for a work of such complexity and brilliance in American letters, *In the American Grain* has been sorely neglected by those whom Williams perhaps wanted most ardently to teach—the critics and scholars who, like Larbaud and Adams, could teach Williams himself something about the American past.

NOTES

1. In his letter on *In the American Grain* to Gregory, Williams tells of "a comical incident" that happened due to his writing in the library: "One day

when I was plugging away on the Ponce de Leon material, I think, I got out my source book but before I opened it (I had been working at the same task the week before) I suddenly got an idea and started to write, furiously. Right at the height of my flight I felt a tap on my shoulder and the son of a bitch of an attendant there, with a British accent (in the American history room!) told me that this was a reading room and that if I wanted to write I would have to go somewhere else. Christ! I could have murdered him" (SL, 186). Williams tells a slightly different version of the same story in his *Autobiography*, imagining that it was the De Soto chapter "burning in my head," and that he didn't even have his source book at hand. He also claims to have replied "I'm writing a thesis" to the attendant (A, 183).

2. James Breslin identifies these verbatim extract chapters as the weakest sections of *In the American Grain*. He accuses Williams of pulling "too simple a rhetorical trick," of taking the easy way out by simply copying his material instead of artistically remaking it as he had done in other chapters (108). But Williams' verbatim extract chapters are very much an integral part of his creation of an American history. Williams, in fact, saw these chapters as one of his major achievements in the book, telling Horace Gregory that in his effort to get as close as possible to the style of past writing he had copied the documents by Mather, Franklin, and Jones "with malice aforethought to prove the truth of the book, since the originals fitted into it without effort on my part, perfectly, leaving not a seam" (SL, 187).

3. Charles Olson, in his *A Bibliography on America*, ed. George F. Butterick (Bolinas, Calif.: Four Seasons Foundation, 1974), includes *In the American Grain* among his list of essential books for studying the historical basis of America. Olson, however, envisions a study that goes back millenia to track migrations of aboriginal American peoples, urging examination of Mayan "codices in which *feet* (like on floor after bath) are as arrows in Klee" (5). And he suggests that Williams, despite the value of his book, didn't have a deep enough historical context for his work on the American past, pointing to *In the American Grain* as "An example of how even one of the best men don't quite make it" (6).

4. Williams actually fuses together parts of two separate sentences by Adams (16–17). Williams' placement of quotation marks makes it seem that he, not Adams, is the one familiar with Wood and Josselyn on the topic of Indian 1883; rpt. New York: Burt Franklin, 1967), 92, 93.

5. Except for the last sentence, the whole of this passage is verbatim from Adams (16–17). Williams' placement of quotation marks makes it seem that he, not Adams, is the one familiar with Wood and Josselyn on the topic of Indian sexuality—an appropriation that indeed characterizes Williams' treatment of Adams in "The May-Pole at Merry Mount."

6. "Powhatan's Daughter," the section of *The Bridge* in which Crane envisions an archetypal female embodiment of the continent—a "bride immortal in the maize" who "is virgin to the last of men," *The Collected Poems of Hart Crane*, ed. Waldo Frank (New York: Liveright, 1933), 22—opens by quoting a shorter portion of the "Pocahuntas" passage. Crane was a profound ad-

mirer of *In the American Grain*, writing to Waldo Frank in 1926 that "Williams' *American Grain* is an achievement that I'd be proud of. A most important and *sincere* book. I'm very enthusiastic." Crane, in fact, found Williams' book so remarkable that he troubled to point out to Frank that he had had to force himself *not* to read it until he had completed substantial work on his own historical vision of America: "I put off reading it, you know, until I felt my way cleared beyond chance of confusions incident to reading a book so intimate to my theme," *The Letters of Hart Crane, 1916–1932*, ed. Brom Weber (Berkeley: University of California Press, 1965), 277–78. Crane was fearful that the structure of his still-emerging *Bridge* might become entangled with the skein of *In the American Grain*. And despite his claim to a delayed reading, Crane was more than indirectly aware of just how "intimate to my theme" Williams' book might prove, for he had undoubtedly read the early chapters that appeared in *Broom*, the magazine that published his "The Springs of Guilty Song" in the same issue as Williams' "The Destruction of Tenochtitlan" (*Broom* 4: 131–32). But the question of just how much Crane might have been influenced by or willfully borrowed from *In the American Grain*, difficult enough as it is, becomes further complicated by the peculiarities of the Williams and Crane relationship—or rather by Williams' obstinate refusal of a relationship with Crane. Yet it is safe to say that on a purely textual level, *The Bridge* and *In the American Grain* diverge much more than converge. Though both works attempt a synthesizing vision of the American past, the two works approach that task in very different ways. Crane's poem doesn't involve a close study of books and records. Williams went to the library to write, while Crane retired in isolation at his family's plantation on the Isle of Pines near Grand Cayman, producing the substance of his work in one tremendous creative explosion over several weeks. Williams had tried to convey that difference to Gregory, telling him that Crane "was searching for something inside, while I was all for a sharp use of the materials. We were just on different tracks" (SL, 186). See Joseph Evans Slate's "William Carlos Williams, Hart Crane and 'The Virtue of History,'" *Texas Studies in Language and Literature* 6 (Winter 1965): 486–511, for a good discussion of the problematic Williams and Crane relationship.

7. Adams actually provides much more material on female chastity among the Indians than Williams is able to use. Adams' notes form a running commentary to both his own one-hundred-page essay and the two hundred and fifty pages of *New English Canaan*, a kind of intertextual subnarrative, woven from Adams' rich knowledge of early American historians. Williams follows a well-marked path through these notes. From 16n2 and 17n1, Williams splices together Parkman's material on Le Jeune and the additional remarks by Parkman himself and Roger Williams. (Adams, 16n2, had quoted more extensively from Williams' *A Key into the Language of America*, as well as from Josselyn's *Two Voyages* and Wood's *New England's Prospect*.) The sentence about "an incident mentioned by Morton," though it seems to be spoken by Williams, is also from Adams' notes, and, in this case, is Adams' own words (17n1). Williams appropriates Adams' statement, then follows the historian's reference "(*Infra*, *32)" to the designated section of *New English Canaan* in which Morton

tells the story of an Indian who may have been cuckolded by an Englishman. Williams quotes that story (Adams, 148), then picks up the thread of Adams' notes on Indian sexuality from that point in Morton's text, leafing back to 145n2, to take the long quotation on Pocahontas from Strachey's *Historie*. The final passage Williams delivers, misleadingly punctuating it as if it were a continuation of the Strachey material, is actually compounded of two separate statements Adams makes in reference to Parkman on Indian sexuality in the same note. One last remark on Williams' theft of Adams' scholarship —the passage Williams quotes from Bradford's *Of Plymouth Plantation* about Morton's Maypole revels (79) isn't a product of Williams' own reading of Bradford's history, but of Adams' quotation from it (18–19). Williams' knowledge of *Of Plymouth Plantation* was limited to the closing chapters of book 1.

8. Williams seems to have been familiar with the *Old South Leaflets* at least as early as his writing of *The Great American Novel* in the fall of 1921. His passages on De Soto in that work (GAN, 192, 204) focus exclusively on the Spaniard's last moments at the Mississippi River, suggesting that Williams was not yet familiar with the complete chronicles of the De Soto expedition that he would eventually use to write "De Soto and the New World," but only with the excerpt "The Death of De Soto, from the 'Narrative of a Gentleman of Elvas' " printed in *Old South Leaflets*, no. 36. Williams dates the beginning of the major period of source reading for *In the American Grain* from the fall of 1922 (SL, 187).

9. "Voyage of the Mayflower," *Old South Leaflets*, no. 153, reprints chapters 7 through 10 of book 1 and the opening passages of book 2 from William Bradford's *Of Plimoth Plantation*, ed. Charles Deane, *Collections of the Massachusetts Historical Society*, 4th ser., vol. 3 (Boston: Little, Brown, 1856), 3: 58–89, omitting only two lengthy letters by John Robinson (the Puritans' dearly beloved minister who remained behind in Leyden) that are separately reprinted as "Words of John Robinson," *Old South Leaflets*, no. 142. Williams thus had access to a goodly section of Bradford's history—represented are events from the departure from Leyden through the arrival and the first winter, including the famous passage that closes chapter 9, Bradford's marvelous icon of loss and removal in a savage land. Williams, however, hardly makes a thorough use of this rich though limited sampling from *Of Plymouth Plantation*. He quotes only two brief passages from early in chapter 9, both concerning Providential acts at sea during the Atlantic crossing—one in which "a proud and very profane younge man, one of ye seamen, of a lustie body," who had tormented the pilgrims by saying "he hoped to cast halfe of them over board before they came to their journey's end," is smitten by God "with a greevous disease, of which he dyed in a desperate manner, and was himself ye first yt was throwne overboard" (64–65), and another in which "a lustie young man (called John Howland)" is washed overboard in a storm and miraculously saved, after which he "lived many years after, and became a profitable member both in church and commone wealth" (66–67). In his early version of "Voyage of the Mayflower," Williams had quoted a third passage from Bradford dealing with the ship's standing to off Cape Cod during a storm

(*Transatlantic Review*, 50). Yet even with this third passage considered, Williams' use of the Bradford material available in the leaflet remains somewhat superficial.

10. "The Founding of Quebec," *Old South Leaflets,* no. 91, reprints *Voyages of Samuel de Champlain,* ed. Edmund F. Slafter, trans. Charles Pomeroy Otis (Boston, Prince Society, 1878; rpt. New York: Burt Franklin, 1967), 2: 158–89. Williams didn't bother to consult Slafter's text directly—he let the leaflet tell him all he wanted to know about Champlain. His references to Champlain's valuable maps and illustrations (70), and to Champlain's birthplace and father (69), are based on information he read in the biographical and bibiographical material appended to the narrative by the Old South editors (19–20). There, too, Williams read the statement by Parkman on Champlain that prompted this outburst: "Parkman says, 'Champlain was a man all for the theme and purpose, nothing for himself.' Good Lord, these historians! By that I understand the exact opposite of what is written: a man all for himself—but gently, with love, with patience, unwilling to endure the smallest fracture of his way of doing. He knew Champlain and followed Champlain in everything. See if I am not right" (69).

11. "Battle between the 'Bon Homme Richard' and the 'Serapis,'" *Old South Leaflets,* no. 152. At first glance, it appears that Williams reproduces the text of the leaflet without alteration, but he cuts two brief sections. The first is a relatively minor excision of Jones's short entries for August 18 to 23. But the second is a fairly significant omission of Jones's entry for September 19, in which he notes the reluctance of Captain Cottineau, the leader of the French contingent, to help him carry out his perhaps overly exuberant plans for terrorizing the English coastline after his attempts to raid Leith and Edinburgh had fallen through: "I proposed another project to Mr. Cottineau, which would have been highly honorable though not profitable. Many difficulties were made, and our situation was represented as being the most perilous. The enemy, he said, would send against us a superior force, and that, if I obstinately continued on the coast of England two days longer, we should all be taken." Fascinatingly, Jones imagines himself, in this narrative of deceptive signals, from the Frenchman's point of view for a moment as he claims it was his fear of Cottineau's reproach that held him back from immediately undertaking his project: "I had thoughts of attempting the enterprise alone after the Pallas had made sail to join the Vengeance. I am persuaded even now that I would have succeeded; and, to the honor of my young officers, I found them as ardently disposed to the business as I could desire. Nothing prevented me from pursuing my design but the reproach that would have been cast upon my character as a man of prudence, had the enterprise miscarried. It would have been said, Was he not forewarned by Captain Cottineau and others?" (6).

12. "Plan for Western Colonies," *Old South Leaflets,* no. 163, reprints two pieces by Franklin from *The Works of Benjamin Franklin,* ed. John Bigelow, 12 vols. (New York: G. P. Putnam's Sons, 1904)—"Plan for Settling Two Western Colonies in North America, with Reasons for the Plan" (*Works,* 3: 148–57), and "Information to Those Who Would Remove to America" (*Works,* 9: 432–44).

13. "Cortes's Account of the City of Mexico," *Old South Leaflets*, no. 35, reprints 110–25 of Folsom's translation of Cortez's letters, the very passage upon which Williams bases "The Destruction of Tenochtitlan."

14. "The Death of De Soto," *Old South Leaflets*, no. 36, reprints portions of Halkluyt's English translation of the Fidalgo's relation, first published in London in 1609 as *Virginia Richly Valued by the Description of the Mainland of Florida, Her Next Neighbor,* and subsequently republished in numerous historical collections. Williams might have first learned of the availability of the additional relations by Hernandez de Biedma and Ranjel through the detailed bibiliographical notes appended to the leaflet, but he didn't discover his particular source—Bourne's *Narratives of the Career of Hernando De Soto in the Conquest of Florida,* the only collection in which all three of these narratives were available (and in modern translations as well)—through the leaflet, for Bourne's work did not appear until 1904, some dozen years after the leaflet was published.

15. "The First Voyage to Roanoke," *Old South Leaflets*, no. 92, reprints three pieces from *Sir Walter Ralegh and His Colony in America,* ed. Increase N. Tarbox (Boston: Prince Society, 1884; rpt. New York: Burt Franklin, 1967): Arthur Barlowe's account to Raleigh of the first explorations of Virginia in 1584 (107–27); the "Charter in Favor of Sir Walter Ralegh, Knight, for the Discovery and Planting of New Lands in America" granted him by Elizabeth (95–105); and an extract from Ralph Lane's letter to Richard Hakluyt, written from Virginia in 1585 (143). "The Invention of Ships," *Old South Leaflets*, no. 166, reprints "A Discourse of the Invention of Ships, Anchors, Compass, & c.," from *The Works of Sir Walter Raleigh,* 8 vols. (Oxford: Oxford University Press, 1829; rpt. New York: Burt Franklin, 1967), 8: 317–34. Williams incorporates portions of Barlowe's relation in his chapter. The paragraph beginning "What might he have known, what seen, O Muse?" (61), is—with the exception of the first sentence—made up entirely from Barlowe's description of the Virginia coastline and the reception accorded the expedition by Granganimeo, the King's brother, and his wife (2–8). The second and third paragraphs of "Sir Walter Raleigh" ("The truth is that all nations . . . and they are all of them idolators in one kind or another," 59–60), are verbatim from "The Invention of Ships" (3). Williams' energetic depiction of Raleigh as a seer and visionary in the English colonization of the New World might owe much to the enthusiastic praise of Raleigh in the biographical notes appended to these two leaflets (no. 92: 19–20; no. 166: 15–16).

16. "Manners and Customs of the Indians," *Old South Leaflets*, no. 87, reprints chapters from book one of Morton's text in a substantially different order than they are given in Adams' edition of *New English Canaan*: chap. 4 (Adams, 134–38); chap. 6 (Adams, 141–45); chap. 8 (Adams, 148–50); chaps. 11–13 (Adams, 154–61); chap. 15 (Adams, 165–66); chaps. 9–10 (Adams, 150–54); chap. 14 (Adams, 161–65); chap. 3 (Adams, pp. 130–34); chap. 5 (Adams, 139–41); chaps. 16–20 (Adams, 167–78).

17. *Old South Leaflets*, no. 36: 11.

Index

Note on the Author

Bryce Conrad received his Ph.D. in 1988 from the University of Iowa, where he currently teaches. He has also taught at Grinnell College and at California State University, Chico. His previous publications include articles on William Carlos Williams, Herman Melville, and Richard Henry Dana, Jr.